Inside Writing

A Writer's Workbook

FIRST CANADIAN EDITION

Inside Writing

A Writer's Workbook

WILLIAM SALOMONE

STEPHEN McDONALD

MARK EDELSTEIN

FIRST CANADIAN EDITION

WILLIAM GOEDE

Capilano College

Nelson Canada

I(T)P An International Thomson Publishing Company

Toronto • Albany • Bonn • Boston • Cincinnati • Detroit • London • Madrid • Melbourne
Mexico City • New York • Pacific Grove • Paris • San Francisco • Singapore • Tokyo • Washington

I(T)P⁻

International Thomson Publishing
The ITP logo is a trademark under licence

© Nelson Canada
A division of Thomson Canada Limited, 1995

Published in 1995 by
Nelson Canada
A division of Thomson Canada Limited
1120 Birchmount Road
Scarborough, Ontario M1K 5G4

Canadian Cataloguing in Publication Data
Main entry under title:
  Inside writing

Includes index.
ISBN 0-17-604271-7

1. English language - Rhetoric. 2. English language -
Rhetoric - Problems, exercises, etc. 3. English
language - Grammar. 4. English language - Grammar -
Problems, exercises, etc. I. Goede, William.

PE1408.I57 1995   808'.042   C95-930297-2

Acquisitions Editor	Andrew Livingston
Senior Production Editor	Tracy Bordian
Developmental Editor	Joanne Scattolon
Art Director	Liz Harasymczuk
Cover and Interior Design	Kevin Connolly
Composition Analyst	Zenaida Diores
Input Operators	Elaine Andrews and Michelle Volk
Senior Production Coordinator	Sheryl Emery

Printed and bound in Canada

1 2 3 4 (WC) 99 98 97 96

OTABIND The pages in this book open easily and lie flat, a result of the Otabind bookbinding process. Otabind combines advanced adhesive technology and a free-floating cover to achieve books that last longer and are bound to stay open.

Bound to stay open

Table of Contents

Chapter Three
Improving Sentence Patterns

Chapter Four
Lining Up the Parts of a Sentence

Preface

This first Canadian version carries on the wonderful work of William Salomone, Stephen McDonald, and Mark Edelstein. The format is essentially the same: the student examines the structure of English expression and then puts it straight into practice.

The landscape of the book has, however, been substantially altered. Canadian students now work within the Canadian context. Personal names in examples reflect our cultural mosaic. Wherever possible, explication of writing concepts is made with an awareness that many Canadian students bring ESL problems into the classroom. Much of the instructional materials has been modified to make the book more useful for Canadians. For instance, Chapter Six has been greatly expanded to include a broader discussion of style and usage. Finally, in response to the wishes of instructors and reviewers, all the sections on paragraph and essay composition have been materially expanded and deepened.

The design of the American edition is maintained throughout. The first three sections of each chapter detail a certain structure of the English language. Instructors should, above all, insist on students working carefully and methodically through the instructions by completing the "practice" sections at home and cross-checking their answers against the correct answers provided at the end of each chapter. This step is crucial. We feel students must learn this material themselves. The instructor then meets with students and evaluates their understanding of these structures. Instructors need to be inventive and enthusiastic at this stage. As a last step in the process, we anticipate that instructors will move to the exercise sections to evaluate the progress of the class in each section of the chapter.

Each chapter concludes with a practice test covering the work of the entire chapter.

The fourth section of each chapter is devoted to sentence combining, which, we feel, is the heart of the workbook. Here students make sentences out of what what they have learned in the chapter and begin to write with more authority.

The fifth section of each chapter relates to paragraphs and the essay proper. These sections develop cumulatively, building on each other throughout the book.

This is a big book. Instructors can be selective. Some exercises contain fifteen sentences; the instructor can opt for ten. One hearty recommendation: Chapter One, which is principally a study of parts of speech, can be omitted as a class undertaking. The Chapter One Practice Test may be used as a diagnostic instrument, and the instructor can hold separate, individual sessions with people who do poorly on it. *However, be careful not to skip Section Four and Five of Chapter One, since these sections introduce the concept of sentence combining and the first steps of the writing process.*

Starting with Chapter Two, a study of clauses and sentence construction errors, is, we believe, an excellent launch into the course. We could not omit Chapter One, however, because it is so basic to an understanding of the rest of the book.

William Goede
Capilano College

Acknowledgments

I want to thank my good friends and colleagues at Capilano College for their enthusiastic assistance and intelligent recommendations for improving the workbook: Melanie Fahlman Reid, Rosemary Coupe, Crystal Hurdle, Gladys Hindmarch, Jean Clifford, Tim Acton, Andrea Westcott, and Bill Schermbrucker. I am grateful, too, for the support of Joanne Scattolon, Developmental Editor at Nelson Canada, and the warm direction of Tracy Bordian, Senior Production Editor. I also want to thank my wife Marilyn Brulhart for her heroic patience and professional assistance in helping me through the intrigues of an often quite mysterious language. Finally, and most important, if it hadn't been for the brainstorm and ensuing initiative of Andrew Livingston, Acquisitions Editor at Nelson Canada, this workbook would not exist, and I would not have had so much fun with my own language. Thank you, Andrew.

Chapter One
Naming the Parts

Most of us find the whole idea of studying the grammatical structure of our language a waste of time. We will do it only if someone can convince us that, being ill, we will feel better if we swallow this bitter pill.

The reason is simple. We believe that language structures have little or nothing to do with writing. The truth is we are correct—partly. Good writers are good not because they know these structures but because they know how to write.

However, most of us find writing to be a constant struggle. We don't seem to be able to improve, or we tinker with this and that and still achieve only a modicum of success. We wonder why.

The whole truth is that structures have a lot to do with writing. We *can* improve our writing if only we understand how language works. One way to become better writers is to learn how to build better sentences and paragraphs, and we can build better sentences and paragraphs by understanding what they are made of and how they work.

It helps a lot to know the names for the elements of sentences and paragraphs in order to discover where we're going wrong. A surgeon can probably perform an operation without knowing the names of the scalpel and the stethoscope, but no competent doctor would lack that knowledge. Carrying the analogy further: if something has gone wrong in the operation, or the surgeon wants to discuss, analyze, and improve upon the way it was performed, knowing the names of the tools would be important.

We begin, then, by examining the tools of our language and building from there. One level leads to the next, and the mastery of one will hopefully lead to the mastery of all; by the same law, the misunderstandings and confusions at one level will carry, unfortunately, on to the next, and so on. Don't let things slide. It is crucial that you master each element along the way before proceeding to the next on your path to becoming a competent writer.

Section One

Subjects and Verbs

Of all the terms presented in this chapter, perhaps the most important are SUBJECT and VERB. They are the foundation stones of the sentence. Sentences come in many forms, and the structures of sentences may be quite complex, but they all have one thing in common: *every sentence must contain a SUBJECT and a VERB.* Like most grammatical rules, this one is based on simple logic: without a subject you have nothing to write about, and without a verb you have nothing to say about your subject.

Subjects: Nouns and Pronouns

Before you can find the subject of a sentence, you need to be able to identify nouns and pronouns because the subjects of sentences will always be nouns or pronouns—or, occasionally, other words or groups of words that function as nouns. You probably already know the definition of a noun:

DEFINITION · | noun | A noun names a person, place, thing, or idea.

This definition works perfectly well for most nouns, especially for those that name concrete things we can *see, hear, smell, taste,* or *touch*. Using this definition, most people can identify words such as *door, road,* or *tulip* as nouns.

EXAMPLES

         N   N   N
Keiko reads her favourite **book** whenever she goes to the **beach**.

      N   N   N
My **brother** likes to watch **hockey** on **television**.

Unfortunately, when it comes to identifying *ideas* as nouns, many people have trouble. Part of this problem is that nouns name more than ideas: they name **emotions, qualities, conditions,** and many other **abstractions.** Abstract nouns such as *fear, courage, happiness,* and *trouble* do not name persons, places, or things, but they are nouns.

Below are a few examples of nouns, arranged by category. Add nouns of your own to each category.

Persons	Places	Things	Ideas
Keiko	Montreal	spaghetti	sincerity
engineer	beach	book	anger
woman	India	sun	democracy
artist	town	bicycle	intelligence
_____	_____	_____	_____
_____	_____	_____	_____
_____	_____	_____	_____

PRACTICE

Place an "N" above all the nouns in the following sentences.

   N   N   N   N
1. Brad noticed a strange bird in the tree in his backyard.

2. My mother has just learned how to bake bread in a microwave oven.

3. The pilot could see the tails of the other planes in the clouds.

4. The students in her class were impressed with her stamina.

5. Monica played the harmonica with little skill but much enthusiasm.

To help you identify all nouns, remember these points:

1. *Nouns can be classified as* **proper nouns and common nouns.** **Proper nouns** name specific persons, places, things, and ideas. The first letter in each of these nouns is capitalized (Betty, Quebec, Toyota, Marxism). **Common nouns** name more general categories. The first letter of a common noun is not capitalized (woman, province, car, economics).

2. *A,* **an,** *and* **the** *are noun markers.* A common noun will always follow one of these words.

                   N   N

EXAMPLES   The young **constable** was given a new police **car**.

     N   N   N   N
The **point** of the **lecture** was that **students** should study the **textbook**.

3. *If you are unsure whether or not a word is a noun, ask yourself if it could be introduced with a, an, or the.*

EXAMPLE
                N   N   N

My **granddaughter** asked for my **opinion** of her new **outfit**.

4. *Words that end in **ment, ism, ness, ence, ance**, and **tion** are usually nouns.*

EXAMPLE
         N   N

Her **criticism** of my **performance** made me very unhappy.

PRACTICE

Place an "N" above all the nouns in the following sentences.

1. Her new Chevrolet with all of its accessories pleased Valerie.

2. The young musician played his flute to the whales.

3. On the diving board the diver shivered in the cold air.

4. The pear had a green leaf attached to its stem.

5. The engineers liked the complexity of the design.

6. The rocking motion of the ship caused nausea in some of the passengers.

7. The constable called his uniform a "bag."

8. Canada is a nation with many different races, religions, and political views.

9. Her parties were famous for delicious food, good humour, and malicious gossip.

10. He refused the position as a matter of principle.

A pronoun takes the place of a noun. The "pro" in pronoun comes from the Latin word meaning "for." Thus, a pronoun is a word that in some way stands "for a noun."

DEFINITION
    | pronoun | A pronoun takes the place of a noun. |

Pronouns perform this task in a variety of ways. Often, a pronoun will allow you to refer to a noun without having to repeat the noun. For instance, notice how the word *John* is awkwardly repeated in the following sentence:

John put on John's coat before John left for John's job.

Pronouns allow you to avoid the repetition:

John put on his coat before he left for his job.

In later chapters we will discuss the use of pronouns and the differences among the various types. For now, you simply need to be able to recognize pronouns in a sentence. The following list includes the most common pronouns. Read over this list several times until you are familiar with these words.

Personal Pronouns

I	we	you	he	she	they	it
me	us	your	him	her	them	its
my	our	yours	his	hers	their	
mine	ours				theirs	

Indefinite Pronouns

some	everyone	anyone	someone	no one
all	everything	anything	something	nothing
many	everybody	anybody	somebody	nobody
each				
one				
none				

Reflexive/Intensive Pronouns

myself	ourselves
yourself	yourselves
himself	themselves
herself	
itself	

Relative Pronouns

who, whom, whose
which
that

Demonstrative Pronouns

that	this
those	these

Interrogative Pronouns

who, whom, whose
which
what

PRACTICE

Place an "N" above all nouns and a "Pro" above all pronouns in the following sentences.

      N   Pro N   N   Pro

1. Erik noticed their boat was drifting toward the falls, so he dropped

   Pro   N

   its anchor.

2. Everyone looked to see if the equipment was in proper order.

3. The astronauts relaxed in their seats and treated themselves to a movie.

4. Which of the waiters served your dessert?

5. The cook himself served mine.

6. Omar found a cauliflower stuck in an air vent.

7. Who will make some of the decorations for our party?

8. Caps with their bills turned around to the back are now in style.

9. Those are the coins from my old trunk in the attic.

10. Anyone who finishes the marathon will be given a bouquet of flowers

    and a shirt with a picture of herself on it.

PRACTICE

In the following sentences, write nouns and pronouns of your own choice as indicated.

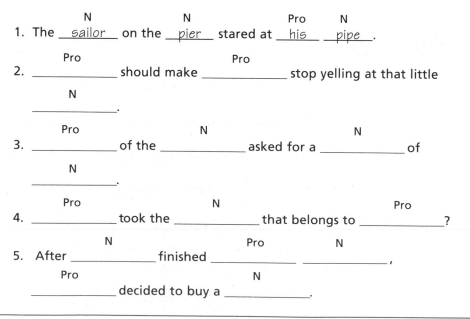

           N   N   Pro   N

1. The __*sailor*__ on the __*pier*__ stared at __*his*__ __*pipe*__.

      Pro   Pro

2. _____ should make _____ stop yelling at that little

    N

   _____.

      Pro   N   N

3. _____ of the _____ asked for a _____ of

    N

   _____.

      Pro   N   Pro

4. _____ took the _____ that belongs to _____?

           N   Pro   N

5. After _____ finished _____ _____,

    Pro   N

   _____ decided to buy a _____.

Verbs

Once you can identify nouns and pronouns, the next step is to learn to identify verbs. Some people have trouble finding verbs. However, it is easy if you can remember the following definition: **A verb either shows action or links the subject to another word.**

DEFINITION | verb | A verb either shows action or links the subject to another word.

This definition identifies two types of verbs. Some are "action" verbs (they tell what the subject is *doing*), and others are "linking" verbs (they tell what the subject is *being*). This distinction leads to the first point that will help you recognize verbs.

Action Verbs and Linking Verbs

One way to recognize verbs is to know that some verbs can do more than simply express an action. Some verbs are action verbs; others are linking verbs.

Action Verbs

Action verbs are usually easy to identify. Consider the following sentence:

The deer leaped gracefully over the stone wall.

If you ask yourself what the **action** of the sentence is, the answer is obviously *leaped*. Therefore, *leaped* is the verb.

Examples of Action Verbs *run, read, go, write, think, forgive, wait, laugh*

PRACTICE

Underline the action verbs in the following sentences.

1. The blind girl <u>leaped</u> over the fence on her way home.

2. Jennifer spent her mornings on the beach at Puerto Vallarte.

3. She covered herself in sunblock and swam for hours.

4. The new vegetarian cookbook arrived yesterday.

5. Susan found a baby rabbit in the back seat of her car.

Linking Verbs

Linking verbs are sometimes more difficult to recognize than action verbs. Think of them as an equal sign (=):

Chantal **is** a woman of unusual integrity.

Chantal = a woman of unusual integrity.

Notice that the sentence does not express action. The verb *is* simply links the word *woman* to the word *Chantal*.

Examples of Linking Verbs forms of *to be*: am, is, are, was, were, be, being, been

---

PRACTICE

Underline the linking verbs in the following sentences.

1. John <u>was</u> a gentleman in every way.

2. "Chrysanthemum" is a hard name to spell and pronounce.

3. Fiona will be happy after her last French class.

4. The dogs were tense before the show.

5. I am a millionaire in training.

Careful! Some linking verbs deal with the **senses**, such as *look, smell, feel, taste,* and *sound*. Others deal with a sense of existence or becoming, such as *appear, seem, get, grow, turn, remain, stay,* and *prove*. You can test whether it is a linking verb if you can substitute a form of *to be* for it:

1. Fiona *seemed* happy after her class. Fiona *was* happy after her class.

2. The dog *grew* tense before the show. The dogs *were* tense before the show.

3. The testimony *proved* false. The testimony *was* false.

Linking verbs can link three types of words to a subject.

1. They can link nouns to the subject:

Mike <u>became</u> a hero to his team. (*Hero* is linked to *Mike*.)

2. They can link pronouns to the subject:

    Cheryl <u>was</u> someone from another planet. (*Cheryl* is linked to *someone*.)

3. They can link adjectives (descriptive words) to the subject:

    The sky <u>was</u> cloudy all day. (*Cloudy* is linked to *day*.)

Verb Tense

Another way to identify verbs is to know that they appear in different forms to show the time when the action or linking takes place. These forms are called **tenses**. The simplest tenses are *present*, *past*, and *future*.

Present		Past	
I walk	we walk	I walked	we walked
you walk	you walk	you walked	you walked
he, she, it walks	they walk	he, she, it walked	they walked

Future

I will walk	we will walk
you will walk	you will walk
he, she, it will walk	they will walk

Note that the verb *walk* can be written as *walked* to show past tense and as *will walk* to show future tense. When a verb adds "d" or "ed" to form the past tense, it is called a **regular verb.**

Other verbs change their forms more drastically to show past tense. For example, the verb *eat* becomes *ate*, and *fly* becomes *flew*. Verbs like these, which do not add "d" or "ed" to form the past tense, are called **irregular verbs.** Irregular verbs will be discussed in Chapter Six. For now, to help you identify verbs, remember this point: *Verbs change their forms to show tense.*

PRACTICE

In the following sentences, first underline the verb and then write the tense (present, past, or future) in the space provided.

Present 1. Rose <u>goes</u> to the movies with her boyfriend every Friday.

_____ 2. The dog with the red collar sat in the front seat of the car.

_____ 3. Richard and Nicole will celebrate their first anniversary soon.

_____ 4. We waited for the sunrise.

_____ 5. Rana often volunteers to serve on committees.

Helping Verbs and Main Verbs

A third way to identify verbs is to know that the verb of a sentence is often more than one word. The MAIN VERB of a sentence may be preceded by one or more HELPING VERBS to show time, condition, or circumstances. The helping verbs allow us the flexibility to communicate a wide variety of ideas and attitudes. For example, note how adding a helping verb changes the following sentences:

I *run* indicates that an action is happening or happens repeatedly.

I *will run* indicates that an action is not now occurring but will occur in the future.

I *should run* indicates an attitude toward the action.

The COMPLETE VERB of a sentence, then, includes a MAIN VERB and any HELPING VERBS. The complete verb can contain as many as three helping verbs.

     MV
He *writes*.

    HV   MV
He *has written*.

    HV HV   MV
He *has been writing*.

    HV   HV   HV   MV
He *might have been writing*.

You can be sure that you have identified all of the helping verbs in a complete verb simply by learning the helping verbs. There are not very many of them.
    These words are **always** helping verbs:

can	may	could
will	must	would
shall	might	should

These words are sometimes helping verbs and sometimes main verbs:

Forms of *have*	Forms of *do*	Forms of *be*		
have	do	am	was	be
has	does	is	were	being
had	did	are		been

In the following examples, note that the same word can be a helping verb in one sentence and a main verb in another:

MV
Annie **had** thirty pairs of shoes.

      HV   MV
The engineers **had** thought about the problem for years.

MV
She **did** well on her chemistry quiz.

HV MV
Bob **did** go to the game after all.

MV
The bus **was** never on time.

HV   MV
He **was** planning to leave in the morning.

When you are trying to identify the complete verb of a sentence, remember that any helping verbs will always come before the main verb; however, other words may occur between the helping verb(s) and the main verb. For instance, you will often find words such as *not, never, ever, already,* or *just* between the helping verb and the main verb. Also, in questions you will often find the subject between the helping verb and the main verb.

HV   S   MV
EXAMPLES   Will the telephone company raise its prices?

S   HV   MV
Nobody has **ever** proved the existence of the Loch Ness Monster.

PRACTICE

In the spaces provided, identify the underlined words as main verbs (MV) or helping verbs (HV).

    HV   1. Chris <u>has</u> run in every marathon the city has held since 1980.

_____   2. His brother sometimes <u>runs</u> with him, but not often.

_____   3. Once, when he <u>was</u> running, a dove landed on his shoulder.

_____   4. Chris <u>was</u> in a state of shock.

_____   5. He <u>did</u> the humane thing.

_____   6. <u>Did</u> he stop?

_____   7. He decided that he <u>would</u> decrease his pace a bit.

_____   8. He <u>had</u> some sunflower seeds in his pocket.

_____ 9. His wife, Beth, <u>had</u> placed them there.

_____ 10. Chris <u>shared</u> the sunflower seeds with the dove.

PRACTICE

A. In the following sentences, place "HV" over all helping verbs and "MV" over all main verbs.

    HV   MV
1. I have come home late each night this week.

2. The Hendersons will enjoy their vacation.

3. Allison is running in the Vancouver marathon this year.

4. Has Farzad found the answer yet?

5. You have been complaining a bit too loudly.

B. In the following sentences, write helping verbs and main verbs of your own choice as indicated.

      MV
6. Emil __*stared*__ at the mouse running across his kitchen floor.

      MV   MV
7. The glass _____ to the floor and _____ into hundreds of small pieces.

      HV   MV
8. A spider _____ slowly _____ along the wall behind my sister.

    HV   MV   HV
9. _____ you _____ the food that I _____

    MV
_____ for tonight's dinner?

          HV   HV   MV
10. The postal carrier _____ not _____ _____ so angry

      MV
when I _____ her to deliver the mail earlier.

Verbals

A fourth way to identify verbs is to recognize what they are not. Some verb forms do not actually function as verbs. These are called VERBALS. One of the most important verbals is the INFINITIVE, which usually begins with the word *to* (*to write, to be, to see*). The infinitive cannot serve as the verb of a sentence because it cannot express the time of the action or linking. *I wrote* communicates a clear idea, but *I to write* does not.

Another common verbal is the "-ing" form of the verb when it occurs without a helping verb (*running, flying, being*). When an "-ing" form without a helping verb is used as an adjective, it is called a PRESENT PARTICIPLE. When it is used as a noun, it is called a GERUND.

EXAMPLES

    MV   Verbal
I hope **to pass** this test.

    HV   MV
I **should pass** this test.

        Verbal   MV
The birds **flying** from tree to tree **chased** the cat from their nest.

        HV   MV
The birds **were flying** from tree to tree.

  Verbal   MV
Jogging is good cardiovascular exercise.

  MV
I **jog** for the cardiovascular benefits of the exercise.

PRACTICE

In the following sentences, write "HV" above all helping verbs, "MV" above all main verbs, and "Verbal" above all verbals.

           HV MV   Verbal
1. Paradise should be a good place to sleep late.

2. Climbing that steep rock, Nico might hurt his ankle.

3. Stooping only slightly, the professor spoke to the Vice President for External Student Affairs.

4. We had planned to begin before today.

5. The skateboarder running down the stairs tripped because of his loose shoelaces.

Place "HV" above all helping verbs and "MV" above all main verbs in the following sentences. Draw a line through any verbals.

         HV   MV

1. Paul had wanted ~~to finish~~ the deck before spring.

2. The aircraft workers have been organizing a protest.

3. Do the Lindsays like to sail in their new boat?

4. Sydney, Australia, has an unusual opera house.

5. The new albino tiger at the zoo has been frightening the visitors by

   leaping at the fence.

6. Mrs. Johnson was planning to get home before dark.

7. Cruising down the river, the gunboat was searching for smugglers.

8. The knight had never been challenged by such an impressive foe.

9. The campers had tried to find the lost dog.

10. Has the concert begun yet?

Identifying Subjects and Verbs

Finding the Subject

Most sentences contain several nouns and pronouns used in a variety of ways. One of the most important ways is as the subject of a verb. In order to identify which of the nouns or pronouns in a sentence is the subject, you need to identify the complete verb first. After identifying the verb, it is easy to find the subject by asking yourself "Who or what (verb)?"

            S   HV   MV

EXAMPLE   The **man** in the green hat **was following** a suspicious-looking stranger.

The complete verb in this sentence is *was following*, and when you ask yourself "Who or what was following?" the answer is "the man." Therefore, *man* is the subject.

    Remember, most sentences contain several nouns and pronouns, but not all nouns and pronouns are subjects.

EXAMPLE

                S   MV
The **people** from the **house** down the **street** often borrow our **tools**.

This sentence contains four nouns, but only *people* is the subject. The other nouns in this sentence are different types of **objects**. The noun *tools* is called a **direct object** because it receives the action of the verb *borrow*. The nouns *house* and *street* are called **objects of prepositions**. Direct objects will be discussed in Chapter Four. Objects of prepositions will be discussed later in this chapter. For now, just remember that not all nouns and pronouns are subjects.

PRACTICE

In the following sentences, place an "HV" above any helping verbs, an "MV" above the main verbs, and an "S" above the subjects.

        S   HV   MV
1. The raccoons have treated themselves to our cat's food every night.

2. Some people like to eat chocolate-covered ants.

3. Cecile might want to attend the concert for the homeless.

4. Ted spent most of his tour in Bali.

5. Their candlelight dinner for their anniversary was especially romantic

   this year.

Subject Modifiers

Words that modify or describe nouns or pronouns should not be included when you identify the subject.

EXAMPLE

            S   MV
The red **wheelbarrow is** in the yard.

The subject is *wheelbarrow*, not *the red wheelbarrow*.
    Remember that the possessive forms of nouns and pronouns are also used to describe or modify nouns, so do not include them in the subject either.

EXAMPLES

                 S   MV
My brother's **suitcase is** very worn.

        S   MV
His **textbook was** expensive.

The subjects are simply *suitcase* and *textbook*, not *my brother's suitcase* or *his textbook*.

Verb Modifiers

Just as words that describe or modify the subject are not considered part of the subject, words that describe or modify the verb are not considered part of the verb. Watch for such modifiers because they will often occur between helping verbs and main verbs and may be easily mistaken for helping verbs. Notice that in the following sentence the words *not* and *unfairly* are modifiers and, therefore, not part of the complete verb.

EXAMPLES

    S   HV   MV

Parents should **not unfairly** criticize their children.

Some common verb modifiers are *not, never, almost, just, completely, sometimes, always, often,* and *certainly.*

PRACTICE

Place "HV" over helping verbs, "MV" over main verbs, and "S" over the subjects of the following sentences.

          S   HV   MV

1. The baseball season has not started yet.

2. His Christmas card list has never changed over the years.

3. Last summer, the heat became almost unbearable.

4. During the thunderstorm, my umbrella would not open.

5. Cleaning up after the flood, we continuously searched for our collection of family videos.

Multiple Subjects and Verbs

Sentences may contain more than one subject and more than one verb.

EXAMPLES

    S   MV

Simon petted the dog.

    S   S   MV

Simon and **Mary petted** the dog.

    S   S   MV   MV

Simon and **Mary petted** the dog and **scratched** its ears.

    S   MV   S   MV

Simon petted the dog, and **Mary scratched** its ears.

    S   S   MV   S   MV

Simon and **Mary petted** the dog before **they fed** it.

Place "HV" over helping verbs, "MV" over main verbs, and "S" over subjects in the following sentences.

                    S   MV

1. After dinner, we walked downtown.

2. The wind and rain were uncomfortable.

3. Our hands and feet shook and ached from the cold.

4. I started a fire, and my friend brewed some coffee.

5. When we were comfortable again, Jim and Irving arrived.

Special Situations

Subject Understood

When a sentence is a command (or a request worded as a polite command), the pronoun *you* is understood to be the subject. *You* is the only understood subject.

             MV

EXAMPLES   **Shut** the door. (Subject is *you* understood.)

                   MV

Please **give** this book to your sister. (Subject is *you* understood.)

Verb Before Subject

In some sentences, such as in questions, the verb comes before the subject.

       MV   S

EXAMPLE   **Is** your **mother** home?

The verb also comes before the subject in sentences beginning with *there* or *here*, as well as in some other constructions.

              MV   S

EXAMPLES   There **is** a **bug** in my soup.

            MV   S

Here **is** another **bowl** of soup.

                   MV   S

Over the hill **strode** the **camel**.

                       MV   S

On the front porch **was** a **basket** with a baby in it.

PRACTICE

Place "HV" over helping verbs, "MV" over main verbs, and "S" over subjects in the following sentences. Verbals and verb modifiers should not be included in the complete verb.

       MV
1. Help me to understand the advantage of more taxes.

2. After the movie came the martial arts demonstration.

3. Will you pass the beets?

4. There is a tired camel in my backyard.

5. Spell your name for me, please.

PRACTICE

Underline all subjects once and complete verbs twice in the following sentences. Remember that the complete verb contains the main verb and all helping verbs and that verbals and verb modifiers should not be included in the complete verb.

1. You certainly wear those baggy shorts with style.

2. Pandas have been placed on the endangered species list.

3. The bicycles at that store are drastically reduced in price.

4. My father's uncle has lived all his life in Romania.

5. Did Jane really read Alice Munro's new book?

6. The guests did not leave until after midnight.

7. Avoid an unnecessary trip to Chula Vista.

8. The newscaster and the producer disagreed about how to cover the story.

9. Here are the instructions for curing the hiccups.

10. The loggers faced the prospect of another day without work.

PRACTICE

Write sentences of your own that follow the suggested patterns. Identify each subject (S), helping verb (HV), and main verb (MV).

1. A statement with one subject and two main verbs (S–MV–MV):

   <u>S   MV   MV</u>
   <u>A large black cat hopped off the fence and crept into our yard.</u>

2. A statement with two subjects and one main verb (S–S–MV):

   _____

   _____

3. A statement with one subject, one helping verb, and one main verb (S–HV–MV):

   _____

   _____

4. A question with one helping verb, one subject, and one main verb (HV–S–MV):

   _____

   _____

5. A command that begins with a main verb (MV):

   _____

   _____

6. A statement that starts with "Here" and is followed by a main verb and a subject ("Here" MV–S):

   _____

   _____

7. A statement with two subjects and two main verbs (S–S–MV–MV):

   _____

   _____

8. A statement with one subject, one helping verb, and one main verb followed by "when" and another subject and another main verb (S–HV–MV "when" S–MV):

    _____

    _____

9. A statement with a subject, a helping verb, and a main verb, followed by ", but" and another subject, helping verb, and main verb (S–HV–MV ", but" S–HV–MV):

    _____

    _____

10. A statement with a subject, a helping verb, and a main verb followed by "if" and another subject and a main verb (S–HV–MV "if" S–MV):

    _____

    _____

    _____

Section One Review

1. A noun names a person, place, thing, or idea.

   a. **Proper nouns** name specific persons, places, things, or ideas. They begin with a capital letter. **Common nouns** name more general categories and are not capitalized.

   b. *A, an*, and *the* are noun markers. A noun always follows one of these words.

   c. If you are unsure whether or not a word is a noun, ask yourself if it could be introduced with *a, an,* or *the*.

   d. Words that end in *ment, ism, ness, ence, ance,* and *tion* are usually nouns.

2. A **pronoun** takes the place of a noun.

3. A **verb** either shows action or links the subject to another word.

4. Verbs appear in different **tenses** to show the time when the action or linking takes place.

5. The **complete verb** includes a main verb and any helping verbs.

6. **Verbals** are verb forms that do not function as verbs.

   a. The **infinitive** is a verbal that begins with the word to.

   b. The "-ing" form of the verb without a helping verb is called a **present participle** if it is used as an adjective.

   c. The "-ing" form of the verb without a helping verb is called a **gerund** if it is used as a noun.

7. To identify the **subject** of any sentence, first find the verb. Then ask "Who or what (verb)?"

8. **Subject modifiers** describe or modify the subject. They should not be included when you identify the subject.

9. **Verb modifiers** describe or modify verbs. They are not considered part of the verb.

10. Sentences may contain **multiple subjects** and **multiple verbs**.

11. When a sentence is a command (or a request worded as a polite command), the pronoun *you* is understood as the subject. *You* is the only understood subject.

12. In some sentences the verb comes before the subject.

EXERCISE

Exercise 1A

In the spaces provided, indicate whether the underlined word is a subject (write "S"), a helping verb (write "HV"), or a main verb (write "MV"). If it is none of these, leave the space blank.

1. ___MV___ Jack <u>scorched</u> his armadillo-and-beet soup.

2. _____ The youthful thief dropped the <u>money</u> and ran.

3. _____ The <u>constable</u> wrote down the license plate number of the vehicle.

4. _____ The fire <u>burned</u> brightly in the large fireplace.

5. _____ The marble <u>arches</u> framed the entrance to the museum.

6. _____ Through his <u>window</u> the boy could see the moon.

7. _____ Before sunrise the loons <u>began</u> to call their mates.

8. _____ The coach <u>was</u> obviously angry when she addressed her players.

9. _____ Even if you <u>have</u> already eaten, you must try my escargot.

10. _____ The <u>door</u> opened suddenly, and a well-dressed robot entered the room.

11. _____ Frustrated by the bad weather, <u>Icarus</u> cancelled his flight.

12. _____ The young boy was stubborn and <u>gave</u> his parents a great deal of trouble.

13. _____ <u>Somebody</u> left Nizar off the party invitation list.

14. _____ The students <u>learned</u> quickly how to use the new computer.

15. _____ If the key <u>is</u> not found in time, we will miss *Wrestling Mania*.

Exercise 1B

A. Underline all subjects once and complete verbs twice in the following sentences. Remember that a sentence may have more than one subject and more than one verb.

1. Two <u>outfielders</u> <u><u>were running</u></u> after the fly ball.

2. Has the writer finished his novel yet?

3. The victims should have acted ignorant.

4. Out of the fog loomed a huge battleship.

5. The bride smiled, but the groom was trembling slightly.

6. His only brother lived in Winnipeg and never visited him.

7. Nick had been playing classical guitar for five years.

8. Private golf or skiing lessons are expensive, but they are well worth the price.

9. Because Laszlo could hit a baseball long distances, he made millions of dollars.

10. Mansour's uncle is known to be very rich.

B. Write sentences of your own that follow the suggested patterns. Identify each subject (S), helping verb (HV), and main verb (MV).

11. A statement with two subjects and one main verb (S–S–MV):

              S   S   MV
    <u>The baseball player and his agent decided to meet for lunch.</u>

12. A statement with one subject, one helping verb, and one main verb (S–HV–MV):

    _____

    _____

13. A question that begins with a main verb followed by the subject (MV–S):

    _____

    _____

14. A statement with a subject, two helping verbs, and one main verb
(S–HV–HV–MV):

_____

_____

15. A statement with a subject and main verb followed by a comma and
"but" and another subject and main verb (S–MV, "but" S–MV):

_____

_____

EXERCISE

Exercise 1C

In the following paragraph, underline all subjects once and complete verbs twice.

1. During World War II, a Chinese <u>seaman</u> <u><u>experienced</u></u> one of the most amazing survival adventures of the war. **2.** He survived alone for 133 days aboard a small life raft in the South Atlantic. **3.** On November 23, 1942, Poon Lim's ordeal began when his ship was torpedoed by a German submarine 565 miles off the coast of Africa. **4.** After he was thrown overboard, Poon Lim watched as his ship and its passengers disappeared into the sea. **5.** He had been swimming for two hours when he saw a wooden raft bobbing in the wreckage. **6.** He crawled into the raft. **7.** It was eight feet square and held a few tins of biscuits, a container of water, a flashlight, and a rope. **8.** These few rations lasted only sixty days before he was forced to improvise. **9.** To catch small fish, he made a hook from a wire spring from the flashlight, and then he attached some hemp from a rope to the hook. **10.** Sometimes he used bits of fish to lure sea gulls, which he caught and killed with his bare hands. **11.** His life jacket provided him with material to make a receptacle to catch rain water. **12.** To keep physically fit, Poon swam in the ocean daily. **13.** On April 5, 1943, after Poon Lim had survived by his own ingenuity for 133 days, a fishing boat off Brazil picked him up. **14.** Poon Lim's rescuers were amazed because he had lost only twenty pounds from his five-foot-five frame and could walk without aid. **15.** Because his survival was such a feat, Poon Lim was awarded the British Empire Medal. **16.** Poon Lim's record of 133 days alone on a raft still stands today.

Section Two

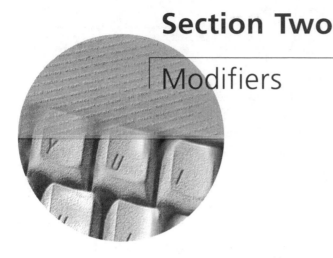

Modifiers

Subjects and verbs form the backbone of sentences, but many other words appear in a sentence and serve a variety of purposes. One such group of words includes **the modifiers**, which limit, describe, intensify, or otherwise alter the meaning of other words. The word *modify* simply means "change." Notice, for instance, how the modifiers change the meaning of *power* in each of the following sentences.

The dictator had **total** power.

The dictator had **great** power.

The dictator had **little** power.

The dictator had **no** power.

As you can see, the word *power* is significantly changed by the different modifiers in these sentences.

Although modifiers can change the meaning of words in many different ways, there are basically only two types of modifiers, ADJECTIVES and ADVERBS. You will be able to identify both types of modifiers more easily if you remember these three points:

1. *Sentences often contain more than one modifier.*

EXAMPLE   The **new** moon rose **slowly** over the desert.

In this example, the word *new* modifies *moon*; it describes the specific phase of the moon. The word *slowly* modifies *rose*; it describes the speed with which the moon rose. The arrows point from the modifiers to the words being modified.

2. *Two or more modifiers can be used to modify the same word.*

EXAMPLE   The moon rose **slowly** and **dramatically** over the desert.

In this example the words *slowly* and *dramatically* both modify *rose*. *Slowly* describes the speed, and *dramatically* describes the manner in which the moon rose.

3. *All modifiers must modify something.* You should be able to identify the specific word that is being modified as well as the modifier itself.

EXAMPLE   **Slowly** the **new** moon rose over the desert.

In this example, notice that the word *slowly* still modifies *rose*, though the two words are not close to each other.

PRACTICE

Draw an arrow from the underlined modifier to the word it modifies.

1. Merchants <u>once</u> sold <u>pink</u> ducklings at Easter.

2. My uncle is <u>wealthy</u> and <u>generous</u>.

3. Simone <u>sometimes</u> works <u>eighteen</u> hours on Saturdays.

4. The <u>fur</u> coat was <u>warm</u>.

5. <u>Huge</u> chunks of hail <u>steadily</u> rattled on the roof.

Adjectives

An adjective modifies a noun or a pronoun. In English most adjectives precede the noun they modify.

DEFINITION | adjective | An adjective modifies a noun or pronoun. |

EXAMPLE   The **young** eagle perched on the **rocky** cliff.

In this example, the word *young* **modifies** *eagle*, and the word *rocky* **modifies** *cliff*.

Although most adjectives precede the noun or pronoun they modify, they may also follow the noun or pronoun and be connected to it by a linking verb.

EXAMPLE   **Poisonous** plants are **dangerous**.

In this example, the word *poisonous* describes the noun *plants*. Notice that it **precedes** the noun. However, the word *dangerous* also describes the noun *plants*. It is **linked** to the noun by the linking verb *are*. Both *poisonous* and *dangerous* are adjectives that modify the noun *plants*.

Many different types of words can be adjectives, as long as they modify a noun or pronoun. Most adjectives answer the questions which? what kind? or how many? Here are the most common types of adjectives.

1. *Descriptive words*

E X A M P L E S   I own a **blue** suit.

That is an **ugly** wound.

2. *The words a, an, and the*

E X A M P L E   **An** apple and **a** pear fell to **the** floor.

3. *Possessive nouns and pronouns*

E X A M P L E   I parked **my** motorcycle next to **John's** car.

4. *Limiting words and numbers*

E X A M P L E S   **Some** people see **every** movie that comes out.

Two accidents have happened on **this** street.

5. *Nouns that modify other nouns*

E X A M P L E   The **basketball** game was held in the **neighbourhood** gym.

PRACTICE

A. In the following sentences, circle all adjectives and draw an arrow to the noun or pronoun each adjective modifies.

1. (Strange) wildcats have appeared on (our) (front) lawn recently.

2. The baseball season began last April.

3. Five grey pelicans glided above the busy beach.

4. After their morning paper had been stolen for the third time, Sharon and her husband decided to cancel their subscription.

5. Last Christmas Ming wanted a cowboy hat and some black socks with purple clocks on them.

B. Add two adjectives of your own (other than *a*, *an*, or *the*) to each of the following sentences.

                                        dusty   *broken*

6. The garage was filled with ∧boxes and ∧tools.

7. Snow fell from the sky and covered our lawn.

8. Mr. Medina pointed his finger at the stranger wearing a mask.

9. The aroma from the ham in the oven filled the kitchen.

10. People were worried about the fog that had blanketed our city for

      days.

Adverbs

An adverb modifies a verb, adjective, or another adverb. Adverbs are sometimes more difficult to recognize than adjectives because they can be used to modify three different types of words—verbs, adjectives, and other adverbs. They can either precede or follow the words they modify and are sometimes placed farther away from the words they modify than are adjectives.

DEFINITION

adverb	An adverb modifies a verb, adjective, or another verb.

EXAMPLES

                  Adv

The president **quickly** walked across the room.

The president walked **quickly** across the room.

The president walked across the room **quickly**. (adverb modifying a verb)

                Adv   Adv

The president seemed **unusually** nervous. (adverb modifying an adjective)

           Adv   Adv

The president left **very** quickly after the press conference. (adverb modifying an adverb)

    Because adverbs are often formed by adding "ly" to adjectives such as *quick* or *usual*, many adverbs end in "ly" (*quickly* and *usually*). However, you cannot always use this ending as a way of identifying adverbs because some words that end in "ly" are *not* adverbs and because some adverbs do not end in "ly," as the following list of common adverbs illustrates:

already	now	still
also	often	then
always	quite	too
never	seldom	very
not	soon	well

Here are two ways to help you identify adverbs:

1. *Find the word that is being modified.* If it is a verb, adjective, or adverb, then the modifier is an adverb.

E X A M P L E   Thelma **seriously** injured her finger during the tennis match.

My brother and I have **completely** different attitudes toward tennis.

Sophie **almost** always arrives on time for work.

2. *Look for words that answer the questions* **when? where? how? or to what extent?**

E X A M P L E S   My grandparents **often** bring gifts when they visit. (**when?**)

The turnips were grown **locally**. (**where?**)

Rachel **carefully** removed the paint from the antique desk. (**how?**)

Homer is **widely** known as a trainer in a flea circus. (**to what extent?**)

NOTE: *Adverbs are not considered part of the complete verb, even if they come between the helping verb and the main verb. Some common adverbs that come between the helping verb and the main verb are* not, never, ever, already, *and* just.

HV Adv   MV

E X A M P L E   He has **not** failed to do his duty.

PRACTICE

A. In the following sentences, circle all adverbs and draw an arrow to the word that each adverb modifies.

1. The detective (quietly) stepped into the corridor and (slowly) raised his revolver.

2. She quite certainly knew that she would never go to Medicine Hat with that man.

3. The praying mantis sometimes practises a rather brutal mating rite.

4. The guitar player leaped deftly onto a speaker and frantically shook his long hair.

5. Sophocles stared tragically at his completely blank tablet.

B. Add one adverb of your own to each of the following sentences.

slowly

6. The full moon moved ∧ across the sky.

7. Kathy visits her father on Saturdays.

8. The shutters creaked as they swung in the wind.

9. Jean gazed into Walter's bloodshot eyes.

10. The lake glistened in the sunlight as we rowed our boat across it.

Section Two Review

1. **Modifiers** limit, describe, intensify, or otherwise alter the meaning of other words.
   a. Sentences often contain more than one modifier.
   b. Two or more modifiers can be used to modify the same word.
   c. All modifiers must modify *something*.

2. An **adjective** modifies a noun or a pronoun.

3. Most adjectives answer the questions **which? what kind?** or **how many?**

4. Common types of adjectives are the following:
   a. *Descriptive words*
   b. *The words **a**, **an**, and **the***
   c. *Possessive nouns and pronouns*
   d. *Limiting words and numbers*
   e. *Nouns that modify other nouns*

5. An **adverb** modifies a verb, adjective, or another adverb.

6. There are two ways to identify adverbs:
   a. *Find the word that is being modified. If it is a verb, adjective, or adverb, then the modifier is an adverb.*
   b. *Look for words that answer the questions **when? where? how?** or **to what extent?***

EXERCISE

Exercise 2A

In the following sentences, write "Adj" above all adjectives and "Adv" above all adverbs. For extra practice, underline all subjects once and all verbs twice.

                     Adj Adj   Adv
1. <u>Michelle</u> <u><u>played</u></u> her new saxophone intensely.

2. From his pocket he carefully pulled a tattered old map.

3. Our company was quite successful this year.

4. The dirty snow covered the city's streets.

5. The painful decision did not bother the brave contestant.

6. The curtain slowly rose, and the young actress graciously accepted a bouquet of beautiful red roses.

7. The grey heron landed gracefully on the top of a tall pine.

8. Alaine was unhappy with the judge's decision and protested angrily.

9. Gary Payton leaped incredibly high but nearly missed his shot.

10. The sailor often said that he would never re-enlist.

11. The young candidate walked confidently onto the platform and began her speech.

12. The salesman spoke rapidly and enthusiastically about his new product.

13. Three police officers on yellow rollerblades glided easily among the crowd.

14. His uncertain future stretched ominously before him.

15. The normally quiet child cried loudly because he was hungry.

EXERCISE

Exercise 2B

A. Add two adjectives to each of the following sentences. Try to think of adjectives that make the sentence more colourful or descriptive.

EXAMPLE

enraged   terrified

The ∧ bull charged toward the ∧ spectators.

1. The wrestler decided to quit his profession.

2. The rancher and his daughter rode into town.

3. On the street the people walked in front of the stores.

4. The tractor was sitting near the fence.

5. The surfer turned and paddled his board toward the wave.

B. Add an adverb to each of the following sentences. Again, try to make the sentence more colourful or descriptive by your addition.

EXAMPLE

cautiously

The guide ∧ led the group along the trail.

6. He walked into the store and demanded service.

7. The shortstop grabbed her bat and walked up to home plate.

8. Because he was hungry and cold, he went home.

9. The hippopotamus waded into the river and rolled over on its back.

10. Through the night the wind howled.

C. Add an adjective and an adverb to each of the following sentences.

EXAMPLE

carefully   wooden

Gipetto worked ∧ on the ∧ shoes all night.

11. Twenty thousand fans cheered as the ball sailed into the stands.

12. In cities people have difficulty finding housing.

13. The coach gathered her players around her to tell them how to improve their performance.

14. The engineers were angry because they believed that the building was unsafe.

15. Near the pier the sailors stood in a group and discussed the voyage.

EXERCISE

Exercise 2C

In the following sentences, identify each of the underlined words as noun (N), pronoun (Pro), verb (V), adjective (Adj), or adverb (Adv).

1. In 1984 China was emerging from twenty $\overset{\text{N}}{\underline{\text{years}}}$ of economic and political upheaval, and $\overset{\text{Pro}}{\underline{\text{you}}}$ would have found few foreigners in the country. **2.** They lived in hotels and could not <u>travel</u> out of clearly <u>defined</u> sectors. **3.** It <u>was</u> in that very year that a young Canadian named Michael Buckley and <u>his</u> friend Robert <u>decided</u> to ride bicycles halfway across China, from Shanghai to Xian. **4.** <u>Chinese</u> officials informed <u>them</u> they could travel only by the main road during the day, and they <u>had</u> to register at a hotel in a <u>large</u> city by nightfall. **5.** It was forbidden for a foreigner to be out at <u>night</u>. **6.** For a while <u>everything</u> was fine, except for the heat, <u>muddy</u> roads, flies, and <u>hordes</u> of peasants who, never having seen a foreigner, <u>crowded</u> around them at every pit stop. **7.** Once, <u>darkness</u> fell on them when they were 90 kilometres from their destination, Kaifeng, and they <u>had</u> to hide out in a <u>wheatfield</u>. **8.** Shortly after that, it <u>began</u> to rain hard. **9.** They spent <u>several</u> days in a hotel in Kaifeng waiting for the rains to stop. **10.** All the <u>way</u> to the next city, Zhengzhou, they <u>pedalled</u> their way through <u>waterlogged</u> roads. **11.** After the <u>storms</u>, the heat intensified <u>quickly</u> as they climbed into the <u>mountains</u>. **12.** Just before reaching Xian, they stopped to visit the Tomb of the Terracotta Warriors, which was <u>discovered</u> in 1974 and <u>contains</u> over six thousand full-sized <u>clay</u> soldiers. **13.** In Xian they sold <u>their</u> bicycles and travelled by <u>rail</u> and truck to Lhasa, the capital of <u>Tibet</u>. **14.** There, they made <u>plans</u> to <u>cycle</u> from Lhasa up over the <u>top</u> of the Himalayas and <u>down</u> to Katmandu.

Section Three

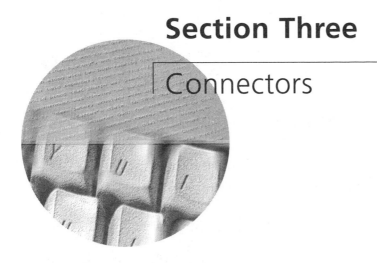

Connectors

The final group of words consists of the connectors. These are signal words that indicate the relationship of one part of a sentence to another. The two types of connectors are **conjunctions** and **prepositions**.

Conjunctions

A conjunction joins two parts of a sentence. The word *conjunction* is derived from two Latin words meaning "to join with." The definition is easy to remember if you know that the word *junction* in English refers to the place where two roads come together.

DEFINITION | conjunction | A conjunction joins two parts of a sentence.

The two types of conjunctions are **coordinating** and **subordinating**. In Chapter Two we will discuss the subordinating conjunctions. You will find it much easier to distinguish between the two types if you memorize the coordinating conjunctions now.

The **coordinating conjunctions** are *and, but, or, nor, for, yet,* and *so.*

NOTE: An easy way to learn the coordinating conjunctions is to remember that their first letters can spell **BOYSFAN** *(But Or Yet So For And Nor).*

Coordinating conjunctions join elements of the sentence that are *equal* or *parallel.* For instance, they may join two subjects, two verbs, two adjectives, or two parallel groups of words.

EXAMPLE
    S   Conj   S   MV   Conj   MV
Robin **and** Batman often disagree **but** never fight each other.

In this example the first conjunction joins two subjects and the second conjunction joins two verbs.

                       S   MV   Adj   Conj   Adj   Conj   MV
E X A M P L E   Setsuko often felt awkward **or** uncomfortable **yet** never showed it.

In this example the first conjunction joins two adjectives, and the second joins two verbs.

Coordinating conjunctions may even be used to join two entire sentences, each with its own subject and verb.

                      S   HV MV   S   MV
E X A M P L E   The rain had fallen steadily all week long. The river was close to overflowing.

                      S   HV MV   Conj   S   MV
The rain had fallen steadily all week long, **so** the river was close to overflowing.

Notice that the coordinating conjunctions have different meanings and that changing the conjunction can significantly change the meaning of a sentence. *A person should never drink **and** drive* communicates a very different idea from *A person should never drink **or** drive*.

• The conjunction *and* indicates **addition.**

E X A M P L E   Jules **and** Jim loved the same woman.

• The conjunctions *but* and *yet* indicate **contrast.**

E X A M P L E S   She wanted to go **but** didn't have the money.

I liked Brian, **yet** I didn't really trust him.

• The conjunctions *or* and *nor* indicate **alternatives.**

E X A M P L E S   You can borrow the record **or** the tape.

He felt that he could neither go **nor** stay.

• The conjunctions *for* and *so* indicate **cause** or **result.**

E X A M P L E S   The plants died, **for** they had not been watered.

Her brother lost his job, **so** he had to find another.

PRACTICE

A. In the following sentences, circle all coordinating conjunctions. Underline all subjects once and all complete verbs twice.

1. The <u>cook</u> (or) the <u>waiter</u> <u><u>will clear</u></u> the tables.

2. Ed did not know the difference between inflation and recession, but he had no trouble balancing his chequebook.

3. The musicians in the band could not play in tune or together, yet the audience did not seem to mind at all.

4. The rhinoceros charged Martin, so he jumped behind his wife.

5. The sports car was flashy yet practical, so Sylvia decided to buy it.

B. In the following sentences, add coordinating conjunctions that show the relationship indicated in parentheses.

6. We can go to the baseball game, _____*or*_____ we can see a movie, but we can't do both. (alternatives)

7. Laura loves to eat steak, _____ Chad never eats any beef at all. (contrast)

8. The cat grabbed the toy mouse _____ carried it into the back-yard. (addition)

9. Rico was irritated at the mail order company _____ he had never received what he had ordered. (cause)

10. Fog covered the airport, _____ the plane could not land. (result)

Prepositions

A preposition relates a noun or a pronoun to some other word in the sentence. Prepositions usually indicate a relationship of **place** (in, near), **direction** (toward, from), **time** (after, until), or **condition** (of, without).

DEFINITION

| preposition | A preposition relates a noun or pronoun to some other word in the sentence. |

EXAMPLE

Prep
He fired the puck **toward** the goal.

Notice how the preposition *toward* shows the relationship (direction) between *fired the puck* and *goal*. If you change prepositions, you change the relationship.

EXAMPLES

Prep
He fired the puck **near** the goal.

Prep
He fired the puck **across** the goal.

Prep
He fired the puck **into** the goal.

Here are some of the most common prepositions:

above	before	for	on	under
across	behind	from	onto	until
after	below	in	over	up
among	beside	in spite of	past	upon
around	between	into	through	with
as	by	like	till	without
at	during	near	to	because of
except	of	toward		

NOTE: For *can be used as a coordinating conjunction, but it is most commonly used as a preposition.* **To** *can also be used as part of an infinitive, in which case it is not a preposition.*

PRACTICE

Write "Prep" above the prepositions in the following sentences.

1. Mr. Duong sat in the waiting room and thought about his wife.
   <small>*Prep* .... *Prep*</small>

2. We parked and walked across the street to the Vietnamese restaurant.

3. During the hurricane the police led people to shelters.

4. Roland saw a scorpion under the stairs near his baby sister.

5. Most of the archers shot their arrows into their own feet.

Prepositional Phrases

The word *preposition* is derived from two Latin words meaning "to put in front." The two parts of the word (pre + position) indicate how prepositions usually function. They are almost always used as the first words in **prepositional phrases**.

A prepositional phrase consists of a preposition plus a noun or a pronoun, called the object of the preposition. This object is almost always the last word of the prepositional phrase. Between the preposition and its object, the prepositional phrase may also contain adjectives, adverbs, or conjunctions. A preposition may have more than one object.

DEFINITION

prepositional phrase	Preposition + Object (noun or pronoun) = Prepositional Phrase.

EXAMPLES

Prep   Obj
after a short **lunch**

Prep   Obj   Obj
with his very good **friend** and his **brother**

Prep Obj   Obj
to you and **her**

Prep   Obj
through the long and dismal **night**

Although prepositions themselves are considered connectors, prepositional *phrases* actually act as modifiers. They may function as adjectives, modifying a noun or pronoun, or they may function as adverbs, modifying a verb.

EXAMPLES

The cat **(from next door)** caught a gopher.

The burglar jumped **(from the window)**.

In the first example, the prepositional phrase functions as an adjective, modifying the noun *cat*, and in the second example, the prepositional phrase functions as an adverb, modifying the verb *jumped*.

NOTE: *If you can recognize prepositional phrases, you will be able to identify subjects and verbs more easily **because neither the subject nor the verb of a sentence can be part of a prepositional phrase.***

In the following sentence it is difficult at first glance to determine which of the many nouns is the subject.

In a cave near the village, a member of the archaeological team found a stone axe from an ancient civilization.

If you first eliminate the prepositional phrases, however, the true subject becomes apparent.

                                               S
(In a cave) (near the village), a member (of the archaeological team)

     MV
found a stone axe (from an ancient civilization).

PRACTICE

A. Place parentheses around the prepositional phrases and write "Prep" above all prepositions and "Obj" above the objects of the prepositions.

   Prep   Obj Prep Obj
1. The Trembleys walked (through the streets) (of Florence.)

2. By the river they found an ancient coin in the shallow water.

3. Near him on a dirty bench, an old pigeon stared at Brad.

4. Blinded by his love for Michelle, Nizar lost his sense of balance.

5. Abner Snopes looked for his matches and found them under the rug.

B. Add two prepositional phrases to each of the following sentences.

        from China   in the morning
6. The students ∧ will visit the zoo ∧ .

7. A long snake moved slowly.

8. Ginger grabbed the orange and threw it.

9. The brush fire approached the house.

10. Everyone has seen the latest movie.

Section Three Review

1. A **conjunction** joins two parts of a sentence.

2. The **coordinating conjunctions** are *and, but, or, nor, for, yet,* and *so.*

3. A **preposition** relates a noun or pronoun to some other word in the sentence.

4. A **prepositional phrase** consists of a **preposition** plus a noun or a pronoun, called the **object of the preposition**.

5. Neither the subject nor the verb of a sentence can be part of a prepositional phrase.

EXERCISE

Exercise 3A

Place all prepositional phrases in parentheses and circle all conjunctions. For additional practice, underline all subjects once and all complete verbs twice.

1. <u>Silvie</u> (and) three <u>teammates</u> <u>drove</u> (to the orphanage.)

2. The fugitive and his children have not been seen for several months.

3. The maple leaf in the middle of the flag is the national symbol.

4. A total of thirty thousand people saw that play, but not one of them liked it.

5. Below the water a strange fish had attached itself to the sailboat.

6. The manager took the papers from his desk and placed them in a filing cabinet.

7. The old house had been empty for twenty years.

8. The witness must have been telling the truth, for he had passed the lie detector test.

9. After the trial, Chen talked to his son.

10. The lawyer took the contract from his briefcase and examined it.

11. On his back was a tattoo of Wonder Woman with her magic lasso.

12. The city planned to redevelop its downtown, but the provincial government refused to provide funds for the project.

13. Her bookshelves probably contained the finest collection of first editions of Mavis Gallant and Emily Dickinson.

14. No one respected the president of that company because of his greed and dishonesty.

15. Sharon had searched all day for her lost schedule book, but she had found nothing except two misplaced business receipts.

EXERCISE

Exercise 3B

Add two prepositional phrases to each of the following sentences.

EXAMPLE   Suddenly a man ᴧ appeared ᴧ .

(above: in a pink tuxedo   at the door)

1. The shaggy elk crossed the road.

2. The surprised man turned.

3. Melodie liked the book.

4. Farzad enthusiastically taught humanities.

5. The happy woman drove her car.

In each of the spaces below, construct a sentence using the coordinating conjunction indicated. Include at least one prepositional phrase in each sentence. Place prepositional phrases in parentheses.

6. (and) _____

_____

7. (or) _____

_____

8. (nor) _____

_____

9. (for) _____

_____

10. (so) _____

_____

11. (but) _____

_____

12. (yet) _____

_____

EXERCISE

Exercise 3C

In the following sentences, identify each of the underlined words as noun (N), pronoun (Pro), verb (V), adjective (Adj), adverb (Adv), conjunction (Conj), or preposition (Prep).

1. On March 25, 1944, Nicholas Alkemade reserved a place for <u>himself</u> [Pro] in <u>aviation</u> [Adj] history. 2. He was in the tail of a plane flying at 5.5 km when the plane was hit by anti-aircraft <u>fire</u>. 3. Alkemade <u>looked</u> for his parachute only to find that he could <u>not</u> reach it because the plane was on fire. 4. He knew that he had <u>two</u> choices: burn alive in the tail of the plane or jump out without his parachute. 5. Believing he would be unconscious before he hit the ground, he <u>decided</u> to jump out. 6. As he plummeted <u>toward</u> the ground, he <u>had</u> no sensation of falling. 7. In fact, he <u>later</u> said that he felt as if he were floating on a soft cloud up to the <u>point</u> when he passed out. 8. Moments after he had jumped from the plane, Alkemade's <u>unconscious</u> body was falling <u>to</u> the earth at a speed of 200 km per hour. 9. However, before he hit the ground, Alkemade crashed into a forest of <u>fir</u> trees where thick branches broke <u>his</u> fall. 10. Then, below the trees, he came to rest in half a metre of soft snow that <u>acted as</u> a cushion. 11. When he <u>finally</u> regained <u>consciousness</u> several hours later, Alkemade was being cared for by a German patrol. 12. He told <u>them</u> his incredible story, <u>but</u> they did not believe that he had fallen from a plane without a parachute. 13. After all, Alkemade had <u>very</u> little to show as a <u>result</u> of his 5.5 km fall. 14. He had a burned hand, a strained back, a <u>scalp</u> wound, <u>and</u> a twisted knee. 15. Nicholas Alkemade's story was later verified, and his fall <u>became</u> part of the folklore <u>of</u> aviation history.

REVIEW

Chapter One Review

Remember that each sentence must contain at least one subject and one verb. Once you have identified the verb, you can find the subject simply by asking yourself "Who or what _(verb)_?" The subjects, of course, will always be nouns, pronouns, or words that function as nouns.

Remember also that the names of the various types of words describe how a word functions in a sentence. Many words can function in various ways, depending on how they are used in a particular sentence. For instance, the word *light* can be used as a noun, a verb, or an adjective.

EXAMPLES

Sarah turned on the <u>light</u> above her bed. (noun)

At dusk the campers <u>light</u> a fire. (verb)

He preferred <u>light</u> meals in the summer. (adjective)

Similarly, the word *for* can serve either as a preposition or as a coordinating conjunction.

EXAMPLES

The lawyer did not take the case just <u>for</u> the money. (preposition)

She left early, <u>for</u> she hated to be late. (conjunction)

PRACTICE

Identify the underlined words by writing one of the following abbreviations in the blank: noun (N), pronoun (Pro), verb (V), adjective (Adj), adverb (Adv), conjunction (Conj), preposition (Prep).

___V___ 1. The continual disruptions <u>anger</u> the musicians.

___N___ His <u>anger</u> was sometimes uncontrollable.

_____ 2. The <u>throw</u> from the catcher was not in time.

_____ The Andersons <u>throw</u> wonderful parties.

_____ 3. He would always <u>brown</u> the mushrooms in butter before serving them.

_____ The <u>brown</u> horse looked much faster than the black one.

_____ <u>Brown</u> was the colour of my true love's hair.

_____ 4. The doctor has not arrived <u>yet</u>.

_____ He needed a vacation, <u>yet</u> he didn't have the time.

_____ 5. John's older sisters <u>like</u> to tease him.

_____ The room was small and smelled <u>like</u> an old sock.

_____ 6. Using your knife that way will <u>dull</u> the blade.

_____ The movie was so <u>dull</u> that Peter fell asleep.

_____ 7. Mr. Jackson asked his lawyer to draw up a new <u>will</u>.

_____ Mansour <u>will</u> leave for Ottawa as soon as possible

_____ 8. The surgeon was <u>so</u> exhausted he could hardly finish his last operation.

_____ She wanted to save money, <u>so</u> she decided to repair the car herself.

_____ 9. He knew that one day his <u>past</u> would be discovered.

_____ The <u>past</u> weeks have been very difficult for Marie.

_____ 10. The soldier's <u>wound</u> quickly became infected.

_____ Words may <u>wound</u> a person more deeply than a knife will.

Section Four

Sentence Practice: Embedding Adjectives, Adverbs, and Prepositional Phrases

You have now learned to identify the basic parts of a sentence, but this skill itself is not very useful unless you can **use** it to compose clear and effective sentences. Obviously, you have some flexibility when you compose sentences, but that flexibility is far from unlimited. The following sentence has a subject, a verb, five modifiers, one conjunction, and two prepositional phrases, but it makes no sense at all.

> Architect the quickly president for the drew up building new and plans the them to showed company.

With the parts arranged in a more effective order, the sentence, of course, makes sense.

> The architect quickly drew up plans for the new building and showed them to the company president.

There is no single correct pattern for the English sentence. The patterns you choose will be determined by the facts and ideas you wish to convey. For any given set of facts and ideas, there will be only a few effective sentence patterns and an enormous number of ineffective ones. Knowing the parts of the sentence and how they function will help you choose the most effective patterns to communicate your thoughts.

Assume, for example, that you have four facts to communicate:

1. *Moby Dick* was written by Herman Melville.
2. *Moby Dick* is a famous novel.
3. *Moby Dick* is about a whale.
4. The whale is white.

You could combine all these facts into a single sentence:

> *Moby Dick* was written by Herman Melville, and *Moby Dick* is a famous novel, and *Moby Dick* is about a whale, and the whale is white.

Although this sentence is grammatically correct, it is repetitious and sounds foolish.

If you choose the key fact from each sentence and combine the facts in the order in which they are presented, the result is not much better:

Moby Dick was written by Herman Melville, a famous novel about a whale white.

A much more effective approach is to choose the sentence that expresses the fact or idea you think is most important and to use that as your base sentence. Of course, the sentence you choose as the base sentence may vary depending upon the fact or idea you think is most important, but, whichever sentence you choose, it should contain the essential fact or idea that the other sentences somehow modify or explain. Once you have found the base sentence, you can embed the other facts or ideas into it as adjectives, adverbs, and prepositional phrases.

For example, let's use "*Moby Dick* is a famous novel" as the **base sentence** since it states an essential fact about *Moby Dick*—that it is a famous novel. The idea in sentence number one can now be embedded into the base sentence as a **prepositional phrase**:

> by Herman Melville
> *Moby Dick* ∧ is a famous novel.

The idea in sentence three can then be embedded into the expanded base sentence as another **prepositional phrase**:

> about a whale
> *Moby Dick* by Herman Melville is a famous novel ∧ .

Finally, sentence number four contains an adjective that modifies the noun *whale*, so it can be embedded into the sentence by placing it before *whale*:

> white
> *Moby Dick* by Herman Melville is a famous novel about a ∧ whale.

Thus, your final sentence will read:

Moby Dick by Herman Melville is a famous novel about a white whale.

The same facts could be embedded in a number of other ways. Two of them are:

Moby Dick, a famous novel by Herman Melville, is about a white whale.

Herman Melville's *Moby Dick* is a famous novel about a white whale.

This process of embedding is called **sentence combining.** The purpose of practising sentence combining is to give you an opportunity to apply the grammatical concepts you have learned in the chapter. For instance, in the above example the base sentence was expanded into a more interesting sentence by means of prepositional phrases and an adjective. Practising this process will also help you develop greater flexibility in your sentence structure and will show you how to enrich your sentences through the addition of significant details. After all, the use of specific details is one of the most important ways of making writing interesting and effective. Now let us practise!

PRACTICE

a. The farmer was old.

b. The farmer waited in front of the bank.

c. The farmer was in overalls.

d. The overalls were faded.

e. The farmer was patient.

1. In the space below, write the base sentence, the one with the main idea.

_____

_____

2. Embed the **adjective** from sentence A into the base sentence by placing it before the noun that it modifies.

_____

_____

3. Embed the **prepositional phrase** from sentence C into the sentence by placing it after the word that it modifies.

_____

_____

4. Embed the **adjective** from sentence D into the sentence by placing it before the noun that it modifies.

_____

5. Change the **adjective** in sentence E into an **adverb** (add "ly") and embed it into the sentence by placing it after the verb that it modifies.

_____

_____

EXERCISE

Sentence Combining: Exercise A

In each of the following sets of sentences, use the first sentence as the base sentence. Embed into the base sentence the adjectives, adverbs, and prepositional phrases underlined in the sentences below it.

EXAMPLE

a. A man strode into the nightclub.

b. The man was <u>young</u>.

c. He was <u>in a bright orange bathrobe</u>.

d. He strode <u>confidently</u>.

e. The nightclub was <u>fashionable</u>.

A young man in a bright orange bathrobe strode confidently into the

fashionable nightclub.

1. a.   The editor fired the reporter.

b.   The editor was <u>enraged</u>.

c.   The reporter was <u>incompetent</u>.

_____

_____

2. a.   The thunder frightened the children.

b.   The thunder was <u>deafening</u>.

c.   The children were <u>in the house</u>.

d.   The house was <u>next door</u>.

_____

_____

3. a.   The town used to be a vacation spot.

b.   The town is <u>empty</u>.

c.   The town is <u>in the middle of the Prairies</u>.

d.   The vacation spot was <u>popular</u>.

_____

_____

4. a.   The bullfighter waved his cape.
   b.   The bullfighter was waving <u>at the bull</u>.
   c.   The bullfighter was <u>young</u>.
   d.   The bullfighter was <u>in the arena</u>.
   e.   The bull was <u>angry</u>.

   _____

   _____

5. a.   The room contained a painting.
   b.   The room was <u>in the gallery</u>.
   c.   It was the <u>smallest</u> room.
   d.   It was a <u>new</u> gallery.
   e.   The painting was <u>of a man</u>.
   f.   It was a man <u>with one ear</u>.

   _____

   _____

EXERCISE

Sentence Combining: Exercise B

First, choose a base sentence and circle the letter next to it. Then, using adjectives, adverbs, and prepositional phrases, embed the other facts and ideas into the base sentence.

EXAMPLE
a. The mountains were tall.
b. The mountains were snow-covered.
(c.) The mountains towered over the hikers.
d. There were three hikers.
e. The hikers were from France.
f. The hikers were lost.
g. The mountains towered menacingly.

The tall, snow-covered mountains towered menacingly over the three lost

hikers from France.

1. a. The skier was disappointed.
   b. The skier gazed at the mountain.
   c. The mountain was bare.
   d. The mountain was rocky.
   e. The mountain was above her.

   _____

   _____

2. a. They leaped out of the water.
   b. They leaped in arcs.
   c. The dolphins leaped.
   d. The arcs were graceful.
   e. The arcs were long.

   _____

   _____

3. a. They played in the square.
   b. The violinist and his daughter played.
   c. The square was crowded.
   d. They played beautifully.
   e. The violinist was blind.

   _____

   _____

4. a. The swing was that strong.
   b. It was a swing of the bat.
   c. One swing sent the baseball flying.
   d. It was flying out of the ballpark.
   e. The ballpark was his favourite.

   _____

   _____

5. a. The lagoon was black.
   b. The monster was green.
   c. The monster was slow.
   d. The monster walked out of the lagoon.
   e. The monster was ugly.

   _____

   _____

6. a. A person has invented a talking tombstone.
   b. The person is imaginative.
   c. It was invented recently.
   d. The talking tombstone is solar-powered.

   _____

   _____

7. a. The statement is tape-recorded.

    b. The case is Plexiglas.

    c. A statement is placed in a case.

    d. It is a case that sits in an area of the tombstone.

    e. The area is hollowed-out.

    _____

    _____

8. a. The speaker is small.

    b. A speaker and a panel are installed.

    c. It is a solar panel.

    d. The speaker and panel are on the tombstone.

    e. It is a three-inch panel.

    _____

    _____

9. a. The recording can be activated with the correct key.

    b. One can activate the recording and listen to a statement.

    c. The recording is in the case.

    d. The statement is from the grave's occupant.

    _____

    _____

10. a. The sunlight must be enough.

    b. With sunlight, the recording will run.

    c. The recording will run for as long as two hours.

    d. The recording is in the tombstone.

    e. The tombstone is $10,000.

    _____

    _____

Section Five

The Process of Writing

If you have ever sat for hours before a blank sheet of paper or stared for what seemed like forever at a blank computer screen, you know how difficult and frustrating it can be to write a paper. In fact, some people have such trouble simply *starting* their papers that for them writing becomes a truly agonizing experience.

Fortunately, writing does not have to be so difficult. If you learn how to use the steps involved in the process of writing, you can avoid much of the frustration and enjoy more of the satisfaction that comes from writing a successful paper.

In this section, you will practise using the three general activities that make up the writing process—**prewriting, writing,** and **rewriting**—to produce a paragraph based on the following assignment.

Writing Assignment: Narration

Exercises 1C (page 25), 2C (page 36), and 3C (page 47) of Chapter One are about three unusual events: Poon Lim's record-setting ordeal in a life raft, Michael Buckley's bicycle ride across China, and Nicholas Alkemade's 5.5 km fall from an airplane without a parachute. Few of us have had such dramatic experiences. Yet, we all have had experiences that we remember with either warm, positive feelings or uncomfortable, negative ones.

For this writing assignment, you will use the writing process explained in the following pages to describe something that happened to you. You do not need to have jumped from an airplane without a parachute or survived for weeks in a life raft. Ask yourself, "What events—either from the distant past or from more recent times—have happened to me that I remember well?" Perhaps it was your first day at school, your first traffic ticket, or your first child. Perhaps it was the day you felt betrayed by a close friend or read a novel in which the meaning of life came through like lightning. Do you have such an event in your mind? Good. Now, before we look at the writing process you will follow in writing your paragraph, jot the idea of this experience down in one or two sentences.

The Stages of the Writing Process

Prewriting

Prewriting is the part of the writing process that will kick-start you into creating a piece of writing. Often, the most difficult step in the process is getting started. We don't seem to be able to start. Nothing works. We stare at the blank page. This is called "writer's block."

Prewriting consists of any technique that will generate ideas and get you started. Three of the most successful prewriting techniques are **freewriting, brainstorming,** and **clustering.**

1. **Freewriting** is based on one simple but essential idea: When you sit down to write, you write. You don't stare at your blank page or look out the window, wondering what in the world you could write about. Instead, you write down your thoughts even if you have no idea what topic you should focus on. In addition, as you freewrite, you do not stop to correct spelling, grammar, or punctuation errors. After all, the purpose of freewriting is to generate ideas, not to write the final draft of your paper.

    Here is how some freewriting might look for the assignment described above.

    To describe an event? What could I write about that? I don't have a lot of

    "events" that I can think of—but I suppose I must have some. What do I

    remember? How about recently? Have I gone anywhere or has anything

    happened to me? I went skiing last month and took a bad fall—but so

    what? That wouldn't be very interesting. How about something I remember

    that I didn't like—like what? Death? Too depressing. Besides, I have never

    been closely involved in death. I was in a car accident once, but that was

    too long ago, and it doesn't really interest me. How about—what? I'm

    stuck. How about events I have good memories about—wait—I remember

    almost drowning when I was practising for water polo in high school. That

    was a wild event. I could do it. Any other possibilities? How about good

    memories—like the time I made that lucky catch in Little League. That

    would be good. Or the fish I caught with my dad when I was a kid. Lots of good memories there. Any others? Yeah—I joined a softball league

recently—that was a real experience, especially because it'd been so long

since I'd played baseball. But I can't think of any particular thing I'd write

about it.—Of all these, I think I like the drowning one best. I really remem-

ber that one and all the feelings that went with it.

You can tell that the above writer was not trying to produce a clean, well-written copy of his paper. Instead, he wrote down his thoughts as they occurred to him, and the result was a very informal rush of ideas that eventually led him to a topic, a near-drowning that occurred when he was in high school. Now that he has his topic, he can continue to freewrite to generate details about the event that he can use in his paper.

2. **Brainstorming** is another prewriting technique that you can use to generate ideas. It is similar to freewriting in that you write down your thoughts without censoring or editing them, but it differs in that the thoughts usually appear as a *list of ideas* rather than as *separate sentences*. Here is an example of how the above freewriting might have looked as brainstorming.

> An event I remember well—what could I use?
> > recently?
> > > fall while skiing—no
> >
> > things I didn't like
> > > death? too depressing
> > > car accident I was in? too long ago
> > > almost drowned at practic—good one
> >
> > good memories?
> > > lucky catch in Little League
> > > fishing with Dad
> >
> > <u>Use the one about almost drowning.</u>

3. **Clustering** is a third prewriting technique. It involves the free association of ideas in a nonlinear form. Like roses, grapes, cherries, freckles, and oysters, ideas and images often come in clusters when you let your mind roam freely. Once you map these clusters of ideas on paper, you will perceive patterns and meanings that can yield a more natural form of writing.

    We begin with *the nucleus*. The nucleus is the centre of the cluster, the stone you throw into the pond of your thoughts. It may be a word, a phrase, or an idea. It may be the topic of your paper. You write this word, phrase, or idea in the middle of a blank page and circle it. Next, you let go of any attempt to judge or plan what to do. You let the word out, so to speak, by writing other words in a circle around the nucleus. You now circle those words and connect them with a line to the nucleus. You must fight down a feeling of foolishness and defeat any desire to impose order over the process at this point. Relax and let your mind freely associate as you meditate over the words you have written. Let these new words act in turn as nuclei and spill out the words they suggest. Circle these words and draw lines to the nuclei. Add arrows, if you wish, to show the direction of thought.

You will know to stop clustering when at last you sense an order to all this. Do not hurry the process. The order will suggest itself. Here is how the brainstorming material used above might have looked if it were "clustered."

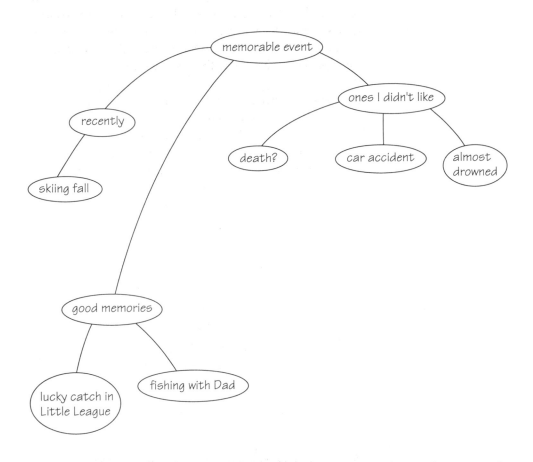

Freewriting, brainstorming, and clustering are only three of many techniques to help you start writing. When you use them, you should feel free to move from one to the other at any time. And, of course, your instructor may suggest other ways to help you get started. Whatever technique you use, the point is to *start writing*.

Writing Application
Use freewriting, brainstorming, or clustering (or a combination of the three) to find a topic idea that you can use for the assignment to describe an event. Once you have decided upon your topic, continue to prewrite to decide what

details you will include in your paper. Remember that you should not correct spelling or sentence errors as you prewrite.

Writing

Writing the draft of your paper is the second step in the writing process. The trick to writing your first draft without getting stuck is to remember that what you write now is not your final copy, so you can allow yourself to make mistakes and to write awkward sentences. Don't worry about how "correct" your writing is. Instead, just describe your experience as thoroughly as you can.

Here is a sample first draft of the paper on drowning. As you read it, notice that the writer has not yet corrected any errors it may contain.

I almost drowned when I was sixteen. It all happened one day at practice for water polo. It was my second year on the Kearney Highschool water polo team. One day I volunteered for the dreaded "Challenge Set." I had just finished the first lap underwater. I still felt good. As I come to the wall, I make the decison to go for another lap, I keep swimming, but my lungs collapse. I took a few more strokes, and then it happend. I blacked out. All I remember was seeing black. I felt completely relaxed. Then I remember hearing voices. Suddenly, starting to cough violently. When I opened my eyes, the first person I saw was my coach. He told me what had happened, I was a little shaken. I couldn't believe that I almost died. This was really a frightening experience that I remember whenever I go for a swim.

The above first draft is far from perfect. It contains writing errors and could use more descriptive details. However, it has accomplished its purpose: *It has given the writer a draft to work with and to improve with revision.*

Writing Application

Now write the first draft of your paragraph. Remember that your goal is not to write an error-free draft. Rather, it is to write a *first* draft that you will then improve.

Rewriting

Rewriting consists of two stages: **revising** and **editing**. In the **revising** stage of the writing process, you work on the "larger" areas of your paper—its content, organization, and sentence structure. Here are some suggestions.

1.   *Improve your opening sentence.*

     You can often improve your opening sentence after you have written your first draft because now you really have something to introduce. In fact, if you look at the *concluding* sentences of your first draft, you may find a clearer statement of the central point of your paragraph than the one you have in your opening sentence. If that is the case, rewrite your opening sentence to include that statement.

     Opening sentences that identify your topic and state your central point about that topic are called *topic sentences*. They will be discussed in more detail in Chapter Two, Section Five.

2.   *Add more details.*

     After you have written the first draft, add any further details that might improve your paper. Use prewriting techniques to help yourself think of more details.

3.   *Reorganize the details in the first draft.*

     There are many ways to organize a paper, but one of the most common ones is to save the most important details for last. Another way to organize details, especially if you are describing an event, is to list the details in chronological order. Whichever way you choose, now is the time to make any changes in the order of your material.

4.   *Combine related sentences and ideas.*

     Combine sentences that are obviously related. Where possible, use sentence combining techniques to embed material from one sentence into another.

Editing is the final stage of the writing process. When you edit, you correct the spelling, grammar, and punctuation errors that you find. Careful editing is an important step whenever you write, but remember not to edit too soon. As you can see, *most* of the writing process is spent on prewriting, writing, and revising.

The paragraph on the next page illustrates how the student who nearly drowned revised and edited his first draft.

Revised opening sentence includes writer's reaction to the event

When I was sixteen, I had a frightening experience that I still remember whenever I go for a swim. This event took place when I was in my second year on the Kearney High School water polo team. One day at practice, I volunteered to try the dreaded "Challenge Set."

Added details

It consisted of about three to four players attempting to swim fifty yards, two laps of the pool, on a single breath. I started out full of confidence, but I had no idea what was about to happen. When I

Combined sentences

came to the wall at the end of the first lap, I still felt good, so I made the decision to go for another lap. I made the flip turn and pushed off the wall. I still felt fine, but without my knowing it, my lungs had started to collapse.

Added details

I remember seeing the blue hash marks, the halfway markers, so I knew I had just a little way to go. I took

Combined sentences

a few more strokes, but then it happened. I blacked out. **All I remember was seeing black and feeling completely relaxed. Then, just as I began to hear voices, I started to cough violently.** When I opened

Added details

my eyes, the first person I saw was my coach, **a state beach lifeguard. I was lying in his arms, not knowing where I was or what had happened to me.** When he told me what had happened, I was really shaken.

Added details

I couldn't believe I had almost died. **I got out of the pool, got dressed, and sat in the stands waiting for practice to end.** I don't think I'll ever forget the day I nearly drowned.

Writing Application

Now revise and edit your first draft. As you do so, remember that thorough revisions may involve several new drafts, not just one. Once you have a draft that you are satisfied with, prepare a clean final draft, following the format your instructor has asked for.

Chapter One Practice Test

A. In the spaces provided, indicate whether the underlined word is a subject (S), a helping verb (HV), or a main verb (MV). If it is none of these, leave the space blank.

_____ 1. The recent rains <u>have</u> caused many mud slides in our city.

_____ 2. Every morning Ashley <u>puts</u> on a new pair of shoes and goes for a walk.

_____ 3. The duck <u>waddling</u> up the driveway looked as if it had lost its best friend.

_____ 4. I have <u>never</u> played golf, and I don't think I ever will.

_____ 5. From the orbiting space shuttle, the <u>earth</u> looked like a large blue ball.

_____ 6. Where did that <u>dog</u> put my shoe?

_____ 7. From the <u>sky</u> fell a large chunk of space debris that just barely missed Alix's head.

_____ 8. Alberto <u>is</u> a great skier, but he is also a braggart.

_____ 9. <u>Leave</u> the room as soon as you have finished your work.

_____ 10. The driver who caused the accident <u>should</u> have signalled before changing lanes.

B. Underline all subjects once and all complete verbs twice in the following sentences.

11. Amy and her cousin visited Spain last year.

12. There are three blind mice in our basement.

13. Some of the people at the concert wore spiked hair and nose rings.

14. Henry should not have eaten that mouldy peach.

15. Everyone knew the man in grey, but none of his friends trusted him.

16. After she passed the bar exam, Karen joined a local law firm.

17. A white toy poodle barked loudly at the intruder and then ran into the back room.

18. Did Tai leave already, or is he still in the house?

19. The candidate was disappointed because she had not won the election.

20. After he had practised figure skating for ten years, Alan finally made the team.

C. Write sentences of your own that follow the suggested patterns.

21. A statement with one subject, one helping verb, and one main verb (S–HV–MV):

_____

_____

22. A question with one helping verb, one subject, and one main verb (HV–S–MV):

_____

_____

23. A statement with two subjects joined by "and" and two main verbs joined by "and" (S "and" S–MV "and" MV):

_____

_____

24. A statement with one subject, two helping verbs, and a main verb (S–HV–HV–MV):

_____

_____

25. A statement with a subject and a main verb followed by "because" and another subject and main verb (S–MV "because" S–MV):

_____

_____

D. Add an adjective (other than _a_, _an_, or _the_) and an adverb of your own to each of the following sentences.

26. Louis whispered to the dog in the kennel.

27. Nick turned to his grandmother and asked her why she had bought the Porsche.

28. The pilot announced that an object was flying close to the wing of the airplane.

29. A goose swam to the edge of the pond, hopped out, and pecked at the visitor.

30. Nicole heard a noise in the basement, so she opened the door to investigate.

E. In the following sentences, place all prepositional phrases in parentheses.

31. Two parakeets with blue wings flew into the house.

32. Ahmed decided to leave during the intermission so he could get home before midnight.

33. Above the table floated two yellow balloons that had been given to the birthday boy.

34. Igor opened the door and stared at the package of spiders that had just arrived from Transylvania.

35. Dr. Rinaldo smiled broadly, unaware of the spinach stuck between his two front teeth.

F. In the following sentences, add coordinating conjunctions that show the relationship indicated in the parentheses.

36. Marla wrote the cheque, _____ Jackie mailed it. (addition)

37. Mathieu had a terrible headache, _____ he took two aspirin and went to bed. (result)

38. The spaghetti was delicious, _____ the garlic bread was stale. (contrast)

39. That mess on our lawn must have been caused by the dog next door _____ by the one down the street. (alternative)

40. I'm sure the baby is hungry, _____ it has been crying for the past fifteen minutes. (cause)

G. Identify the underlined words in these sentences by writing one of the following abbreviations above each word: noun (N), pronoun (Pro), verb (V), adjective (Adj), adverb (Adv), conjunction (Conj), preposition (Prep).

41. The <u>local</u> mountains have more snow this year than <u>they</u> have had in the past five years.

42. Our <u>neighbour</u> has <u>named</u> her two new dogs Popcorn and Kernel.

43. The recent rains have turned Rudy's backyard <u>into</u> a <u>swamp</u>.

44. The tiny sailboat headed <u>swiftly</u> toward land.

45. No one had <u>remembered</u> Dr. Norman Bethune's adventures in Spain until someone made a movie <u>about</u> him.

46. Sidney had <u>always</u> wanted to see Hawaii, but he was never able to save enough money to go there.

47. Last night, <u>someone</u> broke into Manon's house and stole her entire <u>collection</u> of Elvis Presley records.

48. The experimental play was <u>lifeless</u> and dull, <u>so</u> we left at the intermission.

49. Keiko's tooth ached <u>for</u> three days, but she <u>refused</u> to call the dentist.

50. When she had <u>finally</u> finished mowing the lawn, Evelyn poured <u>herself</u> a tall glass of iced tea.

ANSWERS

Answers to Practices in Chapter One

Page 3:

2. mother, bread, oven
3. pilot, tails, planes, clouds

4. students, class, stamina
5. Monica, harmonica, enthusiasm

Page 4:

2. musician, flute, whales
3. board, diver, air
4. pear, leaf, stem
5. engineers, complexity, design
6. motion, ship, nausea, passengers

7. constable, uniform, bag
8. Canada, nation, races, religions, views
9. parties, food, humour, gossip
10. position, matter, principle

Page 6:

2. *nouns*: equipment, order
   pronouns: Everyone, its
3. *nouns*: astronauts, seats, movie
   pronouns: their, themselves
4. *nouns*: waiters, dessert
   pronouns: Which, your
5. *noun*: cook
   pronouns: himself, mine
6. *nouns*: Omar, cauliflower, vent

7. *nouns*: decorations, party
   pronouns: Who, some, our
8. *nouns*: Caps, bills, back, style
   pronoun: their
9. *nouns*: coins, trunk, attic
   pronouns: Those, my
10. *nouns*: marathon, bouquet, flowers,
    shirt, picture
    pronouns: Anyone, who, herself, it

Page 6:

Answers will vary. Here are some possible ones.

2. <u>You</u> should make <u>him</u> stop yelling at that little <u>dog</u>.
3. <u>One</u> of the politicians asked for a <u>donation</u> of <u>$10,000</u>.
4. <u>Someone</u> took the <u>paper</u> that belongs to <u>me</u>.
5. After <u>Mr. Merino</u> finished <u>his</u> painting, <u>he</u> decided to buy a <u>frame</u>.

Page 7:

2. spent
3. covered, swam

4. arrived
5. found

Page 8:

2. is
3. will be

4. were
5. am

Page 9:

2. *verb*: sat
   tense: past
3. *verb*: will celebrate
   tense: future

4. *verb*: waited
   tense: past
5. *verb*: volunteers
   tense: present

Pages 11–12:

2. MV
3. HV
4. MV

5. MV
6. HV
7. HV

8. MV
9. HV
10. MV

Page 12:

A.

2. HV: will
   MV: enjoy
3. HV: is
   MV: running

4. HV: Has
   MV: found
5. HV: have been
   MV: complaining

B. Answers will vary. Here are some possible ones.

7. The glass <u>fell</u> to the floor and <u>shattered</u> into hundreds of small pieces.
8. A spider <u>was</u> slowly <u>crawling</u> along the wall behind my sister.
9. <u>Did</u> you <u>eat</u> the food that I <u>had bought</u> for tonight's dinner?
10. The postal carrier <u>should</u> not <u>have become</u> so angry when I <u>asked</u> her to deliver the mail earlier.

Page 13:

2. HV: might
   MV: hurt
   Verbal: Climbing
3. MV: spoke
   Verbal: Stooping

4. HV: had
   MV: planned
   Verbal: to begin
5. MV: tripped
   Verbal: running

Page 14:

2. HV: have been
   MV: organizing
3. HV: Do
   MV: like
   Verbal: to sail
4. MV: has
5. HV: has been
   MV: frightening
   Verbal: leaping
6. HV: was
   MV: planning
   Verbal: to get

7. HV: was
   MV: searching
   Verbal: Cruising
8. HV: had been
   MV: challenged
9. HV: had
   MV: tried
   Verbal: to find
10. HV: has
    MV: begun

Page 15:

2. S: people
   MV: like
3. S: Cecile
   HV: might
   MV: want

4. S: Ted
   MV: spent
5. S: dinner
   MV: was

Page 16:

2. S: list
   HV: has
   MV: changed
3. S: heat
   MV: became

4. S: umbrella
   HV: would
   MV: open
5. S: we
   MV: searched

Page 17:

2. S: wind, rain
   MV: were
3. S: hands, feet
   MV: shook, ached
4. S: I
   MV: started
   S: friend
   MV: brewed

5. S: we
   MV: were
   S: Jim, Irving
   MV: arrived

Page 18:

2. S: demonstration
   MV: came
3. S: you
   HV: Will
   MV: pass

4. S: camel
   MV: is
5. S: You (understood)
   MV: Spell

Page 18:

2. *subject*: Pandas
   verb: have been placed
3. *subject*: bicycles
   verb: are reduced
4. *subject*: uncle
   verb: has lived
5. *subject*: Jane
   verb: did read
6. *subject*: guests
   verb: did leave

7. *subject*: You (understood)
   verb: avoid
8. *subjects*: newscaster, producer
   verb: disagreed
9. *subject*: instructions
   verb: are
10. *subject*: loggers
   verb: faced

Pages 19–20:

Answers will vary. Here are some possible ones.
2. The <u>doctor</u> and the <u>attorney</u> <u>left</u> the building.
3. His <u>car was stolen</u> last night.
4. <u>Did</u> <u>she</u> <u>find</u> the missing briefcase?
5. <u>Leave</u> the building now.
6. Here <u>are</u> the artichoke <u>hearts</u>.
7. The <u>man</u> from Peru and his <u>son</u> <u>flew</u> to Los Angeles and <u>rented</u> an apartment.
8. <u>Stanley</u> <u>was cleaning</u> the table when <u>he</u> <u>heard</u> the siren.
9. <u>She</u> <u>has finished</u> her homework, but she <u>has</u> not fully <u>understood</u> the concepts of the lesson.
10. I <u>will cook</u> dinner if <u>he</u> <u>cleans</u> up afterwards.

Page 27:

2. *Wealthy* and *generous* modify *uncle*.
3. *Sometimes* modifies *works*, and *eighteen* modifies *hours*.
4. *Fur* and *warm* modify *coat*.
5. *Huge* modifies *chunks*, and *steadily* modifies *rattled*.

Pages 28–29:

A.

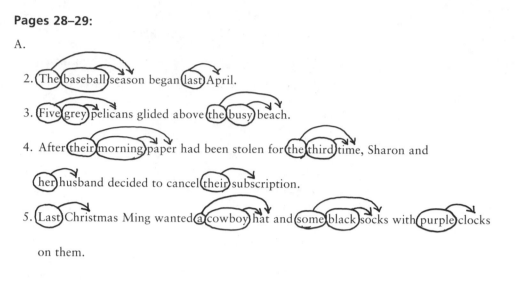

2. The baseball season began last April.

3. Five grey pelicans glided above the busy beach.

4. After their morning paper had been stolen for the third time, Sharon and her husband decided to cancel their subscription.

5. Last Christmas Ming wanted a cowboy hat and some black socks with purple clocks on them.

B. Answers will vary. Here are some possible ones.

              dark   brown
7. Snow fell from the ∧sky and covered our ∧lawn.

                    stubby   black
8. Mr. Medina pointed his ∧finger at the stranger wearing a ∧mask.

   wonderful   warm
9. The ∧aroma from the ham in the oven filled the ∧kitchen.

Many   thick
10. ∧people were worried about the ∧fog that had blanketed our city for days.

Pages 30–31:

A.

2. She quite certainly knew that she would never go to Medicine Hat with him.

3. The praying mantis sometimes practises a rather brutal mating rite.

4. The guitar player leaped deftly onto a speaker and frantically shook his long hair.

5. Sophocles stared tragically at his completely blank tablet.

B. Answers will vary. Here are some possible ones.

        often
7. Kathy ∧visits her father on Saturdays.

                        slowly
8. The shutters creaked as they swung ∧in the wind.

lovingly

9. Jean gazed ʌ into Walter's bloodshot eyes.

Yesterday

10. ʌ the lake glistened in the sunlight as we rowed our boat across it.

Page 39:

A.

2. *subject*: Ed
   verb: did know
   subject: he
   verb: had
   conjunctions: and, but

3. *subject*: musicians
   verb: could play
   subject: audience
   verb: did seem
   conjunctions: or, yet

4. *subject*: rhinoceros
   verb: charged
   subject: he
   verb: jumped
   conjunction: so

5. *subject*: car
   verb: was
   subject: Sylvia
   verb: decided
   conjunctions: yet, so

B.

7. but

8. and

9. because

10. so

Page 40:

2. across, to

3. during, to

4. under, near

5. of, into

Page 42:

A.

2. Prep   Obj
   (By the river)

   Prep   Obj
   (in the shallow water)

3. Prep   Obj
   (Near him)

   Prep   Obj
   (on a dirty bench)

   Prep Obj
   (at Brad)

4. Prep   Obj
    (by his love)

    Prep Obj
    (for Penny)

    Prep Obj
    (of balance)

5. Prep   Obj
   (for his matches)

   Prep   Obj
   (under the rug)

B. Answers will vary. Here are some possible ones.

7. A long snake <u>with a diamond-shaped head</u> moved slowly <u>toward the child</u>.

8. Ginger grabbed the orange <u>from her sister</u> and threw it <u>into the crowd</u>.

9. <u>During the night</u> the brush fire approached the house <u>at an alarming speed</u>.

10. Everyone <u>in our family</u> has seen the latest movie <u>on television</u>.

Pages 48–49:

2. N
   V
3. V
   Adj
   N
4. Adv
   Conj
5. V
   Prep
6. V
   Adj

7. N
   V
8. Adv
   Conj
9. N
   Adj
10. N
    V

Page 52:

1. The farmer waited in front of the bank.
2. The **old** farmer waited in front of the bank.
3. The old farmer **in overalls** waited in front of the bank.
4. The old farmer in **faded** overalls waited in front of the bank.
5. The old farmer in faded overalls waited **patiently** in front of the bank.

Chapter Two

Understanding Sentence Patterns

The grammatical terms you learned in Chapter One will help you understand how *single words* and *word groups* function in a sentence. Knowing how these words and word groups function in a sentence will in turn help you to write and revise your own sentences more effectively and systematically.

But then, what is a sentence, anyway? Here are two definitions. Which is more accurate?

1. A sentence is a group of words that expresses a complete thought.

2. A sentence is a group of words that contains a subject and a verb.

Neither, really. Some sentences do not seem to express "a complete thought." Consider, for example, the sentence "*It fell.*" Do these two words convey a complete thought? In one sense they do: An action is communicated, and a subject, though indefinite, is identified. However, the sentence raises more questions than it answers. What fell? Why did it fall? Where did it fall? Are we talking about apples, stars, the sky, or the Roman Empire?

The second definition is no more satisfactory. The words *"Because my father was sleeping"* do not make sense all by themselves. Why? We have a subject (*father*) and a verb (*was sleeping*). All sentences must contain a subject and a verb, but this example shows that just because we have a subject and a verb, we do not necessarily have a sentence.

The only definition of a sentence that is *always* correct is the following one:

DEFINITION

| sentence | A sentence is a group of words that contains at least one main clause. |

You will agree with this definition, of course, only if you know what a *clause* is and can identify a *main clause* when you see it. If you cannot, you will never be sure that you are writing complete sentences.

Section One

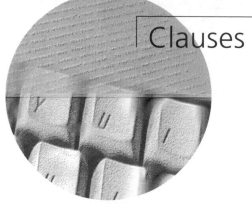

Clauses

Main Clauses and Subordinate Clauses

A clause is a group of words that contains at least one subject and at least one verb.

DEFINITION

clause	A clause is a group of words that contains at least one subject and at least one verb.

The two types of clauses are **main clauses** and **subordinate clauses.**

1. A **main clause** is a group of words that contains at least one subject and one verb and that *expresses a complete idea.*

2. A **subordinate clause** is a group of words that contains at least one subject and one verb but that *does not express a complete idea.* All subordinate clauses begin with **subordinators.**

               sub. clause   main clause

EXAMPLES   [Although <u>he</u> seldom <u>plays</u>,] [<u>Simon</u> <u>is</u> an excellent golfer.]

This example contains two clauses, each with a subject and a verb. As you can see, the clause *Simon is an excellent golfer* could stand by itself as a sentence. But the clause *Although he seldom plays* cannot stand by itself (even though it has a subject and a verb) because it needs the main clause to complete its thought and because it begins with the subordinator *although.*

Subordinators

Subordinators indicate the relationship between the subordinate clause and the main clause. Learning to recognize the two types of subordinators—subordinating conjunctions and relative pronouns—will help you identify subordinate clauses.

Subordinating Conjunctions

<u>after</u>	so that
although	than
<u>as</u>	though
as if	unless
as long as	<u>until</u>
because	when
<u>before</u>	whenever
even though	where
if	wherever
<u>since</u>	while

Relative Pronouns

that	who(ever)
which	whom(ever)
	whose

NOTE: Some of the words in the above list of subordinators are underlined (after, as, before, since, until). These words are used as prepositions when they do not introduce a subordinate clause.

E X A M P L E S   prepositional phrase: *after dinner*
subordinate clause: *after I eat dinner*

The following are examples of sentences containing subordinate clauses. (Note that each subordinate clause begins with a subordinator.)

sub. clause   main clause
E X A M P L E S   [**Before** his horse had crossed the finish line,] [the jockey suddenly stood up in his saddle.]

main clause   sub. clause
[Sea urchin is a dish] [**that** few people love.]

main clause   sub. clause
[Monique won the spelling bee] [**because** she spelled *penicillin* correctly.]

PRACTICE

Identify the following word groups as main clauses (MC) or subordinate clauses (SC) or neither (N).

1. When the moon shone on the river.   _SC_

2. His dog cried all night.   _____

3. Yesterday the rain washed away the sign.   _____

4. After that evening.   _____

5. Before Jack groomed his rat.   _____

6. We were all very happy.   _____

7. Which Sheri did not want to do.   _____

8. Finally, we could get some sleep.   _____

9. That she had made a three-point shot.   _____

10. The night before.   _____

PRACTICE

Identify the following word groups as subordinate clauses (SC) or prepositional phrases (PP).

1. Since the dampness was harmful.   _SC_

2. Since the party last Saturday night.   _____

3. Since the Christmas office party.   _____

4. As a fairy princess.   _____

5. As the whole class stared at me.   _____

6. After the game had ended.   _____

7. After the nomination meeting of the Rhinoceros Party.   _____

8. After the season's first game.   _____

9. Until the Berlin Wall fell.   _____

10. Until next spring.   _____

PRACTICE

Underline the subordinate clauses in the following sentences and circle the subordinators. Not all sentences contain subordinate clauses.

1. A misanthrope is a (person) who does not like people.

2. Elena wants to tour Europe when she graduates from college.

3. After the sudden thunderstorm, many of the fans left.

4. The study skills centre offers help for students who are having trouble in their math classes.

5. If you will go up in a balloon, I will go, too.

6. The storm uprooted a tree that had stood in the town square for fifty years.

7. At first British Columbia appeared to be unapproachable from the rest of Canada because of the Rocky Mountains.

8. Martin did not know the driver whose car had won the race.

9. Hampton decided to take a nap after he had eaten his carrot.

10. The cook put the food exactly where it belonged.

Adverb and Adjective Subordinate Clauses

Subordinate clauses may function as adverbs, adjectives, or nouns in their sentences. Therefore, they are called **adverb clauses, adjective clauses,** or **noun clauses.** We will be discussing adverb and adjective clauses, but not noun clauses. Although we frequently use noun clauses in our writing, they seldom present problems in punctuation or clarity.

Adverb Clauses

Like single-word adverbs, adverb subordinate clauses can modify verbs. For example, in the sentence *Clare ate a big breakfast because she had a busy day ahead of her,* the adverb clause *because she had a busy day ahead of her* modifies the verb *ate.* It explains *why* Clare ate a big breakfast. Another characteristic of adverb clauses is that they begin with a **subordinating conjunction,** not a relative pronoun (see page 77). In addition, in most cases an adverb clause can be moved around in its sentence, and the sentence will still make sense.

EXAMPLES   [**When** she ate the mushroom,] Alice grew taller.
Alice grew taller [**when** she ate the mushroom.]
Alice, [**when** she ate the mushroom,] grew taller.

PUNCTUATION NOTE: When the adverb clause begins the sentence, it is followed by a comma, as in the first example. When the adverb clause ends a sentence, no comma is needed. When the adverb clause interrupts the main clause, it is enclosed by commas.

PRACTICE

Underline the adverb clauses in the following sentences. Circle the subordinating conjunctions.

1. (If) you leave Pompeii now, you will miss the eruption of Mount Vesuvius.

2. Jacques feels ill whenever he eats liver.

3. Ridley was disgusted because one of the aliens was drooling on her.

4. The car, when the chains came off, began to slide across the icy road.

5. When in one race Roger Bannister and John Landy both broke the four-minute mile, he knew that a miracle had occurred.

PRACTICE

Add adverb clauses of your own to the following main clauses in the spaces indicated. Use commas where they are needed.

1. He laid his daughter Regan down for a nap _because she had been acting_

   tired all morning.

2. _____ Marilyn's parents

   spend Christmas in Puerto Vallarte.

3. His teacher liked his essay about rap music _____.

   _____

4. Gloria _____ sat

   patiently in the front seat of the car and waited.

5. _____ they gave

   the leftover cabbage and beets to Buttons.

Adjective Clauses

Adjective subordinate clauses modify nouns or pronouns just as single-word adjectives do. Adjective clauses follow the nouns or pronouns they modify, and they usually begin with a **relative pronoun**—*who, whom, whose, which,* *that* (and sometimes *when* or *where*). As you can see in the examples below, relative pronouns sometimes serve as subjects of their clauses. We will discuss the rules for punctuating adjective clauses in Chapter Three.

EXAMPLES   The horse [**that** Mr. Lee liked best] was named Traveler. (The adjective clause modifies *horse*.)

On the top shelf was the trophy [**that** Kathy had won for her model of the Battle of the Plains of Abraham]. (The adjective clause modifies *trophy*.)

Hampton, [**which** is Michelle's hooded rat,] resides at the foot of her bed. (The adjective clause modifies *Hampton*, and the relative pronoun *which* is the subject of the clause.)

NOTE: *As you can see in the example above, the adjective clause often appears between the subject and the verb of the main clause. In addition, as you can see in the following example, sometimes the relative pronoun is left out.*

EXAMPLES   The man [I met yesterday] works for the RCMP. (Here the adjective clause modifies the noun *man*, but the relative pronoun *whom* is left out.)

A note about relative pronouns:

1. Use *who* or *whom* to refer to people only.
2. Use *which* to refer to nonhuman things only, such as animals or objects.
3. Use *that* to refer to either people or nonhuman things.

PRACTICE

Underline the adjective clauses in the following sentences and circle the relative pronouns.

1. Cafe Ian, (which) is on Columbia Street, is the favourite coffee shop in town.

2. The poet whom we all admire always has his breakfast there.

3. In fact, all of the people who want to chat with us seem to prefer meeting us at Cafe Ian.

4. A barber's pole, which the owners have painted brown and cream instead of red and white, stands at the entrance.

5. A black cat that everyone has named "Cappuccino" roams around the cafe begging for bites of pastry.

PRACTICE

Add adjective clauses of your own to the following main clauses.

1. My horse especially likes doughnuts.

   My horse especially likes doughnuts that have been dunked in coffee.

2. About 9:00 every evening a strange group of people gathers in the back of the cafe.

   _____

   _____

3. Some of the men wear bizarre ties.

   _____

   _____

4. Some of the women wear interesting shirts.

   _____

   _____

5. Each person has his or her own special style of dress or speech.

   _____

   _____

PRACTICE

In the following sentences, underline the subordinate clauses and identify them as adverb clauses (Adv) or adjective clauses (Adj).

1. <u>After Humbert saw Lolita</u>, he was never the same.   Adv

2. The formerly popular premier was not re-elected

   because the economy had declined during his first term.   _____

3. Hiding in the flowerpot, Peter Cottontail thought of

   the advice that his mother had given him.   _____

4. As he enters an expensive restaurant, Mr. Jackson

   invariably blows his nose loudly several times.   _____

5. Winnipeg is a city that has one of the best ballet

   companies in the world.   _____

PRACTICE   Add subordinate clauses of your own to the following main clauses and indicate
whether you have added an adverb clause or an adjective clause.

1. Rupert decided to sell his stamp collection.

   Rupert, who was desperate for extra money, decided to sell his stamp

   collection. (Adj)

2. Kristine wrote a thank-you note to her track coach.

   _____

   _____

3. After the rodeo Elvia was presented a first-place buckle for calf roping.

   _____

   _____

4. Chen took me on a tour of his new art gallery.

   _____

   _____

5. Byron wanted us to go to the new coffee house.

   _____

   _____

Section One Review

1. A **clause** is a group of words that *contains at least one subject and at least one verb.*

2. A **main clause** is a group of words that contains at least one subject and one verb and that *expresses a complete idea.*

3. A **subordinate clause** is a group of words that contains at least one subject and one verb but that *does not express a complete idea.*

4. **Subordinate clauses** begin with *subordinators.*

5. **Adverb subordinate clauses** usually modify verbs and begin with *subordinating conjunctions.*

6. **Adjective subordinate clauses** modify nouns or pronouns and begin with *relative pronouns.*

EXERCISE

Exercise 1A

Underline all subordinate clauses and circle the subordinators. In the spaces provided, indicate whether the subordinator is a subordinating conjunction (SC) or a relative pronoun (RP). If a sentence contains no subordinate clause, do nothing to it.

1. The chairman suggested a solution (that) he thought would help the homeless people in his town.   RP

2. As the wind increased, the sailboats turned back toward the harbour.   _____

3. After his long nap, Papa Bear woke the rest of the family.   _____

4. Crowds of Japanese tourists, who love the Rockies, visit Banff in the winter.   _____

5. If you will fry the beets, I will boil the dandelions.   _____

6. Stan awoke in the middle of the night because he felt ashamed of his earlier behaviour.   _____

7. The driver who stops to read the billboards along the highway will not get the job.   _____

8. When the storm moved east, it dropped four feet of snow in the Prairies.   _____

9. Whenever Michelle picks up Hampton, he crawls into her pocket.   _____

10. Before going out to dinner, George went to the bank to get some money.   _____

11. She chose a Subaru because she lives in a snowbound cabin near Val-des-Bois.   _____

12. Parliament sat to consider the bill that was proposed by

the Member from Cornwall-Rosemont.   _____

13. Although leopards are never supposed to change their

spots, Hubert was eager to change his.   _____

14. Kim wanted to redecorate her house within her budget

if she could manage it.   _____

15. Cathy maintained her dignity even though someone

had tied the laces of her shoes together.   _____

EXERCISE

Exercise 1B

A. Join the pairs of sentences below by making one of them either an adverb or an adjective subordinate clause. You may need to delete or change some words.

  1. The zookeeper comforted the frightened king cobra. The cobra had been attacked by a mongoose.

     The zookeeper comforted the frightened king cobra that had been

     attacked by a mongoose.

  2. Larry quickly finished solving the crossword puzzle. He had ripped the crossword puzzle from the Sunday paper.

     _____

     _____

  3. Alix learned that she had been accepted for graduate school. She called her mother and father and went out for dinner.

     _____

     _____

  4. Jenny was angry with her coach. Jenny's coach had suspended her from the team for missing practice three times.

     _____

     _____

  5. Two reporters rushed excitedly into the newsroom. The reporters breathlessly told of the kidnapping of the editor.

     _____

     _____

B. Write subordinate clauses (adjective or adverb) in the blanks as indicated in parentheses at the beginning of the sentence. Make sure your clauses have subjects and verbs.

  6. (Adv) *After his apartment had been trashed*, Joe decided to install a security system.

  7. (Adj or Adv) Lester played a video game called "Crystal Quest" ____

     _____

8. (Adj) The hummingbird is a small bird _____

_____

9. (Adv) _____
two police cars screeched to a stop in front of the bank.

10. (Adj or Adv) The conductor waved his light and signalled to the

engineer of the train _____

_____

C. To the main clauses below, add the types of subordinate clauses indicated in parentheses. Add your clause at any place in the sentence that you feel is appropriate. For instance, you may add an adjective clause to any noun in a sentence.

11. (Adv) Driving your car along the Quebec side of the Ottawa River is a beautiful trip.

   If you take the time to enjoy the view, driving your car along the Quebec

   side of the Ottawa River is a beautiful trip. _____

12. (Adj) The Spectre stopped and threateningly pointed his vegetable disintegrator.

_____

_____

13. (Adj) The winning football coach did not see the large container of cold water.

_____

_____

14. (Adv or Adj) The couple told their butler to chip away certain parts from their classical statues.

_____

_____

15. (Adv) The butler saved the parts in a shoebox.

_____

_____

EXERCISE

Exercise 1C

Underline all subordinate clauses and identify the type of clause (adjective or adverb) in the spaces provided.

1. When in 1915 Little Rock, Arkansas, built a new school for Black students, they named it "Mifflin Wistar Gibbs High School." __Adv__

2. Today, few Americans and Canadians know that Gibbs was the first Black city councillor in Victoria, British Columbia. _____ 3. In the 1850s he owned a boot store in San Francisco, which had become a haven for Blacks escaping persecution in the American South. _____ 4. After being attacked by a white customer, he went to the police station to lay a charge. _____

5. The police told him that Blacks cannot take white people to court. _____

6. Soon afterward, Gibbs, who had already helped many slaves escape to Canada, left San Francisco for Victoria in 1858. _____ 7. There, he opened a store that outfitted miners heading up the Fraser River, and soon he became a leading citizen. _____ 8. Gibbs and several other Blacks petitioned for the right to vote in elections, and Governor James Douglas gave consent.

_____ 9. Amor de Cosmos, who was a newspaperman running for election, sought the support of Gibbs and the other Blacks. _____ 10. All of the Blacks having voted against him, de Cosmos lost. 11. He was embittered, and when eventually he got into power, de Cosmos attempted to turn the population against all Blacks. _____ 12. However, Gibbs, who in time was elected to City Council, served as mayor of Victoria for a short time. _____

13. After his wife and children returned to the United States, Gibbs felt lonely and left Canada to live with them. _____

Section Two

Simple, Compound, Complex, and Compound–Complex Sentences

Sentences are categorized according to the number and types of clauses they contain. The names of the four kinds of sentences are **simple, compound, complex,** and **compound–complex.** You need to be familiar with these sentence patterns for a number of reasons:

1. **Variety.** Varying your sentence patterns creates interest and avoids monotony. Repeating a sentence pattern endlessly will bore even your most interested reader.

2. **Emphasis.** You can use these sentence patterns to emphasize the ideas that you think are more important than others.

3. **Grammar.** A knowledge of the basic sentence patterns of English will help you avoid the major sentence structure errors discussed in Section Three.

Being able to recognize and use these sentence patterns will help you control your writing and thus express your ideas more effectively.

The Simple Sentence

The introduction to this chapter points out that a sentence must contain at least one main clause. A sentence that contains only one main clause and no other clauses is called a **simple sentence.** However, a simple sentence is not necessarily uncomplicated or short because, in addition to its one main clause, it may also contain a number of phrases and modifiers.

The basic pattern for the simple sentence is subject–verb (SV). This pattern may vary in several ways:

EXAMPLES
                                  S   V

subject–verb (SV): The plane flew over the stadium.

                                         V   S

verb–subject (VS): Over the stadium flew the plane.

                                                    S   S   V

subject–subject–verb (SSV): The plane and the helicopter flew over the stadium.

                                   S   V   V

subject–verb–verb (SVV): The plane flew over the stadium and turned north.

                                            S   S   V

subject–subject–verb–verb (SSVV): The plane and the helicopter flew over the

                V

stadium and turned north.

                                      S   V

A simple sentence can be brief: *It rained.*

                                                                           V

Or it can be rather long: *Enraged by the taunting of the boys, the huge gorilla*

            V   V

leaped from his enclosure and chased them up a hill and down a path-way to the exit gates.

    The important thing to remember about the simple sentence is that it has only one main clause and no other clauses.

PRACTICE

Write your own simple sentences according to the instructions.

1. A simple sentence with the pattern subject–subject–verb:

   Two supermarkets and a department store collapsed in the recent

   earthquake.

2. A simple sentence that begins with a prepositional phrase and has the pattern subject–verb:

   _____

   _____

3. A simple sentence that begins with *There* and has the pattern verb–subject:

   _____

   _____

4. A simple sentence with the pattern subject–verb–verb:

_____

_____

5. A simple sentence with the pattern verb–subject–subject that begins with a prepositional phrase:

_____

_____

_____

The Compound Sentence

Simply put, a **compound sentence** contains two or more main clauses but no subordinate clauses. The basic pattern of the clauses may be expressed subject–verb/subject–verb (SV/SV). The main clauses are always joined in one of three ways:

1. *Two main clauses may be joined by a comma and one of the seven coordinating conjunctions* (and, or, nor, but, for, so, yet).

        S   V   S   V

EXAMPLE   Maria registered for all of her classes by mail, **but** Brad was not able to do so.

Remember, the two main clauses must be joined by **both a comma and a coordinating conjunction,** and the comma always comes before the coordinating conjunction.

2. *Two main clauses may be joined by a semicolon (;).*

        S   V   S   V

EXAMPLE   Maria registered for all of her classes by mail; Brad was unable to do so.

3. *Two main clauses may be joined by a semicolon and a conjunctive adverb or transitional phrase.* [These terms will be explained shortly.] Conjunctive adverbs and transitional phrases are followed by a comma.

        S   V   S   V

EXAMPLE   Maria registered for all of her classes by mail; **however,** Brad was unable to do so.

A list of the most commonly used conjunctive adverbs and transitional words and phrases follows. These words or phrases are **not** coordinating or subordinating conjunctions, which introduce dependent clauses and join independent clauses.

accordingly	hence	next	thus
also	however	nonetheless	undoubtedly
besides	instead	otherwise	for instance
consequently	meanwhile	similarly	for example
finally	moreover	still	on the other hand
further	namely	then	that is
furthermore	nevertheless	therefore	

PRACTICE   Write compound sentences of your own according to the instructions.

1. A compound sentence that uses a comma and *but* to join two main clauses:

    I was very hungry after the game, but I decided not to eat anything.

2. A compound sentence that joins two main clauses with a semicolon:

3. A compound sentence that joins two main clauses with a semicolon and an appropriate transitional word or phrase followed by a comma:

4. A compound sentence that joins two main clauses with a comma and *and*:

5. A compound sentence that joins two main clauses with a semicolon followed by the transitional words *however* or *therefore*:

PRACTICE

In the following sentences, write S above each subject and V above each verb. Then, in the spaces provided, identify each sentence as either **simple** or **compound**.

1. $\overset{S}{\text{The alligators}}$ and $\overset{S}{\text{the crocodiles}}$ $\overset{V}{\text{met}}$ in the arena to

    settle the feud.   _simple_

2. This battle was fierce, so we left for a nearby flea circus.   _____

3. We were eager to arrive, for it was the first flea circus in

    town since the 1950s.   _____

4. Flea circuses began in England in the 1500s.   _____

5. These circuses were enjoyable, but the best ones were

    produced in the 1800s in London by L. Bertolotto.   _____

6. Mr. B. had flea orchestras playing flea music.   _____

7. Cats and dogs must have enjoyed these tunes.   _____

8. Four fleas at a time played cards, and flea dance

    companies presented flea concerts.   _____

9. Sometimes good flea managers allowed their performers

    to enjoy a meal on their arms.   _____

10. The size of an audience was limited by the size of the

    performers, so theaters were limited to a small table

    and a few chairs.   _____

The Complex Sentence

The **complex sentence** has the same subject–verb pattern (SV/SV) as the compound sentence. However, the complex sentence features only one main clause and always contains at least one subordinate clause and sometimes more than one. The subordinate clauses in a complex sentence may occur at any place in the sentence.

EXAMPLES   **Before a main clause**:
$$\overset{S}{\underline{\text{When}}} \overset{V}{\underline{\text{spring arrives}}}, \text{the waters on the Red } \overset{S}{\text{River}} \text{ seem}$$
to have a life of their own.

After a main clause: Rugby is a sport
$$\overset{S}{\underline{\text{that I}}} \overset{V}{\underline{\text{have played}}} \text{ only once.}$$

Interrupting a main clause: Yuan's grandfather,
$$\overset{S}{\underline{\text{who}}} \overset{S}{\underline{\text{fought}}} \overset{V}{\text{in World}}$$
$$\overset{V}{\underline{\text{War II}}}, \text{ told him about his experiences during the war.}$$

Before and after a main clause:
$$\underline{\text{When the } \overset{S}{\text{pianist}} \overset{V}{\text{sat down}} \text{ at the piano}},$$
$$\overset{S}{\text{she}} \overset{V}{\text{played}} \text{ a melody } \underline{\text{that } \overset{S}{\text{she}} \overset{V}{\text{had written}} \text{ recently}}.$$

PRACTICE

Write complex sentences of your own according to the instructions.

1. A sentence with a main clause followed by an adjective clause beginning with *who*:

   <u>Nancy searched for three days to find the person who had lost the</u>

   <u>German shepherd.</u>

2. A sentence with a subordinate clause beginning with *because* followed
   by a main clause:

   _____

   _____

3. A sentence that contains a noun modified by a subordinate clause
   beginning with *which*:

   _____

   _____

4. A sentence that contains a main clause and a subordinate clause beginning with *although*:

_____

_____

5. A sentence that contains one main clause, one adjective subordinate clause, and one adverb subordinate clause:

_____

_____

_____

The Compound–Complex Sentence

The **compound–complex sentence** is a combination of the compound and the complex sentence patterns. It is made up of two or more main clauses and one or more subordinate clauses. Therefore, it must contain a minimum of three sets of subjects and verbs (*at least* two main clauses and *at least* one subordinate clause).

EXAMPLES

                                    main clause   sub. clause
On the day-long bicycle trip, [Monique ate the food] [that she had packed,]

           main clause
[but Farzad had forgotten to bring anything to eat.]

           sub. clause   main clause
[Although he was exhausted,] [Ernesto cooked dinner for his mother,]

           main clause
[and after dinner he cleaned the kitchen.]

           main clause   sub. clause
[The travellers were excited] [when they arrived in Paris;]

           main clause
[they wanted to go sightseeing immediately.]

PRACTICE   Write compound–complex sentences of your own according to the instructions.

1. A sentence that contains two main clauses joined by *and* and one adjective clause beginning with *who*.

   Murphy, who works at the Mazda dealership, sold ten Miatas last

   month, and this month he plans to sell even more.

2. A sentence that contains a main clause and an adverb clause followed by a semicolon and another main clause.

   _____

   _____

3. A sentence that contains two main clauses joined by a semicolon and a transitional word or phrase. Modify one of the nouns in either main clause with an adjective clause beginning with *which* or *that*.

   _____

   _____

4. A sentence that contains two main clauses joined by *but* and one adverb subordinate clause beginning with *if, after,* or *because*.

   _____

   _____

5. A compound–complex sentence about yourself with a pattern of your own choice.

   _____

   _____

In the following sentences, write S above each subject and V above each verb. Then, in the spaces provided, identify the sentences as simple (S), compound (C), complex (CX), or compound–complex (C–CX).

1. Nowadays an assassin is the killer of a politically important

    person.   ___S___

2. During the late Middle Ages, an assassin was a

    member of a secret sect that murdered leaders of

    the Crusades.   _____

3. The word *assassin* comes from *hashshashin,* which means

    "hashish users"; reputedly, members of the secret sect

    used hashish.   _____

4. They would work themselves into a frenzy under the

    influence of hashish, and then they would commit their

    assassinations.   _____

5. Assassin bugs are large, brightly colored insects that kill

    and devour other insects.   _____

6. In Roman times, the intersection of three roads often

    served as a place where people would stop and talk

    before they continued their journeys.   _____

7. They would talk about events of the day; their conversation

    would be about ordinary, commonplace matters.   _____

8. In Latin, *tri* means "three," and *vium* means "road"

    or "way"; hence, an intersection of three roads was

    called a *trivium.*   _____

9. Soon, unimportant conversation at a *trivium* was called "trivial" conversation.   _____

10. Although "trivial" conversation literally means "three-roads" talk, today we use the word *trivial* to mean anything that is unimportant or insignificant.   _____

Section Two Review

1. A **simple sentence** contains only one main clause and no other clauses.

2. A **compound sentence** contains two or more main clauses that are joined by a comma and a coordinating conjunction *or* a semicolon *or* a semicolon and a transitional word or phrase.

3. A **complex sentence** contains only one main clause and one or more subordinate clauses.

4. A **compound–complex sentence** contains two or more main clauses and one or more subordinate clauses.

EXERCISE

Exercise 2A

Identify the following sentences as simple (S), compound (C), complex (CX), or compound–complex (C–CX).

___CX___ 1. The wood carvers of the northwest coast nations have produced art that is unsurpassed in North America, perhaps even in the world.

_____ 2. The totem pole stands as the most profound expression of the carver's art.

_____ 3. Arriving on the northwest coast of North America in the late 1800s, British sailors found galleries of tall, carved wooden pillars standing before coastal native settlements and called them "totem poles."

_____ 4. The sailors believed that they contained some kind of voodoo meaning.

_____ 5. Today we know that these poles are more like history books that record the history of a great person or an influential family and trace a lineage back to its origins.

_____ 6. The creatures carved upon the totem pole are visual statements, or symbols, and they express something about persons or families.

_____ 7. These totemic symbols are called "crests."

_____ 8. The creatures carved into the crests are supernatural beings that were encountered by members of one's clan or ancestral line.

_____ 9. Among the most powerful are the clans of the thunderbird, beaver, eagle, or killer whale.

_____ 10. Usually, totem poles were erected at ceremonies, when a shaman told the stories behind the creatures of the pole, and dancers and musicians celebrated these stories in song.

_____ 11. Today, we do not know much about the crests, since the carvers hid their meanings inside the crests and created visual puns that only they understood.

_____ 12. The carvers also created house posts, which supported the main beams of the house, and frontal posts, which stood against the house front and usually contained the front doorway.

_____ 13. Other carvings are memorial poles, mortuary poles topped with coffins, grave head markers, and welcome figures to greet guests.

_____ 14. Because poles last only 60 to 100 years in the coastal rains, most of these priceless art treasures have fallen and rotted away, but you can still find a fine collection of them in Vancouver at the University of British Columbia Museum of Anthropology.

EXERCISE

Exercise 2B

A. Combine each pair of sentences according to the instructions. You may need to delete or change some words.

1. A simple sentence with the pattern verb–subject:
    a. The ship was in the harbour.
    b. The ship was a nineteenth-century three-masted schooner.

    <u>In the harbour was a nineteenth-century three-masted schooner.</u>

2. A compound sentence that uses a semicolon as the connector:
    a. Vincent's ear hurt severely.
    b. Vincent was in love.

3. A complex sentence that uses the subordinator *because*:
    a. A violent electrical storm was approaching.
    b. The soccer game was postponed.

4. A simple sentence that uses the pattern subject–subject–verb:
    a. Around midnight the cow jumped over the moon.
    b. The spoon jumped over the moon as well.

5. A compound sentence that uses *and* as the connector:
    a. Marty finally figured out how to turn on the computer.
    b. Then Marty wrote a love poem for Maria.

B. Following the instructions, construct sentences of your own.

6. A compound–complex sentence that uses a semicolon:

7. A complex sentence that uses *who* to begin the subordinate clause:

   _____

   _____

8. A compound sentence that uses a semicolon and the transitional word *however:*

   _____

   _____

9. A simple sentence that uses the pattern subject–verb–verb:

   _____

   _____

10. A complex sentence that uses the subordinator *although:*

    _____

    _____

11. A compound sentence that uses *but* as the connector:

    _____

    _____

12. A simple sentence that begins with a prepositional phrase:

    _____

    _____

13. A complex sentence that uses *which* to begin the subordinate clause:

    _____

    _____

EXERCISE

Exercise 2C

Identify the sentences as simple (S), compound (C), complex (CX), or compound–complex (CC–CX).

1. In 1907 the *New York Times* carried a story about John Sharpe, an old man living at Coal Harbor on Quatsino Sound, an inlet at the north end of Vancouver Island. __*S*__ **2.** A man who visited Sharpe had recognized him as William Clarke Quantrill, known as "the bloodiest man in American history," and he felt now he had to tell the world that this notorious man was still alive and living in Canada. _____ **3.** In 1863, Quantrill's Raiders, among whom were such famous outlaws as Jesse and Frank James and Cole Younger, rode clear across Kansas and burned down the city of Lawrence.

_____ **4.** It was the only successful Southern attack upon a Northern city in the American Civil War. _____ **5.** Some say Quantrill died soon after Union forces ambushed Quantrill's Raiders, who were on their way to assassinate President Lincoln. _____ **6.** However, the inhabitants of Quatsino Sound heard Sharpe's long tales about Lawrence and the Civil War in Missouri, and they knew he was hiding from the law. _____ **7.** Two months after the story appeared in the *New York Times*, an Oregonian named John Edmunson took a steamer from Victoria to Hardy Bay. _____ **8.** He walked to Coal Harbour and went into the small house at the end of the pier in which John Sharpe lived. _____ **9.** According to eyewitnesses, the two men soon began arguing, and around midnight they went into a back bedroom, where a fight broke out. _____ **10.** The following morning Edmunson returned to Hardy Bay and took a steamer back to Victoria.

_____ **11.** Sharpe was near death when some friends on their way to Hardy

Bay discovered him. _____ **12.** He told them about the beating, and soon afterward he died. _____ **13.** Constable Arthur Carter, a provincial policeman, investigated the death and concluded that Edmunson had indeed been sent to assassinate "the bloodiest man in American history," but Edmunson had by then returned to Oregon along with two high-ranking Oregon officials. _____ **14.** Carter told reporters from the *Victoria Colonist* that he had solid proof that Sharpe was Quantrill, but that the Canadian government was viewing the matter as a private American affair. _____ **15.** Years later, scholars were able to provide solid evidence to back Carter's claim. _____ **16.** In 1894 Sharpe had been imprisoned in the New Westminster Gaol for robbing a mail coach, and after serving his sentence there, he had moved to Coal Harbour as a caretaker of an abandoned coal mine. _____ **17.** Biographical details and physical features of the accused bore a disturbing correlation to those of the infamous Quantrill. _____

Section Three

Fragments, Fused Sentences, and Comma Splices

Now that you are combining main and subordinate clauses to write different types of sentences, we need to talk about a few of the writing problems you might encounter. Fortunately, the most serious of these problems—the **fragment**, the **fused sentence**, and the **comma splice**—are also the easiest to identify and correct.

Fragments

The easiest way to identify a **sentence fragment** is to remember that *every sentence must contain a main clause*. If you do not have a main clause, you do not have a sentence. You can define a fragment, then, like this: A sentence fragment occurs when a group of words that lacks a main clause is punctuated as a sentence.

DEFINITION

sentence fragment	A sentence fragment occurs when a group of words that lacks a main clause is punctuated as a sentence.

Using this definition, you can identify almost any sentence fragment. However, you will find it easier to locate fragments in your own writing if you know that fragments can be divided into three basic types.

Three Types of Sentence Fragments

1. *Some fragments contain no clause at all.* This type of fragment is simple to spot. It usually does not even sound like a sentence because it lacks a subject or verb or both.

EXAMPLE   The snow in the street.

2. *Some fragments contain a verbal but still no clause.* This fragment is a bit less obvious because a verbal can be mistaken for a verb. But remember,

neither a participle nor an infinitive is a verb. (See Chapter One, pages 12–13, if you need to review this point.)

EXAMPLES   The snow **falling** on the street. (participle)

To slip on the snow in the street. (infinitive)

3. *Some fragments contain a subordinate clause but no main clause.* This type of fragment is perhaps the most common because it does contain a subject and a verb. But remember, a group of words without a main clause is not a sentence.

EXAMPLES   **After** the snow had fallen on the street.

Because I had slipped on the snow in the street.

Repairing Sentence Fragments

Once you have identified a fragment, you can correct it in one of two ways.

1. *Add words to give it a main clause.*

EXAMPLES

(fragment)	The snow in the street.
(sentence)	**I gazed** at the snow in the street.
(sentence)	The snow **was** in the street.
(fragment)	The snow falling in the street.
(sentence)	The snow falling in the street **covered my car**.
(sentence)	The snow **was** falling in the street.
(fragment)	After the snow had fallen in the street.
(sentence)	**I looked for a shovel** after the snow had fallen in the street.

2. *Join the fragment to a main clause written before or after it.*

EXAMPLES

(incorrect)	I love to see the ice on the lake. And the snow in the street.
(correct)	I love to see the ice on the lake and the snow in the street.
(incorrect)	My back was so sore that I could not stand straight. Because I had slipped on the snow in the street.
(correct)	My back was so sore that I could not stand straight because I had slipped on the snow in the street.

One final point might help you identify and correct sentence fragments. Remember that we all speak in fragments every day. (If a friend asks you how you are, you might respond with the fragment "Fine.") Because we speak in fragments, you may find that your writing seems acceptable even though it contains fragments. When you work on the exercises in this unit, do not rely on your "ear" alone. Look at the sentences. **If they do not contain main clauses, they are fragments, no matter how correct they may sound.**

Underline any fragment you find. Then correct it either by adding new words to give it a main clause or by joining it to a main clause next to it.

1. The small boy wandered slowly down the street. Stopping sometimes to look into the store windows.

   The small boy wandered slowly down the street, stopping sometimes to

   look into the store windows.

2. The athlete who won the new Chevrolet because he was voted player of the year.

   _____

   _____

3. When Mr. Nguyen felt lonely. He called his friend Hal. To talk about their home town.

   _____

   _____

4. Please shut the door. To keep out the cold draft.

   _____

   _____

5. After spending hundreds of hours reading the want ads in all of the newspapers that he could find in the three cities in the region.

   _____

   _____

6. The timer on the oven failed to go off. Probably because I had forgotten to set it.

_____

_____

7. The Chocolate Shoppe owner was turning the sign from the "open" side to the "closed" side. Even as Rupert was dashing across the street begging her to stop.

_____

_____

8. Because I had missed a test, I received a B in the class. Even though I had received As on all of the other tests.

_____

_____

9. To find the word that the minister had used just that morning.

_____

_____

10. The end.

_____

_____

Fused Sentences and Comma Splices

The **fused sentence** and **comma splice** are serious writing errors that you can correct with little effort. Either error can occur when you write a compound or compound–complex sentence. The fused sentence occurs when two or more main clauses are joined without a coordinating conjunction and without punctuation.

| DEFINITION | fused sentence | The fused sentence occurs when two or more main clauses are joined without a coordinating conjunction and without punctuation. |

E X A M P L E   (fused)   Raoul drove by his uncle's house he waved at his cousins.

As you can see, the two main clauses in the above example (*Raoul drove by his uncle's house* and *he waved at his cousins*) have been joined without a coordinating conjunction and without punctuation of any kind.

     The comma splice is a similar error: The comma splice occurs when two or more main clauses are joined with a comma but without a coordinating conjunction.

D E F I N I T I O N

comma splice	The comma splice occurs when two or more main clauses are joined with a comma but without a coordinating conjunction.

E X A M P L E   (comma splice)   The hot sun beat down on the construction workers, they looked forward to the end of the day.

In this example, the two main clauses (*The hot sun beat down on the construction workers* and *they looked forward to the end of the day*) are joined by a comma, but a comma alone is not enough to join main clauses.

PUNCTUATION NOTE: One of the most frequent comma splices occurs when a writer joins two main clauses with a comma and a transitional word rather than with a semicolon and a transitional word.

E X A M P L E   (comma splice)   I wanted a dog for Christmas, however, my parents gave me a cat.

Repairing Fused Sentences and Comma Splices

Because both fused sentences and comma splices occur when two main clauses are joined, you can correct either error using one of five methods. Consider these two errors:

(fused)   Jack left for work early he arrived late.

(comma splice)   Jack left for work early, he arrived late.

Both of these errors can be corrected in one of five ways:

1. *Use a comma and a coordinating conjunction.*

   Jack left for work early, **but** he arrived late.

2. *Use a semicolon.*

   Jack left for work early; he arrived late.

3. *Use a semicolon and a conjunctive adverb, transitional word, or phrase. (See page 92.)*

   Jack left for work early; **however**, he arrived late.

   PUNCTUATION NOTE: Do not use a semicolon before a transitional word that does not begin a main clause. For example, in the following sentence, however *does not need a semicolon.*

   I have not seen my father, **however**, for ten years.

4. *Change one of the clauses to a subordinate clause by beginning it with a subordinator.*

   Although Jack left for work early, he arrived late.

5. *Punctuate the clauses as two separate sentences.*

   Jack left for work early. He arrived late.

NOTE: Sometimes the two main clauses in a fused sentence or comma splice are interrupted by a subordinate clause. When this sentence pattern occurs, the two main clauses must still be connected in one of the five ways.

EXAMPLES   (fused)   Alma bought a new Mercedes even though she could not afford one she fell behind in her monthly payments.

(comma splice)   Alma bought a new Mercedes even though she could not afford one, she fell behind in her monthly payments.

These errors can be corrected in any of the five ways mentioned above.

EXAMPLE   Alma bought a new Mercedes even though she could not afford one; consequently, she fell behind in her monthly payments.

PRACTICE

Identify the following sentences as fused (F), comma splice (CS), or correct (C). Then correct the incorrect sentences. Use a different method of correction each time.

____CS____   1. Butler had wanted to join his brother in New York, his business was going too well for him to leave.

   Butler had wanted to join his brother in New York, but his

   business was going too well for him to leave.

_____   2. I tossed the two pieces of iron into the fire then I reached in and pulled them out with my bare hands.

_____

_____

_____   3. After the Bruins lifted their goalie, the Pocket Rocket scored into an empty net.

_____

_____

_____   4. The wind grew stronger, consequently, the fire soon blazed out of control.

_____

_____

_____   5. For two months Dale practised hard for the marble tournament he developed a blister on his right thumb the day before the tournament.

_____

_____

_____   6. The doorbell rang three times, then someone began to bang on the door.

_____

_____

_____   7. Oscar kept riding his mountain bicycle in the middle of the night although he knew it was dangerous he decided to ride only on nights with a full moon.

_____

_____

REVIEW

Section Three Review

1. A **sentence fragment** occurs when a group of words that lacks a main clause is punctuated as a sentence.

2. There are three types of sentence fragments.
    a. Some contain no clause at all.
    b. Some contain a verbal but still no clause.
    c. Some contain a subordinate clause but no main clause.

3. You can correct a sentence fragment in one of two ways.
    a. Add words to give it a main clause.
    b. Join it to an already existing main clause.

4. The **fused sentence** occurs when two or more main clauses are joined without a coordinating conjunction and without punctuation.

5. The **comma splice** occurs when two or more main clauses are joined with a comma but without a coordinating conjunction.

6. You can correct fused sentences and comma splices in one of five ways.
    a. Use a comma and a coordinating conjunction.
    b. Use a semicolon.
    c. Use a semicolon and a conjunctive adverb, word, or phrase.
    d. Change one of the clauses to a subordinate clause by adding a subordinator at the beginning of it.
    e. Punctuate the clauses as two separate sentences.

EXERCISE

Exercise 3A

Identify each of the following as correct (C), fused (F), comma splice (CS), or sentence fragment (Frag). Then correct each error using any of the methods discussed in this unit.

Frag   1. Because it was so cold and slimy and ugly that Carl was becoming nauseated just looking at it.

   It was so cold and slimy and ugly that Carl was becoming

   nauseated just looking at it.

_____   2. I had forgotten to register my car, as a result, a police officer gave me a ticket.

_____   3. Tell me that story again.

_____   4. After leaving class, I drove home then I realized that I had left my wallet at school.

_____   5. The pigeon, pecking and pecking at the peanut glued to the sidewalk.

_____   6. Computer technology has improved in the past ten years, automotive technology has too.

_____   7. The water leaking into her studio almost ruined Olga's paint-
ings, but luckily she was able to save them.

_____

_____

_____   8. Most people say that hockey is our national pastime however
others say baseball has replaced hockey.

_____

_____

_____   9. Josefina was elated by her grade report she took her son out
for dinner.

_____

_____

_____   10. Last night's snowfall was so heavy that the roof of my house
collapsed.

_____

_____

_____   11. The museum bought the collection of classical statues, the
butler gave the museum the shoebox of missing parts.

_____

_____

_____   12. The votes had been cast, the election was over.

_____

_____

_____ 13. Some say that hockey has become a violent sport, for instance, players intentionally attack each other with their bare fists.

_____

_____

_____ 14. After he had examined each of his tires and cheked the oil, but before leaving to see his mother, who had lived for the past fifteen years in Anchorage, Alaska.

_____

_____

_____ 15. The parrot desperately wanted to join Michelle at dinner, although he pushed and pushed against the door of his cage, he was unable to budge it.

_____

_____

EXERCISE

Exercise 3B

A. Correct the following sentence fragments by adding words to them to make them complete sentences.

1. Shannon, who had been standing in the rain for two hours.

   Shannon, who had been standing in the rain for two hours, finally

   decided to give up and go home.

2. Because I could not wait for the plane to arrive.

   _____

   _____

3. The aroma of the snails sizzling in the pan on the stove.

   _____

   _____

4. That he had understood all of the material.

   _____

   _____

5. In the town that is by the Rio Honda.

   _____

   _____

B. Join the following main clauses by using a comma and a coordinating conjunction, a semicolon, a semicolon and a conjunctive adverb, a transitional word or phrase, or by making one of the clauses a subordinate clause. Use each of these four methods at least once.

6. Anouk looked for bait under the wet stones. Finally, she found a hellgrammite and put it on her hook.

   Anouk looked for bait under the wet stones; finally, she found a

   hellgrammite and put it on her hook.

7. Deborah purchased the car that had been recommended by the salesperson. Scott bought the car that cost the least.

   _____

   _____

8. Maurice used a thesaurus to look up an alternative word. He was quite pleased with the word that he found.

   _____

   _____

9. Four ducks flew above the lake. The lake had been polluted by toxic waste.

   _____

   _____

10. The politicians had planned to avoid personal attacks. They did not succeed in avoiding them.

   _____

   _____

C. Expand each of the following sentences by adding a **clause** to it. Identify the subject and verb of each clause you use and vary the placement of the clauses. (Don't place every clause at the end of its sentence.) When you add the clauses, use each of the following methods at least once: a) use a comma and a coordinating conjunction; b) use a semicolon; c) use a semicolon and a transitional word or phrase; d) make one clause a subordinate clause.

11. Sitting in their patrol car, the police constables tried to comfort the lost child.

   S   V
   Sitting in their patrol car, the police constables tried to comfort the

   S   V
   lost child; however, the child would not stop crying.

12. Pasta tastes delicious.

   _____

   _____

13. With its use of advanced film and animation technology, the movie *Terminator II* was visually interesting and exciting.

   _____

   _____

14. I jog two miles every day.

   _____

   _____

15. The musical group Feeding Like Butterflies has become quite popular lately.

   _____

   _____

Exercise 3C

In the following paragraph, correct any fragments, fused sentences, or comma splices.

1. Any visitors stepping through my front door and into my living room.

2. ~~They~~ will immediately be greeted by a flurry of disorderly impressions.

3. On a stand to the right is an open aquarium containing six inches of sawdust, in it they will see a dog biscuit, an orange peel, and an inverted glass container. 4. They will also see two miniature rats. 5. Vanilla Wafer, a brown and white extrovert who loves to play, and Marshmallow, an albino who is a bit more reticent. 6. Some people think rats are repulsive, however, my seven-year-old daughter, Jenna, loves these friendly creatures. 7. Feeding, cleaning, and playing with them everyday. 8. As our visitors move farther into our living room, they might find an earless stuffed rabbit lying between the couch and the rat aquarium, perhaps they will need to step over a cloth doll. 9. Surrounded by red and white plastic building blocks. 10. These "obstacles" are the treasures of my two-year-old, Chelsea they are the signs of a happy, active little girl. 11. Finally, as our visitors approach the far end of our living room, they will come upon a dining table buried under a scattering of school papers, books, pens and pencils, computer printouts, and loose-leaf notebooks. 12. If our visitors move a few of the papers, they will probably find several dog-eared Nancy Drew novels, they belong to Marste. 13. Who is my eleven-year-old. 14. Many people might describe my livng room as a chaotic mess, it reminds me of my three very active daughters.

Section Four

Sentence Practice: Combining Main and Subordinate Clauses

In this chapter you have learned the basic sentence patterns of English, and you have seen that you can combine the major word groups of a sentence—the clauses—in various ways. Of course, how you present your ideas in your sentences can affect the way a reader perceives your ideas. Take, for instance, the following sentences.

1. Subcompact cars are economical.
2. Subcompact cars are easy to handle.
3. Subcompact cars are simple to park.
4. Full-size sedans are roomier.
5. Full-size sedans are safer.
6. Full-size sedans are quieter.

You can present these ideas in six simple sentences like those above, but doing so makes the writing choppy and simplistic. On the other hand, you can use the sentence patterns discussed in this chapter to combine these six ideas in several ways.

1. You can present these ideas as **two simple sentences.**

EXAMPLE   Subcompact cars are economical, easy to handle, and simple to park. Full-size sedans are roomier, safer, and quieter.

2. Or you can group the ideas into **one compound sentence** by using a comma and a coordinating conjunction.

EXAMPLE   Subcompact cars are economical, easy to handle, and simple to park, but full-size sedans are roomier, safer, and quieter.

Note that the coordinating conjunction *but* allows you to emphasize the contrast between the ideas in the two main clauses.

3. You can also group these ideas into **a compound sentence by using a semicolon as a connector.**

EXAMPLE   Subcompact cars are economical, easy to handle, and simple to park; full-size sedans are roomier, safer, and quieter.

In this sentence the contrast in the ideas is implied rather than directly stated.

4. Of course, you can add a **conjunctive adverb** after the semicolon.

EXAMPLE   Subcompact cars are economical, easy to handle, and simple to park; however, full-size sedans are roomier, safer, and quieter.

Note that *however* now signals the contrast between the ideas in the two clauses.

5. Finally, you can group the ideas into **a main clause** and **a subordinate clause** by adding a subordinator. Now you have a complex sentence.

EXAMPLE   Although subcompact cars are economical, easy to handle, and simple to park, full-size sedans are roomier, safer, and quieter.

Like the other sentences, this sentence shows the reader the contrast between the ideas in the two clauses. However, it also shows the ideas the writer thinks are most important—the ones in the main clause.

EXERCISE

Sentence Combining Exercises

Using the knowledge of sentence patterns that you have gained from this chapter, combine the following lists of sentences into longer sentences according to the directions. *Be sure to punctuate carefully to avoid comma splices or fused sentences.* Remember to look for a base sentence or a main idea to build upon. The most important idea should be in a main clause.

EXAMPLE   First, combine these ideas into a compound sentence, using one of the three methods presented in Section Two of this chapter. Then form a complex sentence, using a subordinator to make one clause subordinate.

1. Montreal often seems dirty.
2. Montreal often seems overcrowded.
3. Montreal often seems full of crime.
4. Montreal has excitement.
5. Montreal has charming ethnic communities.
6. Montreal has a great variety of cultural attractions.

A. Compound sentence:

Montreal often seems dirty, overcrowded, and full of crime; however, it also has excitement, charming ethnic communities, and a great variety of cultural attractions.

B. Complex sentence:

Although Montreal often seems dirty, overcrowded, and full of crime, it also has excitement, charming ethnic communities, and a great variety of cultural attractions.

1. Combine the following sentences into a complex sentence by making sentences b and c into one adjective clause.

   a. Dr. Norman Bethune is a folk hero in modern China.
   b. He was a prominent doctor.
   c. He lived in Montreal.

   _____

   _____

   _____

   _____

2. Combine these sentences into a complex sentence beginning with a prepositional phrase. Form sentences c and d into an adverb clause beginning with *where*.

   a. This happened in China.
   b. Bethune carried the hospital on horseback.
   c. The horses went up to the front lines.
   d. On the front lines he was able to operate on wounded Chinese soldiers.

   _____

   _____

   _____

   _____

3. Combine these sentences into a complex sentence. Form sentences b and c into an adverb clause that begins with *if*.

   a. The soldiers might otherwise have lost their lives.
   b. They had to be transported long distances on horseback.
   c. They had to be taken to army hospitals.

   _____

   _____

   _____

   _____

4. Combine these sentences into a compound sentence.

    a. Bethune was a brilliant inventor.
    b. Bethune was an innovative surgeon.
    c. His colleagues found him difficult.
    d. They found him impatient and self-absorbed.

    _____

    _____

    _____

    _____

5. Combine these sentences into a simple sentence.

    a. His restless search was for better ways of helping mankind.
    b. This search led to his going to Spain in 1936.
    c. He went to Spain as a volunteer to work as a doctor.
    d. It was during the Spanish Civil War.

    _____

    _____

    _____

    _____

6. Combine the following into one sentence. Use the most effective pattern
   you can find. At the end of your sentence, indicate which type of sentence
   you have written.

    a. Bethune invented a mobile blood transfusion service.
    b. This service carried blood plasma to Loyalist soldiers.
    c. These soldiers were wounded in the front lines of the war.

    _____

    _____

    _____

    _____

7. Combine these sentences into one sentence. Use the most effective pattern you can find. At the end of your new sentence, indicate which type of sentence you have written.

   a. Many people frustrated his efforts.
   b. He returned to Canada a bitter man.
   c. He was looking for another cause.

   _____

   _____

   _____

   _____

   _____

8. Combine these sentences into one sentence. At the end of your new sentence, indicate which type of sentence you have written.

   a. He heard about the struggle of the Chinese.
   b. They were struggling against Japan.
   c. Bethune toured Canada.
   d. Bethune was drumming up money.
   e. The money was to set up a hospital in China.

   _____

   _____

   _____

   _____

   _____

9. Combine these sentences into one sentence. Indicate which type of sentence you have written.

   a. Bethune went to China.
   b. Bethune established a mobile hospital.
   c. Bethune spent many years of selfless devotion to the cause.
   d. Bethune weakened and died.
   e. Bethune cut his hand during an operation.

   _____

   _____

   _____

   _____

10. Combine these sentences into one sentence. Indicate which type of sentence you have written.

   a. Chairman Mao said he was a hero.
   b. Chairman Mao said he was one of the heroes of the revolution.
   c. Chairman Mao said this Canadian had taught everyone a lesson.
   d. It was a lesson in selflessness.
   e. It was a lesson the world should learn.

   _____

   _____

   _____

   _____

Section Five

Paragraphs: Topic Sentences and Supporting Detail

Assignment

In Chapter Two you have read paragraphs that describe people as well as places. Exercise 1C (page 89) describes the experiences of Mifflin Gibbs as a Black person in Victoria, Exercise 2C (page 105) describes John Sharpe, who escaped to Vancouver Island after the American Civil War, and Exercise 3C (page 121) describes someone's rather cluttered living room. Your assignment in this writing section is to describe a person who is unusual in one particular way or a place that you remember for one particular reason. As you do so, you will practise limiting your paragraph to one idea that is expressed in a topic sentence and developing your paragraph with details that are both specific and concrete.

Prewriting

1. To find a topic, use freewriting, brainstorming, or clustering (or all three) to generate ideas about people and places that you remember well. You do not need to have known a Mifflin Gibbs or lived in a cluttered living room to find an appropriate person or place to write about. Make a list of any unusual people you have ever known and of the characteristics that made them unusual. Make another list of places you remember well and of the reasons you remember them.

2. From your prewriting, choose the one topic that is most interesting to you. Now, prewrite again, but this time keep your focus on this one topic. You are now looking for as many details as you can remember to describe the person or place you have chosen. Remember, you are prewriting here, so write as much as you can without worrying about mistakes.

3. Once you have decided on your topic and have generated some details to describe that topic, you are ready to focus your paper still further by limiting your description to details that illustrate one central point. This prewriting step is important, for the more you *limit* your topic to one

point, the more likely you will be to describe your topic in a detailed and thorough manner.

To limit your description, reread your prewriting. Look for related details that focus on *one particular reason* that the person you have chosen is unusual or that the place you have chosen is memorable. These related details, and others that you might generate through more prewriting, will form the body of your paragraph.

4. The final prewriting step is to develop a preliminary **topic sentence**.

The Topic Sentence

The topic sentence is the one sentence in your paragraph that states both your *topic* and the *central point* that you intend to make about that topic. Although it can appear in a variety of places within the paragraph, for college writing you should write it as the first sentence of the paragraph so that the point you intend to make is clear from the start.

Even paragraphs of description, like the one you are writing for this assignment, have some point. In history texts, for example, a person or a place might be described in detail to help the reader understand some idea about that person or place. And in your own college papers you will usually be expected to provide examples or case studies of real people, places, and situations to illustrate your points. In short, when you use description in your writing, you need to be able to focus it on *one central point* so that the reason for the description is clear.

Here are some examples of topic sentences drawn from exercises in Chapters One and Two. Note that each contains a topic and a central point.

EXAMPLES

                 topic   central point

On March 25, 1994, **Nicholas Alkemade** <u>reserved a placed for himself in aviation history</u>.

                topic

During World War II, **a Chinese seaman** <u>experienced one of the most</u>

       central point

<u>amazing survival adventures of the war</u>.

                                      topic

Any visitor stepping through my front door and into **my living room** will

                    central point

immediately be greeted by <u>a flurry of disorderly impressions</u>.

As you write your topic sentence, be sure that it contains both a *topic* and a central *point*. Also, write a topic sentence that causes your reader to want more explanation. Here are some examples of sentences that would *not* make effective topic sentences.

1. A sentence that has no central point.

EXAMPLE   My paragraph is about Bass Lake Provincial Park.

In this sentence the topic (Bass Lake Provincial Park) is clear, but no central point about that park is expressed. An improved sentence might be:

EXAMPLE   When I visited Bass Lake Provincial Park last summer, I was distressed at how clean and attractive it was.

In this sentence, a central point—that Bass Lake Provincial Park is clean and attractive—has been clearly expressed.

2. A sentence with a central point that does not cause the reader to want more explanation.

EXAMPLE   I have a brother named Bryan.

This sentence simply states a fact. There is nothing to be explained after the fact is stated. An improved topic sentence might be:

EXAMPLE   Although my brother Bryan is forty-three years old, he lives the same kind of wild life today that he did when he was twenty-three.

This sentence now makes a statement about Bryan that causes the reader to want more explanation.

PRACTICE

In each sentence below, underline the topic once and the central point twice.

1. While travelling to the ball game last night, I had a terrifying experience.

2. Smoking of any kind must be outlawed in all public places.

3. Winning at tennis requires as much mental skill as it does physical skill.

4. Following four simple steps will help you pass any test.

5. I deserve the raise that I have asked for.

PRACTICE

Place a check mark before each sentence that would *not* make a good topic sentence.

_____ 1. Last year I worked as a salesperson.

_____ 2. My paper will be about my job in sales.

_____ 3. The merchandise I sold last year should have satisfied my customers.

_____ 4. The customers who returned the merchandise had poor reasons for doing so.

_____ 5. I have worked in sales for a total of five years.

Writing

Once you have a preliminary topic sentence and a list of related details, it is time to write the first draft of your paragraph. Open your paragraph with your topic sentence, and then write out the details that illustrate the central point of your topic sentence. Do not worry about writing a "perfect" first draft. You will have the chance to improve the draft when you revise it.

Rewriting

1. When you have completed the first draft, read it over to see if your preliminary topic sentence accurately states the central point of your paper. If you can improve the topic sentence, do so now.

2. As you read over your draft, see if you can add still more descriptive details that relate to your central point. Add those that come to mind.

3. Finally, check the words and phrases you have used in your first draft. You will find that many of them can be more descriptive if you make them more *specific* and *concrete*.

Specific Details

A specific detail is limited in the number of things it can refer to. For example, the word *poodle* is more specific than the word *dog*, and the word *elm* is more specific than *tree*. The more specific you can be in your paragraph, the more interesting it will be to read.

Write three specific words for each of the following general words:

building _____ _____ _____

tool _____ _____ _____

car _____ _____ _____

emotion _____ _____ _____

table _____ _____ _____

Concrete Details

A concrete detail appeals to at least one of the five senses. It helps a reader *see*, *hear*, *smell*, *taste*, or *feel* what you describe. For example, rather than writing that your grandmother's kitchen smelled "wonderful," you might write that it was always "filled with the aromas of freshly baked bread and my grandfather's cigar smoke." Or, instead of writing that the lake was "beautiful," you might write that "its clear blue water sparkled in the early morning sunlight."

Rewrite the following sentences to make the underlined words more concrete.

EXAMPLE   The <u>house</u> was <u>run down</u>.

<u>The three-bedroom tract house on the corner of Elm and Vine had</u>

<u>deteriorated into a ruin of broken windows, peeling paint, and splintered,</u>

<u>termite-infested walls.</u>

1. The <u>woman</u> walked through the <u>entrance</u>.

_____

_____

_____

2. The <u>food</u> tasted <u>terrible</u>.

_____

_____

_____

3. The man <u>looked angry</u>.

_____

_____

_____

4. Her bedroom walls were <u>colourful</u>.

_____

_____

_____

The final step in rewriting is to edit your paper. Check the spelling of words you are uncertain about. Examine each sentence closely to be sure it is not a **fragment, comma splice,** or **fused sentence**. If it is, repair the error using the techniques you have studied in this chapter.

Once you have a draft you are satisfied with, prepare a clean final draft, following the format your instructor has asked for.

Exercises for Paragraph Practice

A. Now that you have a final draft, number each of your sentences. Then, in the spaces below, identify each sentence as simple (S), compound (C), complex (CX), or compound–complex (C–CX).

1. _____   2. _____   3. _____   4. _____

5. _____   6. _____   7. _____   8. _____

9. _____   10. _____   11. _____   12. _____

13. _____   14. _____   15. _____   16. _____

17. _____   18. _____   19. _____   20. _____

B. Have you written at least one sentence of each type? If you have not, revise one of your sentences (or combine two or more) to make the sentence type you have not yet used.

Sentence type not used: _____

Revision to make that sentence type:

_____

_____

C. Choose one of your simple or compound sentences. Revise it into a complex or compound–complex sentence by adding more words to it or by combining it with a nearby sentence.

Original sentence (identify as **simple** or **compound**):

_____

_____

Revised sentence (identify as **complex** or **compound–complex**):

_____

_____

D. Choose one of your compound or complex sentences. Add more words to it or combine it with a nearby sentence to make a longer complex or compound–complex sentence.

Original sentence (identify as **compound** or **complex**):

_____

_____

Revised sentence (identify as **complex** or **compound–complex**):

_____

_____

PRACTICE TEST

Chapter Two Practice Test

I. Review of Chapter One

A. In the following sentences, identify the underlined words by writing one of the following abbreviations above the words: noun (N), pronoun (Pro), verb (V), adjective (Adj), adverb (Adv), conjunction (Conj), preposition (Prep).

1. The court <u>ordered</u> the city to remove the cross from <u>public</u> land.

2. The <u>friendly</u> pilot banked <u>quickly</u> to the right.

3. The airplane <u>flew</u> from Thunder Bay <u>to</u> Toronto upside down.

4. The <u>thought</u> of interstellar travel excited the astronaut, <u>but</u> discussions of cosmic strings merely bored her.

5. After <u>she</u> had eaten <u>five</u> double-stuffed Oreos, Diane felt a little woozy.

6. <u>Somebody</u> was standing in the rain <u>under</u> a tattered black umbrella.

7. We did <u>not</u> visit her father at Christmas, <u>nor</u> did she see him during semester break.

8. Bill frowned when he <u>noticed</u> half a <u>worm</u> in the apple he was eating.

9. Ellen had <u>always</u> known that someday she would become a <u>successful</u> attorney.

10. When the cow stuck its head <u>through</u> the fence, <u>it</u> was surprised to see how much greener the grass looked.

B. For the following sentences, underline all subjects once and all complete verbs twice. Place parentheses around all prepositional phrases.

11. Have you seen my new apartment?

12. The deep groan seemed to come from the attic.

13. The man with two heads refused to return to the circus.

14. During the night, someone broke into our house and ate our chocolate chip cookies.

15. There were three reasons for Nizar's silly grin, but he would tell us only one of them.

16. If he had heard the weather forecast, Joss would have stayed at home.

17. Some of the inmates objected to the food, but the guards ignored them.

18. Two lions and a giraffe walked to the bus station and asked for tickets to San Francisco.

19. Three of the children screamed when the trapeze artist pretended to slip.

20. Lise was positive that the man who had robbed the bank was wearing a felt hat with a peacock feather in it.

II. Chapter Two

A. Underline the subordinate clauses and identify the type of clause (adjective or adverb) in the space provided.

21. The dog that bit the bicyclist belongs to my neighbour.   _____

22. Whenever she sees a yellow brick road, Dorothy screams and runs the other way.   _____

23. He decided to give his lottery winnings to the woman who had sold him the ticket.   _____

24. Anne will give you her tickets to the concert if you take her skiing next week.   _____

25. Unless the hurricane changes direction, it will hit the

    coast in one hour.   _____

B. To the main clauses below, add the types of subordinate clauses indicated in parentheses. Add your clause at any place in the sentence that is appropriate.

    26. (adverb clause) Karen decided to leave the concert.

    _____

    _____

    27. (adjective clause) The minister looked worried as he began to speak to his assistant.

    _____

    _____

    28. (adjective clause) The ship sailed across the harbour and toward the pier.

    _____

    _____

    29. (adverb clause) My horse loves to roll in the dirt.

    _____

    _____

    30. (adverb clause) The Pope decided to take a plane anyway.

    _____

    _____

C. In the spaces provided, identify the following sentences as simple (S), compound (C), complex (CX), or compound–complex (C–CX).

    31. If you want to leave today, you had better start to pack.   _____

32. The bridge was rotting and starting to fall apart; however, Hilda was determined to cross it. _____

33. Next to a run-down old building with broken windows and peeling paint stood a newly restored Victorian mansion with seven bedrooms, two dining rooms, a sweeping front lawn, and a circular driveway. _____

34. Sandy promised to take his sister to the movies as soon as he returned, but he did not keep his promise. _____

35. The water will not drain from the yard because the ground is not properly graded. _____

D. Compose sentences of your own according to the instructions.

36. Write a simple sentence that contains two prepositional phrases.

_____

_____

37. Write a compound sentence. Use a coordinating conjunction and appropriate punctuation to join the clauses.

_____

_____

38. Write a compound sentence. Use a transitional word or phrase and appropriate punctuation to join the clauses.

_____

_____

39. Write a complex sentence. Use *after* as the subordinator.

_____

_____

40. Write a compound–complex sentence. Use the coordinating conjunction *but* and the subordinator *because*.

_____

_____

E. Identify each of the following sentences as correct (C), fused (F), comma splice (CS), or fragment (Frag). Then correct any errors by using the methods discussed in Chapter Two.

41. _____   Before she had noticed all of the people who were sitting in the waiting room.

_____

_____

42. _____   I mowed the lawn, then I edged it.

_____

_____

43. _____   Stop making so much noise.

_____

_____

44. _____   A flamingo, standing on one leg in the middle of the pond.

_____

_____

45. _____   Shawna searched through the parking lot three times her car was gone.

_____

_____

46. _____   After everyone had left the theater, the custodian locked all of the doors, it was time to go home.

_____

_____

47. _____   Although she had seen the film four times and had hated it each time.

_____

_____

48. _____   My father's back had hurt for the past three days, however the doctor could find nothing wrong with it.

_____

_____

49. _____   By carefully placing one foot in front of the other, Carla walked across the narrow plank that served as a bridge.

_____

_____

50. _____   The attorney believed that the suspect was lying, on the other hand, he thought his own client was lying too.

_____

_____

ANSWERS

Answers to Practices in Chapter Two

Page 77:

2. MC	7. SC
3. MC	8. MC
4. N	9. SC
5. SC	10. N
6. MC	

Page 78:

2. PP	7. PP
3. PP	8. PP
4. PP	9. SC
5. SC	10. PP
6. SC	

Pages 78–79:

2. Elena wants to tour Europe (when) she graduates from college.

3. After the sudden thunderstorm, many of the fans left.

4. The study skills centre offers help for students (who) are having trouble in their math classes.

5. (If) you will go up in a balloon, I will go too.

6. The storm uprooted a tree (that) had stood in the town square for fifty years.

7. At first British Columbia appeared to be unapproachable from the rest of Canada (because) of the Rocky Mountains.

8. Martin did not know the driver (whose) car had won the race.

9. Hampton decided to take a nap (after) he had eaten his carrot.

10. The cook put the food exactly (where) it belonged.

Page 80:

2. Jacques feels ill (whenever) he eats liver.

3. Ridley was disgusted (because) one of the aliens was drooling on her.

4. The car, (when) the chains came off, began to slide across the icy road.

5. (When) in one race Roger Bannister and John Landy both broke the four-minute mile, he knew that a miracle had occurred.

Page 80:

Answers will vary. Here are possible ones.

2. Because it was always cold and snowy in Toronto, Marilyn's parents spend Christmas in Puerto Vallarte.

3. His teacher liked his essay about rap music even though she did not like to listen to rap herself.

4. Gloria, <u>who hated shopping</u>, sat patiently in the front seat of the car

5. <u>When they had finished eating their breakfast</u>, they gave their leftover cabbage and beets to Buttons.

Page 81:

2. The poet (whom) <u>we all admire</u> always has his breakfast there.

3. In fact, all of the people (who) <u>want to chat with us</u> seem to prefer meeting us at Cafe Ian.

4. A barber's pole, (which) <u>the owners have painted brown and cream instead of red and white</u>, stands at the entrance.

5. A black cat (that) <u>everyone has named "Cappuccino"</u> roams around the cafe begging for bites of pastry.

Page 82:

Answers will vary. Here are some possible ones.

2. About 9:00 every evening a strange group of people <u>who wear black berets</u> gathers in the back of the cafe.

3. Some of the men wear bizarre ties, <u>which they must have bought at secondhand stores</u>.

4. Some of the women <u>who are part of this group</u> wear interesting shirts.

5. Each person <u>who frequents Cafe Ian</u>, has his or her own special style of dress or speech.

Pages 82–83:

2. The formerly popular premier was not re-elected <u>because the economy had declined during his first term</u>. (Adv)

3. Hiding in the flowerpot, Peter Cottontail thought of the advice <u>that his mother had given him</u>. (Adj)

4. <u>As he enters an expensive restaurant</u>, Mr. Jackson invariably blows his nose loudly several times. (Adv)

5. Winnipeg is a city <u>which has one of the best ballet companies in the world</u>. (Adj)

Page 83:

Answers will vary. Here are some possible ones.

2. Kristine wrote a thank-you note to her track coach, <u>who had helped her get a scholarship</u>. (Adj)

3. After the rodeo Elvia, <u>who had never before won an award</u>, was presented a first-place buckle for calf roping. (Adj)

4. <u>While my children played in the back room</u>, Chen took me on a tour of his new art gallery. (Adv)

5. Byron wanted us to go to the new coffee house <u>because a friend of his was playing piano there</u>. (Adv)

Pages 91–92:

Answers will vary. Here are some possible ones.

2. At the front door a man holding a briefcase talked to Herman.
3. There were only 20,123 people at the Canucks' game last night.
4. The 1992 Cadillac swerved across the road and crashed into a telephone pole.
5. On the hot sidewalk walked a barefooted ten-year-old boy and his mother.

Page 93:

Answers will vary. Here are some possible ones.

2. The confused polar bear paced in its cage; it did not look at all happy.
3. The orangutan had escaped from its cage five times; as a result, the zookeeper decided to consult an expert locksmith.
4. Jenna loves to eat cotton candy, and her sister loves ice cream bars.
5. It rained for three hours yesterday; however, today should be sunny.

Page 94:

		S:		V:	
2.	compound:	S:	battle	V:	was fierce
		S:	we	V:	left
3.	compound:	S:	We	V:	were eager
		S:	it	V:	was
4.	simple:	S:	circuses	V:	began
5.	compound:	S:	circuses	V:	were
		S:	ones	V:	were produced
6.	simple:	S:	Mr. B.	V:	had
7.	simple:	S:	Cats, dogs	V:	must have enjoyed
8.	compound:	S:	fleas	V:	played
		S:	companies	V:	presented
9.	simple:	S:	managers	V:	allowed
10.	compound:	S:	size	V:	was limited
		S:	theaters	V:	were limited

Pages 95–96:

Answers will vary. Here are some possible ones.

2. Because the weather had been so bad, we decided to stay home.
3. Chung looked sadly at his new Ford Mustang, which he had just driven into a brick wall.
4. Although he was late for the movie, Cyrus did not try to drive any faster.
5. The dog that was chasing the mail carrier down the street returned to its yard when its owner called it.

Page 97:

Answers will vary. Here are some possible ones.

2. Jodi decided not to leave because her car was not running well; she stayed home all day.
3. The horse that had won the Kentucky Derby died two days later; however, no one suspected foul play.
4. If you do not pay me the money, I won't be able to buy groceries this week, but you probably don't care about that.

5. I saw my sister, who sells real estate, at the concert last night, but I don't think she saw me.

Pages 98–99:

2. complex:		S:	assassin	V:	was
		S:	that	V:	murdered
3. compound–complex:		S:	word	V:	comes
		S:	which	V:	means
		S:	members	V:	used
4. compound:		S:	They	V:	would work
		S:	they	V:	would commit
5. complex:		S:	bugs	V:	are
		S:	that	V:	kill, devour
6. complex:		S:	intersection	V:	served
		S:	people	V:	would stop, talk
		S:	they	V:	continued
7. compound:		S:	They	V:	would talk
		S:	conversation	V:	would be
8. compound:		S:	tri	V:	means
		S:	vium	V:	means
		S:	intersection	V:	was called
9. simple:		S:	conversation	V:	was called
10. complex:		S:	conversation	V:	means
		S:	we	V:	use
		S:	that	V:	is

Pages 109–110:

Answers will vary. Here are some possible ones.

2. *fragment*: The athlete who won the new Chevrolet because he was voted player of the year.
   possible correction: The athlete who won the new Chevrolet because he was voted player of the year received his car today.
3. *fragments*: When Mr. Nguyen felt lonely. To talk about their home town.
   possible correction: When Mr. Nguyen felt lonely, he called his friend Hai to talk about their home town.
4. *fragment*: To keep out the cold draft.
   possible correction: Please shut the door to keep out the cold draft.
5. *fragment*: After spending hundreds of hours reading the want ads in all of the newspapers that he could find in the three cities in the region.
   possible correction: After spending hundreds of hours reading the want ads in all of the newspapers that he could find in the three cities in the region, Bernard finally found a job working as a termite inspector for the county.
6. *fragment*: Probably because I had forgotten to set it.
   possible correction: The timer on the oven failed to go off, probably because I had forgotten to set it.
7. *fragment*: Even as Rupert was dashing across the street begging her to stop.
   possible correction: The Chocolate Shoppe owner was turning the sign from the "open" side to the "closed" side even as Rupert was dashing across the street begging her to stop.

8. *fragment*: Even though I had received As on all of the other tests.

   possible correction: Because I had missed a test, I received a B in the class even though I had received As on all of the other tests.

9. *fragment*: To find the word that the minister had used just that morning.

   possible correction: I was unable to find the word that the minister had used just that morning.

10. *fragment*: The end.

    possible correction: This is the end of the practice.

Pages 112–113:

Answers may vary. Here are some possible ones.

2. (F) I tossed the two pieces of iron into the fire, and then I reached in and pulled them out with my bare hands.

3. (C)

4. (CS) The wind grew stronger; consequently, the fire soon blazed out of control.

5. (F) For two months Daley practised hard for the marble tournament; unfortunately, he developed a blister on his right thumb the day before the tournament.

6. (CS) The doorbell rang three times; then someone began to bang on the door.

7. (F) Oscar kept riding his mountain bicycle in the middle of the night although he knew it was dangerous. He decided to ride only on nights with a full moon.

Page 131:

1. *topic*: travelling to the ball game last night

   central point: I had a terrifying experience

2. *topic*: Smoking of any kind

   central point: must be outlawed in all public places

3. *topic*: Winning at tennis

   central point: requires as much mental skill as it does physical skill

4. *topic*: Following four simple steps

   central point: will help you pass any test

5. *topic*: the raise that I have asked for

   central point: I deserve

Pages 131–132:

The sentences that would not make good topic sentences are 1, 2, and 5.

Chapter Three

Improving Sentence Patterns

Now you have some idea of the **sentence patterns** of English. Sentences fall into four categories according to the number and types of clauses, but you can arrange your ideas in many different ways. You may make a sentence short and to the point:

Eniko sold her netsuke collection.

Or, by adding modifying words, phrases, and additional clauses, you can lengthen it:

After much soul searching and after seeking the advice of her mother, her brother, and her best friend, *Eniko*, a person who always carefully considered important decisions, *sold her netsuke collection*, which was worth several thousand dollars, but she kept one special carving of a frog and a sacred bird.

Sometimes you want to be short and to the point. Sometimes you want to be more explanatory, and then you may need more words.

The difference between the *five* words of the first sentence and the *fifty* words of the second one is the addition of modifying words, phrases, and clauses. These modifiers can help you write more clearly and vividly. Modifying words, phrases, and clauses can, however, be overused and should *never* be substituted for strong verbs and nouns, but most beginning writers err in the opposite direction, leaving their writing limp and colourless. You need to follow certain guidelines when you use the various modifying phrases and clauses.

First, we will discuss the most effective ways to use phrases and clauses in your sentences, and then we will discuss how to avoid the typical errors that writers make in using these devices.

Section One

Modifying with Participial and Infinitive Phrases

Using **participial and infinitive phrases** as modifiers in your sentences can help you to streamline your sentences and achieve sentence variety. In most cases, participial and infinitive phrases take the place of subordinate clauses.

EXAMPLES   (subordinate clause)   **As he drove to work,** Kurt Kelly saw a black cat run in front of his car.

(participial phrase)   **Driving to work,** Kurt Kelly saw a black cat run in front of his car.

As you already know, **a clause is a word group that contains a subject and a verb.** On the other hand, **a phrase is a word group that does not contain a subject and a verb.** You are already aware of prepositional phrases. Other phrases generally called **verbal phrases, include present participial phrases, past participial phrases,** and **infinitive phrases.**

Present Participial Phrases

Remember, the present participle is a verbal. It is the form of the verb that ends in "ing" (*running, typing, looking*). Without a helping verb it cannot be used as the verb of a sentence. Instead, it is used as an adjective. For example, you can use it as a one-word adjective.

EXAMPLE   The **running** man stumbled as he rounded the corner.

In this sentence, the present participle *running* modifies the noun *man*.

You can also use the present participle as part of a phrase that functions as an adjective. Such a phrase is called a **participial phrase,** and it is often used to begin sentences.

EXAMPLE   **Rounding the corner**, the running man stumbled.

In this sentence, the present participial phrase *Rounding the corner* is an adjective phrase modifying the noun *man*. The present participle is *Rounding*. The present participial phrase, then, is an adjective phrase consisting of the present participle plus any other words attached to it.

PUNCTUATION NOTE: When a present participial phrase introduces a sentence, it is always followed by a comma.

Past Participial Phrases

The past participle is the form of the verb that you use with the helping verbs *have*, *has*, or *had* (*have eaten, has defeated, had bought*). Like the present participle, the past participle is a verbal when used without a helping verb. And, like the present participle, it is used as an adjective.

You can use a past participle as a single-word adjective.

EXAMPLE   The **defeated** army retreated into the mountains.

In this sentence, the past participle *defeated* modifies the noun *army*.

Or you can use the past participle as part of a past participial phrase.

EXAMPLE   **Pursued by the enemy**, the army retreated into the mountains.

In this sentence, the past participial phrase *Pursued by the enemy* modifies the noun *army*. Notice that it is followed by a comma. As with the present participial phrase, when the past participial phrase introduces a sentence, you should place a comma after it.

Participial phrases make good introductions to sentences, but you can use them anywhere. To avoid confusion, though, you should place them as closely as possible to the words they modify.

EXAMPLES   All of the students **submitting essays for the contest** used word processors.

The man **bitten by the rattlesnake** walked ten kilometres to the hospital.

The present participial phrase *submitting essays for the contest* modifies the noun *students*. The past participial phrase *bitten by the rattlesnake* modifies the noun *man*.

PRACTICE

Underline the participial phrases in the following sentences and circle the words they modify.

1. Put into the game in the last ten minutes, (Zhang) scored twelve points for her team.

2. The hunter saw the elk trotting into the woods.

3. Turning the corner, the ant saw a dead aardvark.

4. Working as an usher at the Queen Elizabeth Theatre, Sheila met many extraordinary people.

5. Hampton enjoyed the carrots given to him by Michelle.

6. The man injured in the accident was taken to the hospital.

7. Blaise wanted to meet the woman giving the lecture on South Africa.

8. Hurt by her remark, Chris slowly turned red.

9. Watching his team practise, Byron brooded about his sore foot.

10. The plan suggested by the mayor was approved by the city council.

Infinitive Phrases

The infinitive is a verbal that you can use as a noun, an adjective, or an adverb. You form the infinitive by adding *to* to the present tense form of the verb (*to write, to run, to listen*).

You can use the infinitive *by itself*.

EXAMPLE   **To fly**, you must first take lessons and get a license.

Or you can use the infinitive to form *an infinitive phrase*.

EXAMPLE   **To play the saxophone well**, you must practise often.

Notice that the infinitive phrase consists of the infinitive plus any words attached to it. Like the two participial phrases, it is followed by a comma when it introduces a sentence.

PUNCTUATION NOTE: When you use the infinitive as a noun, it can act as the subject of a sentence. In this case, you do not use a comma.

EXAMPLE   **To be a good husband** was Clint's ambition.

The infinitive phrase *To be a good husband* is the subject of the verb *was*.
Generally, like the two participial phrases, the infinitive phrase can appear in a variety of places in a sentence.

EXAMPLE   Carla's motives were hard **to understand at first**.

Here the infinitive phrase *to understand* at first acts as an adverb to modify the adjective *hard*.

EXAMPLE   Ed liked having a sister **to play with** even though she teased him constantly.

Here, the infinitive phrase *to play with* acts as an adjective to modify the noun *sister*.

PRACTICE

Underline the modifying participial and infinitive phrases in the following sentences and circle the words they modify.

1. Helen finally found a (pot) to hold her geraniums.

2. Shivering from the cold, the old dog scratched at the back door.

3. Luckily, William Tell knew the correct way to aim a crossbow.

4. Bored by the tedious speech, the people in the audience drifted away.

5. The city council approved the plan to aid the homeless.

6. Mr. Yee gathered a bunch of carnations to give to his wife.

7. Yelling loudly, the British charged up the hill toward the French troops.

8. Delighted by his daughter's grades, Sam took her out to dinner.

9. Fumiko bought several novels to read on her spring break.

10. The material to build the new albino tiger habitat arrived on Monday.

Section One Review

1. The **present participle** is a verbal that ends in "ing" and that is used as an adjective. (When the "ing" form is used as a noun, it is called a **gerund**.)

2. A **present participial phrase** consists of the present participle plus any words attached to it.

3. A comma follows a **present participial phrase** that introduces a sentence.

4. The **past participle** is the form of the verb used with the helping verbs *have, has,* and *had.*

5. The **past participle** is a verbal used as an adjective.

6. A **past participial phrase** consists of the past participle plus any words attached to it.

7. A comma follows a **past participial phrase** that introduces a sentence.

8. An **infinitive** is formed by adding *to* to the present tense of a verb.

9. The **infinitive** is a verbal that can be used as a noun, an adjective, or an adverb.

10. An **infinitive phrase** consists of the infinitive plus any words attached to it.

11. A comma follows an **infinitive phrase** that introduces a sentence and acts as a modifier.

EXERCISE

Exercise 1A

Underline all participial and infinitive phrases. Circle the words that they modify. In the spaces, identify the phrase as present participle (Pres P), past participle (Past P), or infinitive (Inf).

Inf   1. Lian went to the pharmacy for the (medicine) to help her cough.

_____   2. Moved by his apology, Mary forgave Jim again.

_____   3. The redwood deck built by Paul had many beautiful and subtle touches.

_____   4. The politician spoke to the people standing in the park.

_____   5. Trapping water from the storm in her raincoat, the nun survived for three days in the desert.

_____   6. The committee felt that Clarice was the best person to present the proposal.

_____   7. An important rule to understand thoroughly is the one that says wise men learn much from fools.

_____   8. Frightened by the sudden change in the economy, she sold all of her shares of stock.

_____   9. The cashier blamed for the theft did not steal the money.

_____   10. Standing in the rain, the spectators watched the Nigerian runner as he won the marathon.

_____   11. The loggers are looking for a strategy to break the blockade.

_____   12. The firefighter threw a rope to the boy stranded in the tree in the middle of the river.

_____   13. Aided by a generous donation from a famous actress, the school built a new library.

_____   14. Digging in his garden, Mr. Park uncovered an ancient coin.

_____   15. William wanted some shelves to store his scripts.

Exercise 1B

In the places indicated by (^), add your own participial or infinitive phrases to the following sentences. Use the verbs in parentheses. Be sure to place a comma after any phrase that introduces a sentence.

1. ^ Jalayne checked the tires, the oil level, the coolant, and the amount of gas in her car. (prepare)

   To prepare for her trip across the country, Jalayne checked the tires, the oil level, the coolant, and the amount of gas in her car.

2. ^ People should watch their diets and exercise several times a week. (be)

   _____

   _____

3. The crime ^ was in the headlines of the London newspapers the next day. (commit)

   _____

   _____

4. ^ Richard hid his face. (embarrass)

   _____

   _____

5. Carson found a 1956 Mickey Mantle baseball card ^ when he went into his bedroom. (lie)

   _____

   _____

6. A fast food restaurant is sometimes the best place ^ . (get)

   _____

   _____

7. ∧ The SWAT team was soon able to arrest the suspect. (surround)

_____

_____

8. ∧ Veronica got up to investigate. (hear)

_____

_____

9. The campers ∧ were afraid that the roads would be closed by the snow-

storm. (drive)

_____

_____

10. ∧ Pauline tripped on a fallen tree limb. (hike)

_____

_____

EXERCISE

Exercise 1C

Underline all infinitive and participial phrases and circle the words that they modify.

1. Although many movies and television shows portray (people) <u>living in condominiums</u> as elderly retired couples, my condominium complex houses people of all ages. 2. For example, it is not at all unusual to see young families where I live. 3. In fact, in the condominium next to mine live Meredith and Charlie, a young couple raising four children. 4. Meredith recently told me that she can save money to use for her children's college education because she lives in a "condo" instead of a house. 5. Charlie's younger sister also lives in our complex. 6. Raising two children as a single mother, she appreciates having many people nearby who will babysit for her while she is at work. 7. Other residents of condominiums are often young, single professionals who enjoy the chance to meet other people at the pools, tennis courts, or other recreational facilities. 8. George, who lives behind me, is a single, twenty-five-year-old attorney. 9. Worried about his lackluster social life, George moved here specifically to meet new people. 10. He now is chairperson of our recreation committee, and he has organized a club for people interested in traveling. 11. Finally, there are the elderly residents. 12. Acting as surrogate grandmothers and grandfathers, many of these residents play with the children and give advice to young parents. 13. In addition, they frequently find ways to improve our neighbourhood. 14. As you can see, people coming from a wide range of backgrounds and ages live in condominiums.

Section Two

Modifying with Adjective Clauses and Appositives

Adjective Clauses

We discussed adjective clauses earlier in the section on subordinate clauses. An adjective clause is an important option when you want to modify a noun or pronoun in a sentence. Using an adjective clause instead of single-word adjectives or modifying phrases places more emphasis on what you are saying about the noun or pronoun you are modifying. Consider the following sentences:

EXAMPLES   (adjective)   My **insensitive** neighbour plays his trombone all night long.

(adjective clause)   My neighbour, **who is insensitive**, plays his trombone all night long.

Using the adjective clause *who is insensitive* places more importance on the neighbour's insensitivity. Sometimes you need only single-word modifiers, but it is good to be aware of all of your choices for modifying words.

Here is a brief review of adjective clauses.

1. Adjective clauses follow the noun or pronoun they modify.

2. Adjective clauses begin with the relative pronouns *who, whom, whose, which, that* (and sometimes *when* or *where*).

EXAMPLES   We returned the money to the person **who had lost it**. (*Who* introduces an adjective clause that modifies the noun *person*.)

I remember the time **when Jack and Jill were married at Banff**. (*When* introduces an adjective clause that modifies the noun *time*.)

Sidney decided to move to Saskatchewan, where his family used to spend summer vacations. (*Where* introduces an adjective clause that modifies the noun *Saskatchewan*.)

3. If the adjective clause provides information that is necessary to identify the noun or pronoun, do not set it off with commas.

EXAMPLE   The man **who was sitting next to my uncle at the banquet** is a famous sportswriter.

The information in this adjective clause is necessary to identify which man at the banquet is the famous sportswriter.

4. If the adjective clause provides information that is merely descriptive and is not necessary to identify the noun or pronoun, then set the clause off with commas.

EXAMPLE   Michael Ondaatje, **who is sitting next to the premier,** is a famous novelist.

Michael Ondaatje's name already identifies him, so the adjective clause contains added but unnecessary information. Therefore, you need the commas.

We will discuss the rules for the use of commas with adjective clauses again in Chapter Five.

PRACTICE

Underline all adjective clauses and circle the words they modify. For further practice, try to determine which clauses need commas and add them where necessary.

1. The (woman) who developed the new microchip is from Vietnam.

2. Martina Gonzales who is an excellent pediatrician knows more about my children than I do.

3. None of the operators who answered the phone could speak Lithuanian.

4. The astronaut's home town which has a population of only two hundred honoured her with a parade that featured every citizen of the town.

5. The writer returned to Moose Jaw where his parents live.

6. The sweater that you gave me for Christmas received many compliments.

7. Toots was looking for a place where he could play his tuba in peace.

8. Sarah made Sean a tape that contained his favourite Irish songs.

9. The fans cheered for the team that lost instead of for the one that won.

10. The old man pointed to the place where he had been wounded in the war.

Appositives

Appositives give you another option for adding descriptive detail. An **appositive** is a noun or pronoun, along with any modifiers, that **renames** another noun or pronoun. The appositive almost always follows the word it refers to, and it is usually set off with commas.

Note how the following two sentences can be combined not only by adding an adjective clause but also by adding an appositive:

EXAMPLES   My neighbour plays the trombone all night long.

He is an insensitive man.

(adjective clause)   My neighbour, **who is insensitive,** plays his trombone all night long.

(appositive)   My neighbour, **an insensitive man,** plays his trombone all night long.

In the appositive, the noun *man* renames the noun *neighbour*.

EXAMPLES   The wedding *ring*, **a *symbol* of eternal love,** dates back to 2800 B.C. Egypt. (The noun *symbol* renames the noun *ring*.)

The huge *trout*, **the one still in the river,** would have made an impressive trophy on the wall of Harold's den. (The pronoun *one* renames the noun *trout*.)

The *honeymoon*, **a popular marriage *custom*,** comes from an ancient Northern European practice of stealing brides. (The noun *custom* renames the noun *honeymoon*.)

PUNCTUATION NOTE: The appositive is usually set off by commas; as with the adjective clause, though, if the appositive contains information necessary to identify the word it renames, you do not use commas.

EXAMPLES   The movie **Citizen Kane** is considered a classic. (The appositive *Citizen Kane* is necessary to indicate which movie is a classic.)

Citizen Kane, **a movie directed and acted in by Orson Welles,** is considered a classic. (Here, the movie has been identified by its name, so the appositive is set off by commas.)

PRACTICE

Underline the appositives. Then circle the word in the appositive that renames a noun or pronoun. Then draw an arrow to the noun or pronoun that is renamed.

1. The modem, a (device) for connecting computers, has accelerated communication.

2. The word *matador* means "killer."

3. Myriam Bedard was asked to endorse Coral Tea, a new product.

4. Recently they were featured on Channel 13, a local television station.

5. Martin, usually a chubby fellow, had become much thinner on his diet of broccoli.

6. *The Prince of Tides*, a novel by Pat Conroy, was made into a movie.

7. Barbara Streisand made Pat Conroy's novel *The Prince of Tides* into an award-winning film.

8. Athlete card collecting, once a hobby for boys, has become a popular hobby for people of both sexes and all ages.

9. My cousin Mary enjoys hang gliding.

10. Mary, my favourite cousin, enjoys hang gliding.

PRACTICE

Add an appositive or an adjective clause to each of the following sentences. Use commas when they are needed.

1. The sports car was parked near the school.

   The sports car that had been stolen last week was parked near the

   school.

2. The Spectre took the weapon from the shelf.

   _____

   _____

3. An alarm warned the Chuckling Chef that the Spectre had entered the kitchen.

   _____

   _____

4. The huge cook threw the Spectre into an oven by the door.

   _____

   _____

5. The Spectre found himself covered with a sauce.

   _____

   _____

6. Clyde Merdly crashed his motorcycle into the kitchen.

   _____

   _____

7. The Chuckling Chef rushed into the main dining room.

_____

_____

8. Clyde Merdly rescued the Spectre from the oven and cleaned off the sauce.

_____

_____

9. Clyde and the Spectre slipped on pieces of beets and okra as they chased the Chuckling Chef into the street.

_____

_____

10. The Chuckling Chef ran to the parking lot and escaped in his Beetmobile.

_____

_____

_____

REVIEW

Section Two Review

1. **Adjective clauses** modify nouns and pronouns.

2. **Adjective clauses** follow the nouns or pronouns they modify.

3. **Adjective clauses** begin with *who, whom, whose, which, that* (and sometimes *when* or *where)*.

4. **Adjective clauses** that contain information necessary to identify the words they modify are not set off with commas.

5. **Adjective clauses** that do not contain information necessary to identify the words they modify are set off with commas.

6. **Appositives** are words or word groups containing a noun or pronoun that renames another noun or pronoun in a sentence.

7. **Appositives** usually follow the nouns or pronouns they rename.

8. An **appositive** that contains information necessary to identify the word it renames is not set off with commas.

9. An **appositive** that does not contain information necessary to identify the word it renames is set off with commas.

EXERCISE

Exercise 2A

Underline all adjective clauses and appositives. Circle the words they modify or rename. Indicate whether the modifier is an appositive (AP) or an adjective clause (Adj). Add commas where necessary.

AP   1. *The Babe* is a contemporary movie about (Babe Ruth) the famous baseball player.

_____ 2. Babe Ruth whose pictures usually show him to be somewhat overweight was famous for his appetite.

_____ 3. There are rumours that he could eat more than twenty hot dogs and drink several beers before a game.

_____ 4. The pin-striped uniforms a Yankee trademark were not adopted to make Ruth look thinner.

_____ 5. The Yankees began wearing pinstripes in 1912 which was eight years before Babe Ruth joined the team.

_____ 6. *The Babe Ruth Story* an earlier movie starred actor William Bendix.

_____ 7. Bendix who had been a batboy with the New York Giants knew Ruth well.

_____ 8. Once, before a game, Bendix brought Ruth twelve hot dogs and two quarts of soda which made the Babe sick and sent him to the hospital.

_____ 9. It was a favour that caused the batboy to be fired.

_____ 10. In 1930 and 1931 his top years Ruth made $80,000 per year in salary.

_____ 11. Nowadays, it is not unusual to see players who make over $1 million a year.

_____ 12. Some players make more than $1 million a year just for wearing clothing and equipment that sports companies give them.

EXERCISE

Exercise 2B

A. Add adjective clauses of your own to each of the sentences below. Make sure you use commas where necessary.

1. Chris likes to work on his old motorcycle.

   Chris likes to work on his old motorcycle, which he purchased last year

   from his brother.

2. The television program was about a marriage in Argentina.

   _____

   _____

3. Leonard Cohen was born in Westmount.

   _____

   _____

4. Pamela Sharpe usually waits until Saturday to wash her car.

   _____

   _____

5. The groundhog saw his shadow, so he slipped back into his burrow.

   _____

   _____

6. Collecting aluminum cans to sell to recycling centres has been a good summer job for Erin.

   _____

   _____

7. The man performed balloon tricks for the children at the party.

   _____

   _____

8. The audio tapes helped Mr. Dolphy relieve his boredom on his trip across Canada.

_____

_____

B. Add appositives of your own to the sentences below. Make sure you use commas where necessary.

9. The pilot landed the burning airplane in a muddy field.

   _The pilot, an eighty-five-year-old grandmother, landed the burning_____

   _airplane in a muddy field._____

10. The bird flew for many miles before landing on the steeple of the church.

   _____

   _____

11. The mechanic checked the tires of the old Mercedes-Benz.

   _____

   _____

12. On the next day the inspector declared the airplane unsafe to fly.

   _____

   _____

13. Each winter Erika stays in a cabin at Whistler Mountain and goes cross-country skiing.

   _____

   _____

14. The astronomer discovered a new planet when he used the extremely powerful telescope in Idaho.

   _____

   _____

15. The new wheelchair helped Anton become the star of his basketball team.

_____

_____

EXERCISE

Exercise 2C

Underline all adjective clauses and circle the words they modify. Underline all appositives and circle the words they rename. Add commas where necessary.

1. Many English-speaking people are surprised when they discover the number of everyday (words) that are drawn from different mythologies.

2. For example, the names of several of our weekdays—Tuesday, Wednesday, Thursday, and Friday—derive from Norse mythology. **3.** Tuesday and Thursday refer to Tiu, the Norse god of war, and Thor, the Norse god of thunder. **4.** Wednesday refers to Woden, who was the king of the Norse gods, and Friday refers to Frigga, the Norse goddess of love. **5.** Other common words are derived from Greek mythology. **6.** For instance, the word *tantalize* refers to Tantalus, who was a king condemned to Hades as a punishment for his crimes. **7.** In Hades, he was forced to stand below fruit that was just beyond his reach and in water that he could not drink.

8. Another common Greek word in our language is *atlas*, which refers to a map of the world. **9.** The mythological figure Atlas was a Titan who was condemned to support the heavens on his shoulders. **10.** Finally, Roman mythology, which in many ways parallels Greek mythology, is another source of many English words. **11.** For example, the month of January is named after Janus, the Roman god with two faces. **12.** Janus, whose two faces allowed him to watch two directions at once, was the Roman god of doorways. **13.** June, another of the many months that refer to Roman mythology, is named after Juno, the goddess of marriage and childbirth.

14. These examples are just a few of the hundreds of English words that reflect the many mythologies of the world.

Section Three

Misplaced and Dangling Modifiers

In Chapter Two, when you combined clauses to form various sentence types, you learned that joining clauses improperly can lead to comma splices and fused sentences. As you can probably guess, adding modifiers to sentences leads to an entirely new set of problems. In some cases, these problems are a bit more complicated than those caused by comma splices and fused sentences, but with a little practice, you should have no trouble at all handling them.

Misplaced Modifiers

Misplaced modifiers are exactly what their name says they are—modifiers that have been "misplaced" within a sentence. But how is a modifier "misplaced"? The answer is simple. If you remember that a modifier is nearly always placed just before or just after the word it modifies, then a misplaced modifier must be one that has been mistakenly placed so that it causes a reader to be *confused* about what it modifies. Consider the confusion in the following sentence:

> Albert said **quietly** to move away from the snake.

Was Albert speaking quietly or did he tell us to move quietly? Changing the placement of the modifier will clarify the meaning.

> Albert **quietly** said to move away from the snake. (Here, the word modifies the verb *said*.)

> Albert said to move **quietly** away from the snake. (Here the word modifies the verbal *to move*.)

Sometimes finding the correct placement of a modifier can be a bit difficult. Let's look at a few other typical examples.

Misplaced Words

Any modifier can be misplaced, but one particular group of modifiers causes quite a bit of trouble for many people. These words are *only, almost, just, merely,* and *nearly.* Consider, for example, the following sentences:

> By buying her new computer on sale, Florence **almost** saved $100.

> By buying her new computer on sale, Florence saved **almost** $100.

As you can see, these sentences actually make two different statements. In the first sentence, *almost* modifies *saved.* If you almost saved something, you did not save it. In the second sentence, *almost* modifies *$100.* If you saved *almost* $100, you saved $85, $90, $95, or some other amount close to $100.

Which statement does the writer want to make—that Florence did *not* save any money or that she *did* save an amount close to $100? Because the point was that she bought her computer on sale, the second sentence makes more sense.

To avoid confusion, be sure that you place all of your modifiers carefully.

EXAMPLES	(incorrect)	Her piano teacher encouraged her **often** to practise.
	(correct)	Her piano teacher **often** encouraged her to practise.
	(correct)	Her piano teacher encouraged her to practise **often**.
	(incorrect)	Sophia **nearly** drank a gallon of coffee yesterday.
	(correct)	Sophia drank **nearly** a gallon of coffee yesterday.

PRACTICE

Underline and correct any misplaced words in the following sentences. Some of the sentences may be correct.

1. During breakfast, Marshall ~~nearly~~ drank ^nearly^ a whole quart of orange juice.

2. The doctor told him carefully to sew up the wound.

3. After the battle, the exhausted soldiers wanted only to lie down and rest.

4. The dog that ran down the street quickly jumped over the fence.

5. When she had almost hiked for five hours, Caroline stopped by a small stream.

6. The crocodile nearly swam to the edge of the lagoon before the wire fence stopped it.

7. Although Beatrice had sat before her computer all day, she had just written two pages.

8. The mechanic advised me repeatedly to depress the accelerator.

9. Jack knew he could not make it to Halifax because he only had ten litres of fuel.

10. Terry almost ran twenty kilometres before dropping out of the race.

Misplaced Phrases and Clauses

The phrases and clauses that you studied earlier in this chapter are as easily misplaced as individual words. Phrases and clauses often follow the words they modify.

E X A M P L E S	(prepositional phrase)	The driver **in the blue sports car** struck an innocent pedestrian.
	(present participial phrase)	The dog **chasing the car** barked at the confused driver.
	(past participial phrase)	They gave the bicycle **donated by the shop** to the child.
	(adjective clause)	Lucia gave the money **that she had borrowed** from her sister to the homeless woman.

In each of the above sentences, the modifier follows the word it modifies Notice what happens when the modifier is misplaced so that it follows the wrong word.

E X A M P L E S   The driver struck an innocent pedestrian **in the blue sports car**.

The dog barked at the confused driver **chasing the car.**

They gave the bicycle to the child **donated by the shop**.

Lucia gave the money to the homeless woman **that she had borrowed from her sister**.

Obviously, misplaced phrases and clauses can create rather confusing and sometimes even humorous situations. Of course, not all phrases and clauses follow the words they modify. Many occur before the word they refer to.

E X A M P L E S	(past participial phrase)	**Angered by the umpire's poor call**, Dana threw her bat to the ground.
	(present participial phrase)	**Hoping to win the debate**, Cyrus practised three hours every day.

Regardless of whether the modifier appears before or after the word it modifies, the point is that you should place modifiers so that they clearly refer to a specific word in the sentence.

PRACTICE   Underline and correct any misplaced phrases and clauses in the following sentences. Some of the sentences may be correct.

1. The doctor set the leg of the dog <u>that had been broken in the accident.</u>

   <u>The doctor set the dog's leg that had been broken in the accident.</u>

2. Alice bought a new scarf for her mother covered with red and white

   stripes.

   _____

   _____

3. Chuck avoided his teammates worried about the argument he had just

   had with his wife.

   _____

   _____

4. The ten-year-old boy obeyed his grandmother who had been raised to

   respect his elders.

   _____

   _____

5. George tried to stop the huge purple and black dragon with the fire

   extinguisher and a magic dagger.

   _____

   _____

6. Arthur sold a house to his brother that had leaky plumbing.

7. This change will allow customers to place long-distance calls using an alternative long-distance company by simply dialing 1 + the area code + telephone number.

8. I gave some treats to the dog of the little girl that sat up and begged and rolled over.

9. The fish in the aquarium swam around looking at the people with their mouths opening and closing constantly in the murky water.

10. Cecil gave the antique rifle to his son that he had bought at the auction.

Dangling Modifiers

A **dangling modifier** is an introductory phrase (usually a verbal phrase) that lacks an appropriate word to modify. Since these modifiers usually represent some sort of action, they need a **doer** or **agent** of the action represented.

For example, in the following sentence the introductory participial phrase "dangles" because it is not followed by a noun or pronoun that could be the doer of the action represented by the phrase.

Driving madly down the boulevard, the horse just missed being hit and killed.

The present participial phrase *Driving madly down the boulevard* should be followed by a noun or pronoun that could logically do the action of the phrase. Instead, it is followed by the noun *horse*, which is the subject of the sentence. Was the horse "driving"? Probably not. Therefore, the modifying phrase "dangles" because it has no noun or pronoun to which it can logically refer. Here are some more sentences with dangling modifiers.

Nearly exhausted, the game was almost over. (Was the game exhausted?)

After studying all night, the test wasn't so difficult after all. (Did the test study all night?)

To impress his new girlfriend, Jim's Subaru was polished. (Did the Subaru want to impress Jim's girlfriend?)

As you can see, you should check for dangling modifiers when you use introductory phrases.

PRACTICE

In the following sentences, indicate whether the modifying phrases are correctly used by writing either C for correct or D for dangling modifier in the spaces provided.

_D_ 1. Hurrying to work, Celine's briefcase fell into a puddle.

____ 2. Filled with avocado, sour cream, meat, and tasty spices, Jean enjoyed the sandwich prepared by her brother.

____ 3. Fascinated by the movements of the rattlesnake, Jake's dog just stood and stared at it.

____ 4. Joined by two of her favourite friends, Bianca had lunch at an outdoor cafe.

____ 5. Agreeing on the first part of the contract, the second part was negotiated next.

Correcting Dangling Modifiers

You can correct a dangling modifier in one of two ways.

1. *Rewrite the sentence so that the introductory modifier logically refers to the subject of the sentence it introduces.*

EXAMPLES   Nearly exhausted, **I** hoped the game was almost over. (I was nearly exhausted.)

After studying all night, **Lucille** passed the test easily. (Lucille studied all night.)

To impress his new girlfriend, **Jim** polished his Subaru. (Jim wanted to impress his girlfriend.)

2. *Change the introductory phrase to a clause.*

EXAMPLES   **Because I was nearly exhausted,** I hoped the game was almost over.

After Lucille had studied all night, she passed the test easily.

Because Jim wanted to impress his girlfriend, he polished his Subaru.

NOTE: Do not correct a dangling modifier by moving it to the end of the sentence or by adding a possessive noun or pronoun to a sentence. In either case, it will still "dangle" because it lacks a doer or agent that could perform the action of the modifier.

EXAMPLES   (incorrect)   **After searching for three weeks**, the lost watch was finally found. (There is no doer for searching.)

(still incorrect)   The lost watch was finally found **after searching for three weeks**. (There still is no logical doer.)

(still incorrect)   **After searching for three weeks**, Alfred's lost watch was finally found. (Adding the possessive form *Alfred's* does not add a doer of the action.)

(correct)   **After searching for three weeks**, Alfred finally found his watch. (The noun Alfred can logically perform the action—searching—of the modifying phrase.)

(correct)   **After Alfred had searched for three weeks**, he finally found his watch. (Here again, the doer of the action is clear.)

PRACTICE

Underline and correct any dangling modifiers in the following sentences. Some of the sentences may be correct.

1. <u>Delighted by the victory,</u> the champagne and caviar were quickly consumed.

   <u>Delighted by the victory, the coach and her team quickly consumed the</u>

   <u>champagne and caviar.</u>

2. While watching the five-hour play, Jean's chair seemed to become more and more uncomfortable.

   _____

   _____

3. After running on a hot day, a long soak in the tub is enjoyable.

   _____

   _____

4. Worried about the cost of the concert, I asked John if he had any extra money.

   _____

   _____

5. Crying out for help, a life ring was thrown to the boy who had fallen overboard.

   _____

   _____

6. Talking nervously to the police constable, Thomas's nose began to itch.

   _____

   _____

7. To register people to vote, a table was set up outside the market in the middle of town.

   _____

   _____

8. Looking at the horizon, the sun could be seen reflected on the sea.

   _____

   _____

9. Burned in the explosion, a bandage was placed on Curt's right hand by the paramedic.

   _____

   _____

10. To learn more about Paris, books and videos were checked out from the library by Emile before he left for Europe.

    _____

    _____

Section Three Review

1. A **misplaced modifier** is a modifier that has been mistakenly placed so that it causes a reader to be confused about what it modifies.

2. Commonly misplaced words are *only, almost, just, merely,* and *nearly.*

3. Place modifying phrases and clauses so that they clearly refer to a specific word in a sentence.

4. A **dangling modifier** is an introductory phrase (usually a verbal phrase) that lacks an appropriate word to modify. Since these modifiers usually represent some sort of action, they need a **doer** or **agent** of the action represented.

5. You can correct a dangling modifier in one of two ways.

   a. Rewrite the sentence so that the introductory modifier logically refers to the subject of the sentence it introduces.

   b. Change the introductory phrase to a clause.

6. Do not correct a dangling modifier by moving it to the end of the sentence or by adding a possessive noun or pronoun.

EXERCISE

Exercise 3A

A. Underline and correct any misplaced words in the following sentences. Some sentences may be correct.

1. After <u>nearly</u> chasing his horse for four hours, Roy was almost out of breath.

   <u>After chasing his horse for nearly four hours, Roy was almost out of</u>

   <u>breath.</u>

2. Mr. Ito only wanted a few hours' rest; then he would feel just fine.

   _____

   _____

3. Astrud merely asked for a glass of Perrier, and then she could go on with her Samba.

   _____

   _____

4. Although I stopped at five car dealerships, I was only able to find what I wanted at one of them.

   _____

   _____

5. Mansour needed ten dollars to buy a new mouthpiece for his saxophone, but he just had eight.

   _____

   _____

B. Underline and correct any misplaced phrases or clauses in the following sentences. Some of the sentences may be correct.

6. As Keiko sat down in the bus, she looked over at the man in the next seat <u>with the huge ears.</u>

    <u>As Keiko sat down in the bus, she looked over at the man with the huge ears in the next seat.</u>

7. My sister returned the dog to her neighbour that had chewed up her sofa.

    _____

    _____

8. The Olympic diver stood on the board and looked out at the audience wondering about her father.

    _____

    _____

9. Renata stared at the butterflies on the wallpaper singing a lullaby to her baby.

    _____

    _____

10. The investigators were looking for a man in a black car with a red nose and clown wig.

    _____

    _____

C. Underline and correct any dangling modifiers in the following sentences. Some of the sentences may be correct.

11. Angered by the booing of the fans, bats and helmets came flying out of the Dodger dugout.

    Angered by the booing of the fans, the Dodger players threw bats and helmets out of the dugout.

12. Before leaving for vacation, ask the post office to hold your mail.

    _____

    _____

13. After carefully calculating his savings, John's hopes for buying his dream house in the West End soared.

    _____

    _____

14. To perform well in ballet, constant practice needs to be a way of life.

    _____

    _____

15. Creating a diversion with the fire, the early morning escape was successful.

    _____

    _____

    _____

EXERCISE

Exercise 3B

Underline and correct any misplaced or dangling modifiers in the following sentences. Some of the sentences may be correct.

1. <u>Before leaving for their cross-country trip,</u> the silver was placed in their safety deposit box.

   <u>Before leaving for their cross-country trip, the McDonalds put their silver in their safety deposit box.</u>

2. The dog in the car that was barking loudly was just a puppy.

   _____

   _____

3. The patient only regained consciousness after she was given oxygen.

   _____

   _____

4. Pushing wildly at the crowd, Cheryl tried to make room for her mother to breathe.

   _____

   _____

5. Elated by her sense of success, Joy's arms were raised high in the air.

   _____

   _____

6. My new VCR allows me to watch one channel while I record another with all its unique features.

   _____

   _____

7. After looking forward to the snowstorm, the skiers merely saw a few gray clouds.

_____

_____

8. Before leaving the table, please ask to be excused.

_____

_____

9. The Boy Scouts stopped to look at the snake hiking down the mountain.

_____

_____

10. Having followed the instructions carefully, Ashley's new bicycle was almost fully assembled.

_____

_____

11. Ed gave the fishing rod to his granddaughter that he had bought at the bait shop.

_____

_____

12. To learn a new language well, you almost need to speak it every day.

_____

_____

Exercise 3C

Correct any dangling or misplaced modifiers in the following paragraph.

1. The human body's "flight or fight" reaction to stress is an ancient defence mechanism that can allow people to accomplish remarkable feats of strength or endurance. 2. For example, struck by lightning in August, 1989, Mary O'Leary's life was saved by the "flight or fight" system. 3. She had been hiking alone in Colorado's Roosevelt National Forest when a bolt of lightning struck her in the back, which can carry as much as 100 million volts of electricity. 4. Afterwards, although she was barely conscious and had lost the use of both legs, she pulled herself across the ground to get to a Jeep trail that almost was three kilometres away. 5. At one point, only using her hands, she had to climb over a fallen tree that was eighteen metres long and one metre high. 6. Another example of this defence mechanism at work is Lorraine Lengkeek's experience with a grizzly bear. 7. While camping in Montana, a 225 kg grizzly bear attacked her and her husband. 8. When the bear started to maul her husband, feeling an intense anger, Lorraine rushed at the grizzly. 9. Swinging her binoculars, the bear was struck four times and driven off by the sixty-two-year-old, 160 cm tall woman. 10. Finally, a dramatic example of the body's ability to react to dangerous situations happened to John Thompson, a North Dakota farm boy. 11. While working alone, his arms were severed by a tractor-powered auger. 12. He staggered to his house without arms, used his mouth to turn the doorknob, and dialed for help with a pencil held in his teeth. 13. Then, to avoid getting blood on his parents' carpet, the bathtub was where he sat until help arrived. 14. Doctors who reattached Thompson's arms say that his body's "flight or

fight" system saved his life, which automatically clotted blood in his severed arteries. **15.** These examples and others like them are evidence of the human body's extraordinary ability to protect itself.

Section Four

Sentence Practice: Using Participial and Infinitive Phrases, Appositives, and Adjective Clauses

In this chapter, you have become aware of the many **choices** you have when you want to modify words in your sentences. Your options range from single-word modifiers to modifying phrases to subordinate clauses. Let's explore some of the possibilities with the following sentence.

> The beautiful Dalmatian looked hungrily at the thick steaks cooking on the grill and quietly begged the chef for a bite.

By changing various modifiers, you can express the sentence in several other ways. For instance, *The beautiful Dalmatian*, with its single-word modifier *beautiful* describing *Dalmatian*, could be changed into an appositive.

> The dog, **a beautiful Dalmatian,** looked hungrily at the thick steaks cooking on the grill and quietly begged the chef for a bite.

This version tends to emphasize the beauty of the dog.

If you change the part of the sentence that contains the verb *looked* to a present participial phrase, you will get a different effect.

> **Looking hungrily at the thick steaks cooking on the grill,** the beautiful Dalmatian quietly begged the chef for a bite.

This version places a bit more emphasis on the dog's hungry look.

Another alternative is to change the present participial phrase *cooking on the grill* to an adjective clause.

> The beautiful Dalmatian looked hungrily at the thick steaks **that were cooking on the grill** and quietly begged the chef for a bite.

As you can see, the choices are many, and good writers often try several versions of a sentence before deciding on the one that best expresses their ideas. Experimenting with your sentences in this way is part of the fun and the challenge of writing.

The exercises in this section are designed to give you practice in using various types of modifiers when you compose your sentences.

EXERCISE

Sentence Combining Exercises

Using your knowledge of modifying phrases and clauses, combine the following lists of sentences according to the directions. Avoid dangling and misplaced modifiers. Add commas where necessary.

EXAMPLE   Combine these sentences into one sentence. Use sentence a as a present participial phrase. Use sentence b as an appositive.

> a. Elvira hoped to win the Montreal Marathon.
>
> b. Elvira is a world class runner.
>
> c. Elvira practised running on the beaches.
>
> d. The beaches are in Nova Scotia.

Hoping to win the Montreal Marathon, Elvira, a world class runner,

practised running on the beaches of Nova Scotia.

1. Combine the following sentences into one sentence. Use sentence a as an appositive. Use sentence c as an adjective clause.

   a. Charles Stilwell was the inventor of the brown paper grocery bag.

   b. Charles Stilwell called his invention "S.O.S."

   c. "S.O.S." stood for "self-opening sack."

   _____

   _____

   _____

2. Combine the following sentences into one sentence. Use sentence a as an appositive. Use sentence e as a past participial phrase.

   a. Lucien Rivard was a notorious bank robber.

   b. Studs Rafferty escaped from a Quebec prison.

   c. He was watering a rink.

   d. The rink was used for skating.

   e. The rink was located outside the walls of the prison.

   _____

   _____

   _____

3. Combine these sentences into one sentence. Use sentence b as an adjective clause. Use sentence c as an appositive. Use sentence d as an adjective clause.

   a. The Barbie doll was named after Barbie Handler.

   b. Barbie Handler was the daughter of Ruth and Elliot Handler.

   c. Ruth and Elliot Handler were toy manufacturers.

   d. Ruth and Elliot Handler founded Mattel Toy Co. in 1945.

   _____

   _____

   _____

4. Combine these sentences into one sentence. Use sentences c and d as appositives.

   a. Goldfish swallowing was started by Lothrop Withington, Jr.

   b. It was started in 1939.

   c. It was one of the most unusual fads of our century.

   d. Lothrop Withington, Jr., was a Harvard freshman.

   _____

   _____

   _____

5. Combine the following sentences into one sentence. Use sentence a as an introductory adverb clause. Use sentence b as an adjective clause. Use sentence d as an infinitive phrase.

   a. Withington boasted to friends that he had once eaten a live fish.

   b. His friends attended college with him.

   c. His friends dared him.

   d. The dare was to eat another one.

   _____

   _____

   _____

6. Combine the following sentences into one sentence. Use sentence a as a present participial phrase. Use sentence d as an adjective clause.

   a. Withington accepted the challenge.

   b. He agreed to meet on March 3.

   c. He would meet them in the student dining hall.

   d. He would eat a live goldfish.

_____

_____

_____

7. Combine the following sentences into one sentence. Use sentence c as an appositive phrase. Use sentence d as an adjective clause.

   a. The date arrived.

   b. Withington stood before a crowd of students.

   c. Withington was a natural actor.

   d. The students had heard about the challenge.

   e. Withington grabbed a goldfish from a bowl.

_____

_____

_____

8. Combine the following sentences into one sentence. Use sentence a as a present participial phrase.

   a. He held the fish by its tail.

   b. Withington slowly lowered it into his mouth.

   c. He chewed it for a moment.

   d. He then swallowed it.

_____

_____

_____

9. Combine these sentences into one sentence. Use sentence a as an infinitive phrase. Use sentence c as an adjective clause.

    a. He completed his performance.

    b. Withington pulled out a toothbrush.

    c. He used it to clean his teeth.

    d. Then he said, "The scales caught a bit on my throat."

    _____

    _____

    _____

10. Combine the following sentences into one sentence. Use sentence a as an introductory prepositional phrase. Use sentence c as a past participial phrase.

    a. It was that spring.

    b. College students across the country were gulping down goldfish.

    c. The students were worried about exams.

    d. They were ready for any diversion.

    e. They were gulping as many as forty-two goldfish at one sitting.

    _____

    _____

    _____

Section Five

Paragraphs: Using Examples

For writing practice in the first two chapters of this text, you have written paragraphs about an event, a person, or a place. Such writing is usually called "narrative" or "descriptive" because it either narrates (tells about) an event or describes a person or place. In this chapter you will write an **expository** paragraph. Expository writing **explains** a topic or idea to a reader, or it **informs** the reader about a topic or idea. The topic of an expository paragraph or essay can range from explaining how to conduct an experiment in chemistry to analyzing the causes of World War II. In fact, most of the writing you will do in college classes will be expository.

One common type of expository writing is the paragraph or essay that relies upon examples to make its point. If you look at Exercises 1C, 2C, and 3C of Chapter Three, you will see that they all rely on examples to support the statements made in the topic sentences. Exercise 1C gives examples of the different types of people who live in condominiums. Exercise 2C gives examples of English words that are drawn from mythology. And Exercise 3C gives examples of people whose "flight or fight" reaction has allowed them to accomplish remarkable feats of strength or endurance.

Supporting your ideas with examples is a powerful way to help your readers understand your point. Examples allow your readers to see your topic at work in real-life situations, and they show your readers that your topic idea is based on reality. Of course, examples are also important when you take tests. Your ability to back up general answers with specific examples can show an instructor that you have understood and mastered the material you have been studying.

Assignment

For this chapter, your assignment is to write a paragraph that uses at least three examples to support a statement made in a topic sentence. Develop your paragraph from one of the following suggestions or from an idea suggested by your instructor.

1. Write a paragraph that gives examples of one particular personality characteristic of your own. For example, perhaps you are a hard-working, "Type A" personality. Or perhaps you tend to overeat when you feel stress, or are sometimes too outspoken. Perhaps you are a procrastinator, or maybe you are overly impulsive. Choose one personality characteristic of your own, make a statement about it, and then illustrate that statement with three examples.

2. Have you ever found that at times a lie is more appropriate than the truth? If you have, write a paragraph that gives examples of when lying seemed to be the correct thing to do.

3. Do you derive a particular benefit from some form of exercise, such as jogging, swimming, or aerobic dancing? If you do, write a paragraph that gives examples of times you have experienced that benefit while exercising.

4. Do you find that you enjoy one particular way of relaxing more than any other way? If you do, write a paragraph that gives examples of times you have found that particular way of relaxing most effective.

5. Does a particular habit (of your own or of someone else) bother you? If so, write a paragraph that gives examples of that particular habit.

Prewriting

1. Choose one (or several) of the suggested assignment ideas above and use the prewriting techniques discussed in Chapters One and Two to decide on the one limited topic you will focus your paper on. *Do not choose your "limited" topic too quickly.* Many times the best topic idea may be the third, fourth, or fifth one you think of.

2. After determining your limited topic, prewrite to decide what examples you will use in your paragraph. Again, don't settle for the first three examples that come to mind. Instead, develop a list of many examples. Then choose the three most effective ones.

3. Once you have decided on the topic and the examples you will use, write a preliminary topic sentence as discussed in Chapter Two. Remember, your preliminary topic sentence should state both your topic and the central point that your examples will illustrate regarding that topic.

PRACTICE

Identify the topic sentences in Exercises 1C (page 158), 2C (page 171), and 3C (page 187). Then identify the topic and the central point in each topic sentence.

Writing

1. Write the first draft of your paragraph. Your first sentence should be your preliminary topic sentence. After writing the topic sentence, write the examples that illustrate your point. Devote several sentences to each example, and be as specific and as detailed as you can in each of those sentences. For now, do not be afraid of writing what may appear to be a paragraph that is far too long.

2. To each example, add an introductory word, phrase, or clause that lets your readers know when one example has ended and another is beginning. Such "introductions" are called **transitions**. They are essential for clear writing because they help your readers follow your train of thought as you move from one idea to another. The following sentences are the transitions used to introduce each example in Exercise 1C, page 158.

EXAMPLES   **For example**, it is not at all unusual to see young families where I live.

Other residents of condominiums are often young, single professionals who enjoy the chance to meet other people at the pools, tennis courts, or other recreational facilities.

Finally, there are the elderly residents.

PRACTICE

Examine Exercises 2C (page 171) and 3C (page 187). In each paragraph, identify the transitions that introduce each example.

Rewriting

1. Now that your first draft is complete, read it over to determine how you can improve the examples you have used. In particular, try to make the examples as specific and as concrete as you can. Use actual names of people and places, and refer to specific details whenever possible.

2. As you read your draft, make sure you can tell where each of your examples ends and the next begins. Revise your transitions as needed to make them clearer still.

3. If your preliminary topic sentence can be improved so that it more accurately states the central point of your paragraph, change it now.

4. Examine your draft for sentences that can be combined using participial phrases, appositives, infinitive phrases, or adjective clauses. Combine such sentences the way you did in the Sentence Combining Exercises.

5. Check your draft for any of the following errors:
    Sentence fragments
    Comma splices
    Fused sentences
    Misplaced modifiers
    Dangling modifiers
    Misspelled words

6. Now prepare a clean final draft, following the format your instructor has asked for.

7. Before you turn in your final draft, proofread it carefully and make any necessary corrections.

PRACTICE TEST

Chapter Three Practice Test

I. Review of Chapters One and Two

A. In the following sentences, identify the underlined words by writing one of the following abbreviations above the words: noun (N), pronoun (Pro), verb (V), adjective (Adj), adverb (Adv), conjunction (Conj), preposition (Prep).

1. After ten <u>minutes</u> on the job, Nizar <u>knew</u> he would have to quit.

2. Cecilia wanted to buy the <u>red</u> Mercedes, <u>but</u> her sister talked her out

   of it.

3. Whenever Butch flexed his muscles, his snake tattoo moved

   <u>menacingly</u>.

4. <u>Someone</u> left an envelope containing $2,000 <u>under</u> my desk.

5. Dr. T.J. Eckleburg had <u>never</u> seen so many ashes <u>in</u> one place.

B. In the following sentences, underline the subjects once and the complete verbs twice. Put parentheses around all prepositional phrases.

6. Two snails slithered silently across the sidewalk.

7. Did the owner or the manager of the building call the police?

8. Chad wept during the wedding, but Larry merely munched on a ham

   sandwich.

9. Before Apollo entered his chariot, he covered himself with sunscreen.

10. He rebuilt the engine of his 1971 Volkswagen and then decided to

    replace its transmission.

C. Compose sentences of your own according to the instructions.

11. Write a simple sentence with one subject, two verbs, and at least one prepositional phrase.

_____

_____

12. Write a compound sentence. Use a coordinating conjunction and appropriate punctuation to join the two clauses.

_____

_____

13. Write a complex sentence that starts with a subordinate clause. Use appropriate punctuation.

_____

_____

14. Write a complex sentence that uses the subordinator *who*.

_____

_____

15. Write a compound–complex sentence. Use a semicolon and a transitional word or phrase.

_____

_____

D. Identify the following items as being correct (C), fused (F), comma splice (CS), or fragment (Frag). Then correct the errors. If a sentence is correct, do nothing to it.

_____ 16. Kathy could not eat her food, it tasted like axle grease.

_____

_____

_____   17. Barking loudly, a large Irish setter running down the street after the car that had just rounded the corner.

_____

_____

_____   18. After his unexpected haircut, Samson felt rather lethargic.

_____

_____

_____   19. Pam rocked back and forth and moaned, however no one paid any attention to her.

_____

_____

_____   20. The medicine relieved the pain then it began to make me sleepy.

_____

_____

II. Chapter Three

A. Underline all infinitive and participial phrases and circle the words they modify.

21. Singing softly to herself, Denise walked down the hall.

22. Jamal could not decide which gift to buy for his sister's wedding.

23. Stunned by the crowd's reaction, the gold medalist stood and stared.

24. The kite hanging from the tree belongs to Charlie Brown.

25. The person to see about your problem is not in today.

B. Add infinitive or participial phrases to the following sentences at the places indicated. Use the verbs in parentheses.

26. The money ⌃ belongs to my mother. (find)

_____

_____

27. ⌃ Charlene tied a string to her finger. (remember)

_____

_____

28. The termites ⌃ were Tony's only companions. (live)

_____

_____

29. Clyde thought that Bonnie's plan ⌃ was a good one. (steal)

_____

_____

30. ⌃ The new parents held their baby. (smile)

_____

_____

C. Underline the adjective clauses and appositives in the following sentences and circle the words they modify.

31. Dr. Nguyen, a well-known physicist, will discuss chaos theory

tonight in the auditorium.

32. Caddy was the word that always made Benjy cry the most.

33. Martina Navratilova, who recently settled a lawsuit out of court,

will play in an exhibition match next week.

34. Mischief, my daughter's favourite rat, died last night.

35. After dinner, Dolly and Oscar sat down to watch *Lady and the Tramp*, which they had rented at the video store.

D. Add adjective clauses or appositives to the following sentences and punctuate them correctly.

36. Mr. Chen was worried about his neighbour's dog.

_____

_____

37. The cotton candy was sticky, but Sarah ate all of it.

_____

_____

38. The bank teller gave the money to Gordon Chu.

_____

_____

39. The prime minister spoke to the Commons about the national debt.

_____

_____

40. Mickey trembled when he saw the mousetrap.

_____

_____

E. Underline and then correct any dangling or misplaced modifiers in the following sentences. Do nothing if a sentence is correct.

41. Sylvio was not very impressed with the food in the new restaurant that he had just eaten.

_____

_____

42. Because she had forgotten to set her alarm, Samantha almost missed her bus the next morning.

_____

_____

43. Standing at the top of the hill, the view was magnificent.

_____

_____

44. To hear the speaker, a seat closer to the front was chosen.

_____

_____

45. When he went fishing, he only succeeded in catching one fish.

_____

_____

46. Shivering in the cold, the snow swirled down from the mountain.

_____

_____

47. The man walking the dog reading a paperback novel nearly bumped into a lamppost.

_____

_____

48. Irritated by the pesky mosquitoes, Kurt's hands slapped at his neck.

_____

_____

49. Flying across the Blue Line, Alexei Yashin shot the puck past the goalie and into the net.

_____

_____

50. The child who reached out toward the puppy carefully started to pet it.

_____

_____

ANSWERS

Answers to Practices in Chapter Three

Page 152:

2. The hunter saw the (elk) <u>trotting into the woods</u>.

3. <u>Turning the corner</u>, the (ant) saw a dead aardvark.

4. <u>Working as an usher at the Queen Elizabeth Theatre</u>, (Sheila) met many extraordinary people.

5. Hampton enjoyed the (carrots) <u>given to him by Michelle</u>.

6. The (man) <u>injured in the accident</u> was taken to the hospital.

7. Blaise wanted to meet the (woman) <u>giving the lecture on South Africa</u>.

8. <u>Hurt by her remark</u>, (Chris) slowly turned red.

9. <u>Watching his team practise</u>, (Byron) brooded about his sore foot.

10. The (plan) <u>suggested by the mayor</u> was approved by the city council.

Page 153:

2. <u>Shivering from the cold</u>, the old (dog) scratched at the back door.

3. Luckily, William Tell knew the correct (way) <u>to aim a crossbow</u>.

4. <u>Bored by the tedious speech</u>, the (people) in the audience drifted away.

5. The city council approved the (plan) <u>to aid the homeless</u>.

6. Mr. Yee gathered a bunch of (carnations) <u>to give to his wife</u>.

7. <u>Yelling loudly</u>, the (British) charged up the hill toward the French troops.

8. <u>Delighted by his daughter's grades</u>, (Sam) took her out to dinner.

9. Fumiko bought several (novels) <u>to read on her spring break</u>.

10. The (material) <u>to build the new albino tiger habitat</u> arrived on Monday.

Pages 160–161:

2. (Martina Gonzales) <u>who is an excellent pediatrician</u> knows more about my children than I do.

3. None of the (operators) <u>who answered the phone</u> could speak Lithuanian.

4. The astronaut's (home town) <u>which has a population of only two hundred</u> honoured her with a (parade) <u>that featured every citizen of the town</u>.

5. The writer returned to (Moose Jaw) <u>where his parents live</u>.

6. The (sweater) <u>that you gave me for Christmas</u> received many compliments.

7. Toots was looking for a (place) <u>where he could play his tuba in peace</u>.

8. Sarah made Sean a (tape) <u>that contained his favourite Irish songs</u>.

9. The fans cheered for the (team) <u>that lost</u> instead of for the (one) <u>that won</u>.

10. The old man pointed to the (place) <u>where he had been wounded in the war</u>.

Page 162:

2. The word *matador* means "killer."
3. Myriam Bedard was asked to endorse <u>Coral Tea</u>, a new product.
4. Recently they were featured on Channel 13, a local television station.
5. Martin, <u>usually a chubby fellow,</u> had become much thinner on his diet of broccoli.
6. The <u>Prince of Tides</u>, a novel by Pat Conroy, was made into a movie.
7. Barbara Streisand made Pat Conroy's novel The Prince of Tides into an award-winning film.
8. Athlete card collecting, <u>once a hobby for boys</u>, has become a popular hobby for people of both sexes and all ages.
9. My cousin Mary enjoys hang gliding.
10. Mary, <u>my favourite cousin,</u> enjoys hang gliding.

Pages 163–164:

Answers will vary. Here are some possible ones.

2. The Spectre took the weapon, <u>a large carving knife</u>, from the shelf.
3. An alarm warned the Chuckling Chef that the Spectre, <u>who was his mortal enemy</u>, had entered the kitchen.
4. The huge cook, <u>a 150 kg Sumo wrestler</u>, threw the Spectre into an oven by the door.
5. The Spectre found himself covered with a sauce <u>that smelled of garlic</u>.
6. Clyde Merdly, <u>who wanted to help the Spectre</u>, crashed his motorcycle into the kitchen.
7. The Chuckling Chef rushed into the main dining room <u>where he hoped to find safety</u>.
8. Clyde Merdly rescued the Spectre from the oven, <u>which was beginning to smoke</u>, and cleaned off the sauce.
9. Clyde and the Spectre slipped on pieces of beets and okra <u>that had fallen on the floor</u> as they chased the Chuckling Chef into the street.
10. The Chuckling Chef ran to the parking lot and escaped in his Beetmobile, <u>a souped-up 1965 Chevrolet</u>.

Pages 173–174:

2. The doctor told him <u>carefully</u> to sew up the wound.
   The doctor told him to sew up the wound carefully. (Other answers are possible.)
3. Correct
4. The dog that ran down the street <u>quickly</u> jumped over the fence.
   The dog that ran down the street jumped quickly over the fence. (Other answers are possible.)
5. When she had <u>almost</u> hiked for five hours, Caroline stopped by a small stream.
   When she had hiked for almost five hours, Caroline stopped by a small stream.
6. The crocodile <u>nearly</u> swam to the edge of the lagoon before the wire fence stopped it.
   The crocodile swam nearly to the edge of the lagoon before the wire fence stopped it.

7. Although Beatrice had sat before her computer all day, she had <u>just</u> written two pages.

Although Beatrice had sat before her computer all day, she had written just two pages.

8. The mechanic advised me <u>repeatedly</u> to depress the accelerator.

The mechanic advised me to depress the accelerator repeatedly. (Other answers are possible.)

9. Jack knew he could not make it to Halifax because he <u>only</u> had ten litres of fuel.

Jack knew he could not make it to Halifax because he had only ten litres of fuel.

10. Terry <u>almost</u> ran twenty kilometres before dropping out of the race.

Terry ran almost twenty kilometres before dropping out of the race.

Pages 175–176:

2. Alice bought a new scarf for her mother <u>covered with red and white stripes</u>.

Alice bought a new scarf covered with red and white stripes for her mother.

3. Chuck avoided his teammates <u>worried about the argument he had just had with his wife</u>.

Worried about the argument he had just had with his wife, Chuck avoided his teammates. (Other answers are possible.)

4. The ten-year-old boy obeyed his grandmother <u>who had been raised to respect his elders</u>.

The ten-year-old boy, who had been raised to respect his elders, obeyed his grandmother.

5. George tried to stop the huge purple and black dragon <u>with the fire extinguisher and a magic dagger</u>.

With the fire extinguisher and a magic dagger, George tried to stop the huge purple and black dragon. (Other answers are possible.)

6. Arthur sold a house to his brother <u>that had leaky plumbing</u>.

Arthur sold a house that had leaky plumbing to his brother.

7. This change will allow customers to place long-distance calls <u>using an alternative long-distance company</u> by simply dialing 1 + area code + telephone number.

This change will allow customers <u>using an alternative long-distance company</u> to place long-distance calls by simply dialing 1+ area code + telephone number.

8. I gave some treats to the dog of the little girl <u>that sat up and begged and rolled over</u>.

I gave some treats to the little girl's dog that sat up and begged and rolled over.

9. The fish in the aquarium swam around looking at the people <u>with their mouths opening and closing constantly in the murky water</u>.

With their mouths opening and closing constantly in the murky water, the fish in the aquarium swam around looking at the people. (Other answers are possible.)

10. Cecil gave the antique rifle to his son <u>that he had bought at the auction</u>.

Cecil gave the antique rifle that he had bought at the auction to his son.

Page 177:

2. D
3. C
4. C
5. D

Pages 179–180:

2. <u>While watching the five-hour play</u>, Jean's chair seemed to become more and more uncomfortable.

   While Jean watched the five-hour play, her chair became more and more uncomfortable. (Other correct answers are possible.)

3. <u>After running on a hot day</u>, a long soak in the tub is enjoyable.

   After running on a hot day, many people enjoy a long soak in the tub. (Other correct answers are possible.)

4. Correct

5. <u>Crying out for help</u>, a life ring was thrown to the boy who had fallen overboard.

   The boy who had fallen overboard cried out for help and was thrown a life ring. (Other correct answers are possible.)

6. <u>Talking nervously to the police constable</u>, Thomas's nose began to itch.

   As he was talking nervously to the policeman, Thomas's nose began to itch. (Other correct answers are possible.)

7. <u>To register people to vote</u>, a table was set up outside the market in the middle of town.

   To register people to vote, Isaac and Marge set up a table outside the market in the middle of town. (Other correct answers are possible.)

8. <u>Looking at the horizon</u>, the sun could be seen reflected on the sea.

   Looking at the horizon, we could see the sun reflected on the sea. (Other correct answers are possible.)

9. <u>Burned in the explosion</u>, a bandage was placed on Curt's right hand by the paramedic.

   Because Curt's right hand had been burned in the explosion, a paramedic placed a bandage on it. (Other correct answers are possible.)

10. <u>To learn more about Paris</u>, books and videos were checked out from the library by Emile before he left for Europe.

    To learn more about Paris, Emile checked out books and videos from the library before he left for Europe. (Other correct answers are possible.)

Chapter Four

Lining Up the Parts of a Sentence

The Careful Writer

Good writing is perhaps less a matter of inspiration than it is a prudent regard for detail. Good writers pay close attention to detail. They create sentences that communicate ideas so precisely that readers do not have to stop because they feel lost.

Here are two ways to make sure that your reader does not get lost: first, make sure you construct all your sentences correctly, and, second, check to see that your modifiers clearly and logically modify the right words.

In this chapter, we will look at the special relationship between the two most crucial parts of your sentences, subjects and verbs. We will also learn how to make sure that your pronouns show their proper function in the sentence—is it **I** or **me** or **mine?**—and agree with, and refer to, their proper antecedents.

Section One

Subject–Verb Agreement

One reason you need to be able to identify subjects and verbs accurately is that the form of the verb must match the form of its subject. If the subject of your sentence is singular, your verb must be singular. If the subject is plural, your verb must be plural. This matching of the verb and its subject is called **subject–verb agreement**.

You need to pay special attention to subject–verb agreement when you use present tense verbs. **Most present tense verbs that have singular subjects end in "s." Most present tense verbs that have plural subjects do *not* end in "s."** Here are some examples.

Singular	Plural
The dog barks.	The dogs bark.
He walks.	They walk.
It is.	They are.
The man has.	The men have.
She does.	They do.

Notice that in each case the verb ends in "s" when the subject is singular. This rule can be confusing because an "s" at the end of a noun almost always means that the noun is plural, but **an "s" at the end of a verb almost always means it is singular.**

PRACTICE

Change the subjects and verbs in the following sentences from singular to plural or from plural to singular. You may need to add *a*, *an*, or *the* to some of the sentences that change to singular; you may also need to drop an "s" if you change to plural.

1. At night, the mockingbirds sing too loudly.

   At night, the mockingbird sings too loudly.

2. The balloon from the picnic has not popped yet.

   _____

3. Sometimes, my brothers call me late at night.

   _____

4. Commercial airliners pass over my house every day.

   _____

5. A rain shower always makes the highways slick and dangerous.

   _____

Identifying Subjects: A Review

1. *Make sure you accurately identify the subject.* Sentences usually contain several nouns and pronouns.

EXAMPLE   The **boys** from the private **school** on the other **side** of **town** often use our **gymnasium**.

       This sentence contains five nouns, but only *boys* is the subject.

2. *Remember that a noun or pronoun that is part of a prepositional phrase cannot be the subject.*

EXAMPLE   **Each** of the children takes a vitamin with breakfast.

       The subject is *Each*, not *children*, because *children* is part of the prepositional phrase *of the children*.

3. *Indefinite pronouns can be subjects.* The indefinite pronouns are listed on page 240.

EXAMPLE   **Everyone** sitting at the tables under the trees has a picnic lunch.

       Here, remember, *everyone* is singular; hence, you must use the singular verb *has*.

Subject–Verb Agreement: Points to Know

1. *Two subjects joined by* and *are plural.*

               S   S   V

EXAMPLES   The **boy** <u>and</u> his **dog were** far from home.

S   S   V
Ham <u>and</u> **rye make** a delicious combination.

2.   *However, if a subject is modified by* each *or* every, *it is singular.*

EXAMPLES
S   S   V
<u>Every</u> **boy** and **girl** at the party <u>**was** given</u> a present to take home.

S   S   V
<u>Each</u> **envelope** and **piece** of paper <u>**has**</u> the name of the company on it.

3.   *Indefinite pronouns are usually singular.*

EXAMPLES
S   V
Each of the band members **has** a new uniform.

S   V
Everyone sitting under the trees **is** part of my family.

4.   *A few nouns and indefinite pronouns, such as* none, some, all, most, more, half, *or* part *may sometimes be considered plural and sometimes singular, depending on the prepositional phrases that follow them.*

EXAMPLES   (singular)
S   V
None of the cake **is** left.

(plural)
S   V
None of the people **are** here.

PRACTICE

Place an "S" above the subjects and underline the correct verb form in the parentheses.

1. In the writing lab, a teacher and a student (was <u>were</u>) working on a

   piece of writing.

2. A grilled cheese sandwich with potato chips (does do) sound good right

   now.

3. Every kangaroo and koala (wants want) to escape from the zoo.

4. In the morning, a hot shower and a cup of strong tea (helps help) Sam

   wake up.

5. Most of the pasta in the pots on the stoves (was were) overcooked.

6. Because of the extreme heat, every window and door in the barracks

(was were) open.

7. Somebody high in the mountains (plays play) a horn each evening.

8. The car's upholstery and paint job (make makes) it look almost new.

9. Half of the people at the concert (was were) crying.

10. A large bear with its two cubs (is are) eating the dog food.

---

5. *When* either/or, neither/nor, *or just* or *joins the subjects, the subject closer to the verb determines the form of the verb.*

EXAMPLE

$$\overset{S}{} \qquad \overset{S}{} \quad \overset{V}{}$$

Neither **David** nor his **brothers want** to shop across the border anymore.

Of course, if you reverse the order of the subjects above, you must change the verb form.

EXAMPLE

$$\overset{S}{} \qquad \overset{S}{} \quad \overset{V}{}$$

Neither his **brothers** nor **David wants** to shop across the border anymore.

This rule applies to questions also.

EXAMPLES

$$\overset{HV}{} \quad \overset{S}{} \qquad \overset{S}{} \quad \overset{MV}{}$$

Does David or his **brothers** want to shop across the border?

OR

$$\overset{HV}{} \quad \overset{S}{} \qquad \overset{S}{} \quad \overset{MV}{}$$

Do his **brothers** or **David** want to shop across the border?

NOTE: When you have helping verbs in a sentence, as in the example above, the helping verb—not the main verb—changes form.

6. *Collective nouns usually take the singular form of the verb.*

Collective nouns represent groups of people or things, but they are considered singular. Here are some common collective nouns.

audience	crowd	herd
band	factory	jury
class	family	number
college	flock	school
committee	government	society
company	group	team

EXAMPLES

$$\overset{S}{}\qquad\overset{V}{}$$

The **audience was** delighted when the curtain slowly rose to reveal the orchestra dressed like clowns.

$$\overset{S}{}\qquad\overset{V}{}$$

My **family goes** camping in Prince Albert National Park every summer.

7. *The relative pronouns* that, which, *and* who *may be either singular or plural.* When one of these pronouns is the subject of a verb, you will need to know which word it refers to before you decide whether it is singular or plural.

EXAMPLES

(singular)   I bought the <u>peach</u> **that was** ripe.

(plural)   I bought the <u>peaches</u> **that were** ripe.

(plural)   Colleen is one of the <u>students</u> **who are** taking flying lessons.

(singular)   Colleen is the only <u>one</u> of the students **who is** taking flying lessons.

PRACTICE

Place an "S" above the subjects and underline the correct verb forms in the parentheses.

$$\qquad\overset{S}{}\qquad\qquad\overset{S}{}$$

1. Neither the money nor my excuses for the accident (pleases <u>please</u>) Mr. Levin.

2. A whole society of aphids (has have) taken up residence in my garden.

3. Hampton is one of the rats that quickly (runs run) through the maze.

4. Neither the gorillas nor the tiger at the zoo (was were) very happy with the living quarters.

5. A cold shower or two glasses of lemonade (refreshes refresh) Amanda after her run.

6. Tomorrow the committee on foreign affairs (decides decide) whether or not to ban travel to other countries.

7. The only one of the laughs that (counts count) is the last one.

8. (Has Have) your mother or your brother arrived yet?

9. The softball team that my sister plays for on weekends (was were) late

for the last game.

10. My younger sister is one of the girls who (has have) qualified for the

tournament.

---

8. *A few nouns end in "s" but are considered singular; they take the singular form of the verb.* These nouns include *economics, gymnastics, mathematics, measles, mumps, news, physics,* and *politics.*

	S V
EXAMPLES	World **economics has been** an important international issue for years.

    S   V

Gymnastics is one of the most popular events in the Olympics.

9. *When units of measurement for distance, time, volume, height, weight, money, and so on are used as subjects, they take the singular verb form.*

    S   V

EXAMPLES   Two **teaspoons** of sugar **was** all that the cake recipe called for.

    S V

Five **dollars is** too much to pay for an hour's parking.

10. *In a question or in a sentence that begins with* there *or* here, *the order of the subject and verb is reversed.*

    V   S

EXAMPLES   **Was** the **bus** ever on time?

    V   S

Is there a squeaky **wheel** out there somewhere?

    V   S

There **is** an **abundance** of wildflowers in the desert this spring.

    V   S

Here **are** the **keys** to your new car.

11. *Only the subject affects the form of the verb.*

    S   V

EXAMPLE   Our biggest **problem is** termites in the attic.

The singular verb form *is* is correct here because the subject is the singular noun *problem.* The plural noun *termites* does not affect the form of the verb.

PRACTICE

Place an "S" above the subjects and underline the correct verb forms in the parentheses.

                     S

1. Mathematics (<u>remains</u> remain) one of the hardest subjects for students.

2. Three hundred hectares of grain (produces produce) a good income for some farmers.

3. One of Malvina's favourite recordings (is are) a David Foster album.

4. According to Robert Louis Stevenson, politics (is are) perhaps the only profession for which no preparation is necessary.

5. (Is Are) measles still a problem in some parts of the world?

6. Eight kilometres in two days (does do) sound like a long, hard hike.

7. (Does Do) Charles always bring his bloody cleaver to work?

8. There still (are is) people who believe that the earth is flat.

9. The main problem of this neighbourhood (is are) the planes flying over every half hour.

10. Here (is are) the $525 that I owe you.

REVIEW

Section One Review

1. In the present tense, when the subject is a singular noun or a singular pronoun, the verb form usually will end in "s."

2. Subject–verb agreement: points to know
   a. Two subjects joined by *and* are plural.
   b. If a subject is modified by *each* or *every*, it is singular.
   c. Indefinite pronouns are usually singular.
   d. Sometimes indefinite pronouns like *some, half,* or *part* are considered plural, depending on the prepositional phrases that follow them.
   e. When *either/or, neither/nor,* or just *or* joins two subjects, the *subject closer to the verb* determines the verb form.
   f. When a collective noun, such as *family* or *group*, is the subject, the singular form of the verb is used.
   g. The relative pronouns *that, which,* and *who* may be either singular or plural.
   h. A few nouns, such as *economics* or *news*, end in "s" but are considered singular.
   i. When the subject is a unit of measurement, such as distance, weight, or money, the singular form of the verb is used.
   j. In a question or in a sentence that begins with *there* or *here*, the verb will often come before the subject.
   k. Only the **subject** affects the form of the verb.

EXERCISE

Exercise 1A

Circle the subjects and underline the correct verb forms in the parentheses.

1. (Anyone) with plaid pants and pink shoes (<u>was</u> were) let into the golf tournament free.

2. Either the prime minister or one of his staff members (addresses address) the press each Wednesday.

3. By October 15, the elk herd and the pigeon flock (has have) usually left the higher elevations.

4. The first group to reach the base camp (was were) the Girl Scouts.

5. Angela participates in many sports, but gymnastics (interest interests) her the most.

6. A long-haired dog with many fleas (has have) a hard time during the hot weather.

7. Twenty-five centimetres (is are) the average size of trout at Lake Simcoe this summer.

8. A good used car with a sound engine and good tires (costs cost) about five thousand dollars.

9. "(Has Have) the birdseed and the gerbil food arrived?" asked Mustafa.

10. Every mother and father (was were) proud when the graduates received their diplomas.

11. Too much politics in the news (causes cause) many people to want to turn off their televisions.

12. Somebody down by the trees (was were) calling for more punch.

13. Four weeks (seem seems) too long for Jack to wait for his new computer system to arrive.

14. (Does Do) either the coach or several of the players have to be present

for the scheduling?

15. Anyone from either of the buildings (is are) allowed to use the pool.

EXERCISE

Exercise 1B

Correct any subject–verb agreement errors in the following sentences. If a sentence is correct, do nothing to it. To check your answers, circle the subjects.

1. Neither (Keiko) nor (Natalie) ~~want~~ *wants* to clean up the mess.

2. Last night, everyone watching the boxing matches was dressed in colourful clothes.

3. Every rock and log were turned over in the search for worms.

4. The news at the end of the first day of the negotiations were not positive.

5. The sweet roll and the bagel seem to be stale.

6. Andre, along with his friend Carlos, have been chosen for a managerial position.

7. A bevy of quails cross this road each day at sunset.

8. Do Paul's aunt or her children own the family business?

9. Hector and Ajax from the Greek restaurant help with the shish kabobs at the school fair.

10. In June, the house down by Willow Shores were burglarized while the owners were gone.

11. Oscar and his cowchip-pitching team helps clean the barn out each month.

12. As the sun disappeared over the horizon, somebody over by the trees was playing the flute.

13. The society for the preservation of old TV Guides meet at Kang Jin's house.

14. His association with known meat eaters hurts his reputation.

15. Everybody in both of the fifth-grade classes know who stole the money for the field trip.

EXERCISE

Exercise 1C

Correct all subject–verb agreement errors. Not all sentences will contain errors.

1. Throughout the world, people of many different cultures share the custom of offering a blessing or a word of goodwill when someone sneezes. 2. This custom, practised by so many people today, have derived from a number of historical causes. 3. First, there was the ancient beliefs that a person's life force reside in the head and that a sneeze can dislodge that vital force. 4. Each of these beliefs were reinforced whenever a person died after an illness involving bouts of sneezing. 5. Someone who heard a person sneeze would perform a short ritual that were meant to protect that person's life force. 6. Later, in the fourth century B.C., Greek thinkers explained that sneezing is caused when the body tries to expel foreign substances or irritating material that have come in through the nostrils. 7. However, they also recognized that bouts of sneezing precedes many illnesses, so they gave a blessing to people who sneezed, such as "May you enjoy good health!" 8. Then Roman physicians added to the custom by claiming that a series of strong sneezes actually help rid the body of spirits that causes illnesses. 9. They encouraged people to sneeze to help cleanse the body, and soon one vigorous sneeze as well as several brief sneezes were greeted with "Congratulations!" 10. Finally, the common "God bless you" of today derive from the sixth century. 11. A deadly plague ravaged Italy at that time, and one of its most telling symptoms were severe sneezes. 12. Pope Gregory the Great ordered people to replace "May you enjoy long life" with a more direct plea for God's help in the form of "God bless you." 13. As the plague spread throughout Europe, killing hundreds of thousands of people, the response of "God bless you" to any sudden sneezes were widespread.

Section Two

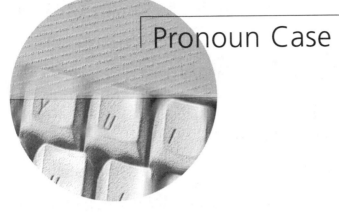

Pronoun Case

Pronouns, like verbs, can appear in a variety of different forms, depending on how they function in a sentence. For example, the pronoun that refers to the speaker in a sentence may be written as *I, me, my,* or *mine.* These different spellings are the result of what is called **pronoun case**.

The three pronoun cases for English are the **subjective**, the **objective**, and the **possessive**. The subjective is used as the **subject** of a verb; the objective is used as the **object** of a verb or preposition; the possessive shows **ownership**.

Subjective Case

Singular	*Plural*
I	we
you	you
he, she, it	they
who	who

Objective Case

Singular	*Plural*
me	us
you	you
him, her, it	them
whom	whom

Possessive Case

Singular	*Plural*
my, mine	our, ours
your, yours	your, yours
his, her, hers, its	their, theirs
whose	whose

Subjective Pronouns

The subjective pronouns are *I, we, you, he, she, it, they,* and *who.* They are used in two situations.

1. *Subjective pronouns are used as subjects of sentences.*

EXAMPLES

S

I will finish the first draft this weekend.

S

They are always trying to outwit me.

2. *Subjective pronouns are used when they follow linking verbs.* Because the linking verb *identifies* the pronoun after it with the subject, the pronoun must be in the same case as the subject.

EXAMPLES

S

It was **she** who won the award for being the best-dressed mud-wrestler.

(The subjective pronoun *she* is identified with the subject *it* by the linking verb *was.*)

S

That was **I** you saw rowing across the lake yesterday.

S

It was **they** who caused the huge traffic jam.

NOTE: These pronouns always sound strange to the ear but are structurally correct.

Objective Pronouns

The objective pronouns are *me, us, you, him, her, it, them,* and *whom.* They are used in three situations.

1. *Objective pronouns are used as objects of prepositions.*

EXAMPLES

Sally loved the chrysanthemums Mr. Kim gave <u>to **her**</u>.

The difficulties <u>between Samantha and **me**</u> continued into the fall.

2. *Objective pronouns are used as direct objects of action verbs.* The noun or pronoun that receives the action of the action verb is called the **direct object**.

For example, in the simple sentence *Jim visited Serena yesterday,* the verb is *visited,* an action verb. The direct object of *visited* is *Serena* because *Serena* receives the action of the verb *visited.* If you substitute a pronoun for *Serena,* it must be the objective pronoun *her*—*Jim visited **her** yesterday.*

EXAMPLES   Brenda married **him** on March 7, 1987.

Last summer Joan beat **me** at tennis every time we played.

Both classes helped clean up the park, and the city rewarded **them** with a picnic.

3. *Objective pronouns are used as indirect objects.* The indirect object indicates **to whom or for whom (or to what or for what) an action is directed,** but the prepositions *to* and *for* are left out.

EXAMPLES   (prepositional phrase)   He threw the ball **to her**.

(indirect object)   He threw **her** the ball.

In the first sentence, *her* is the object of the preposition *to*.
    In the second sentence, the *to* is omitted and the pronoun is moved, making *her* the indirect object. In both sentences, the direct object is *ball*. Here are other examples.

She had already given **me** two chances to make up for my mistakes.

The architect showed **them** a picture of how the new city hall would look.

PRACTICE

In the blanks, identify the underlined pronouns as subjective (sub) or objective (obj).

sub   1. On Saturday, <u>we</u> will leave for our trip to the Grey Cup game.

_____   2. The profits will be shared with <u>him</u>.

_____   3. It was <u>he</u> who gave me my favourite recipe for fried wonton.

_____   4. What the dawn revealed was a pleasant surprise for <u>her</u>.

_____   5. Out of respect, we bowed to <u>them</u> as they passed by.

_____   6. Hoping for good weather, <u>they</u> left for two weeks in Whitehorse.

_____   7. It was <u>they</u> who sailed from Vancouver to Bella Bella.

_____   8. For three years, the father searched for <u>her</u>.

_____ 9. Because <u>he</u> was a misanthrope, he shopped for groceries only after midnight.

_____ 10. She succeeded <u>me</u> as president of the class.

Possessive Pronouns

The **possessive pronouns** are *my, mine, our, ours, your, yours, his, her, hers, its, their, theirs,* and *whose.* They are used in two situations.

1. *Possessive pronouns are used as adjectives to indicate possession.*

EXAMPLES   The old sailor had turned up **his** collar against the wind.

The weary travellers shuffled off to **their** rooms.

The polar bear constantly paced up and down **its** enclosure.

*NOTE: The contraction **it's** means "it is." The word **its** is the only possessive form for it. (In fact, you do not use apostrophes with any of the possessive pronouns. You would not, for example, write hi's, or her's.)*

2. *Some possessive pronouns indicate possession without being used as adjectives.* In this case, they may be used as subjects or objects.

EXAMPLE   I had to borrow Jan's flashlight because **mine** was lost.

Here the possessive pronoun *mine* is the subject of its clause.

EXAMPLE   The Chin house is large, but **yours** is cozy.

In this example, *yours* is the subject of its clause.

EXAMPLE   He didn't have any change for a phone call because he had given **his** to the children begging on the street.

Here the possessive pronoun *his* is a direct object.

Common Sources of Errors in Pronoun Case

Compound Constructions

Compound subjects and objects often cause problems when they include pronouns. If your sentence includes a compound construction, be sure you use the correct pronoun case.

EXAMPLES	(compound subject)	**Sandra and <u>she</u>** will return the car on Monday.
	(compound after linking verb)	That was **my friend and <u>I</u>** whom you saw on the news.
	(compound object of a preposition)	They awarded first place trophies to **both Dolores and <u>me</u>.**
	(compound direct object)	Lim's boss fired **Mark and <u>him</u>** yesterday.
	(compound indirect object)	She had already given **him and <u>me</u>** two chances to make up our minds.

In most cases, you can use a simple test to check whether you have chosen the right pronoun case when you have a compound construction. Simply remove one of the subjects or objects so that only one pronoun is left. For example, is this sentence correct? *Our host gave Erin and I a drink.* Test it by dropping *Erin and. Our host gave I a drink.* Now you can see that the *I* should be *me* because it is an object (an indirect object). The correct sentence should read: *Our host gave Erin and me a drink.*

PRACTICE

Underline the correct pronoun in the parentheses.

1. My brother and (<u>I</u> me) enjoy our rollerblades.

2. Between you and (I me), I think a plate of freeze-dried prunes sounds revolting.

3. Mr. Wambuster sent tickets for the concert to (she her) and (I me).

4. Curt's proudest achievement was the mural that Nicole and (he him) had painted on the library wall.

5. Can you lend Brutus and (I me) your ears?

6. After we were late for work the fifth day in a row, Mr. Bob fined George and (I me).

7. Chin will give his old computer to Colin and (I me).

8. Ms. Matusan said that it was Mary and (she her) at the door.

9. The bridge had been washed out before Corey and (she her) could get across.

10. Your sister and (they them) left for the play an hour ago.

Who and Whom

When to use *who* or *whom* is a mystery to many writers, but you should have no problem with these pronouns if you remember two simple rules.

1. Use the subjective pronoun *who* or *whoever* when it is used as the subject of a verb.

2. Use the objective pronoun *whom* or *whomever* when it is not used as the subject of a verb.

EXAMPLES   After leaving the airport, I followed the man **who** had taken my bags. (*Who* is the subject of *had taken*.)

The letter was sent to the person **whom** we had decided to hire. (*Whom* is not the subject of a verb.)

Please give the money to **whoever** needs it. (*Whoever* is the subject of *needs*.)

PRACTICE   Underline the correct pronoun in the parentheses.

1. The people (who <u>whom</u>) we saw at the concert were having a good time.

2. The people (who whom) were at the concert were having a good time.

3. These certificates are for the people (who whom) donate the most food for the flood victims.

4. Give the flowers to (whoever whomever) the Queen points out.

5. Give the money to (whoever whomever) wins the drawing.

Comparisons

When a pronoun is used in a comparison, you often need to supply the implied words in order to know what pronoun case to use. For example, in the sentence *My brother cannot skate as well as I,* the implied words are the verb *can skate: My brother cannot skate as well as I [can skate].*

EXAMPLE   The constable allowed my friend to leave the scene sooner than me.

You can tell that *me* is the correct case in this sentence when you supply the implied words:

The constable allowed my friend to leave the scene sooner than **[he allowed]** me **[to leave]**.

PRACTICE   Underline the correct pronoun in the parentheses.

1. Oscar usually leaves for work before (I me).

2. Although the crowd cheered both skaters about the same, the judges gave Elvis Stojko higher scores than (he him).

3. Vincent's father likes Sichuan cooking better than (he him).

4. The columnist noticed that many other writers were more proficient with a word processor than (he him).

5. When we missed class, the vice principal punished Vanessa more than (I me).

Appositives

As you will remember from Chapter Three, an appositive is a word group containing a noun or pronoun that renames another noun or pronoun. When the appositive contains a pronoun that does the renaming, be sure that the pronoun is in the same case as the word it renames.

EXAMPLE   Some team members—Joe, Frank, and **I**—were late for practice.

Here *I* is in the subjective case because the appositive *Joe, Frank, and I* renames the word *members,* the subject of the sentence.

EXAMPLE   When the show is over, please send your review to the producers, Mark and **her**.

Here *her* is in the objective case because the appositive *Mark and her* renames *producers*, the object of the preposition *to*.

PRACTICE

Underline the correct pronoun in the parentheses.

1. Alex was disappointed when the authors—Elena, Serena, and (<u>he</u> him)—were not paid well.

2. After the test, the people turned in their answers to the invigilators, Cecil and (I me).

3. Suzanne felt that her team had lost because the pitchers, Bill and (she her), had not played well.

4. Felix was embarrassed when the press praised the guides, Maria and (he him), for saving the hunters from the storm.

5. The winners of the relay—Carlos, Antonio, Broderick, and (I me)—took a victory lap.

PRACTICE

Underline the correct pronoun in the parentheses.

1. The tape will be broken by (<u>whoever</u> whomever) crosses the finish line first.

2. My girlfriend likes beets much more than (I me).

3. The only two cooks, Cecilia and (I me), prepared over four hundred meals.

4. Are Martin and (she her) really ready to give up that soon?

5. You should attend the party with (whoever whomever) you prefer.

6. The trip to Toronto went to the co-winners of the spelling bee, Mordecai and (he him).

7. Place Larry and (she her) on the interview committee.

8. When we were late getting home, my parents punished my sister more

    than (I me).

9. That was a famous actor (who whom) we saw helping to clean the

    streets in Los Angeles after the fires.

10. Will Joy and (she her) be able to join us at the pub tonight?

REVIEW

Section Two Review

1. The **subjective pronouns** are used in two ways:
   a. As the subjects of sentences
   b. After linking verbs

2. The **objective pronouns** are used in three ways:
   a. As objects of prepositions
   b. As direct objects of action verbs
   c. As indirect objects

3. The **possessive pronouns** are used in two ways:
   a. As adjectives to modify nouns to indicate possession
   b. As subjects and objects

4. Some common sources of errors in pronoun case are:
   a. Pronouns in compound constructions
   b. The use of the pronouns *who, whom, whoever,* and *whomever*
   c. Pronouns in comparisons
   d. Pronouns in appositives

EXERCISE

Exercise 2A

Underline the correct pronoun form in the parentheses.

1. The baby seal was barking because it could not find (its it's) mother.

2. Just between you and (I me), I think the yellow car is a much better deal.

3. The class applauded Garfield and (she her) after their presentation on feline eating habits.

4. It was (he him) (who whom) wanted us to push ahead with the swamp project.

5. By the end of the summer, Steve and Pat had cooked many more hamburgers than (I me).

6. Tell the Keenes and (they them) that the plans are almost complete.

7. The people (who whom) the band encouraged to rush the stage blocked our view.

8. Will Ya Li and (she her) play tennis with us?

9. No matter how many times Keiko dropped the cat, it always landed on (its it's) paws.

10. Was it (they them) that we spent a few days with in the summer of 1980?

11. The prize goes to (whoever whomever) throws a cowchip the farthest.

12. Wang told his grandmother that he wanted to buy a new condominium for his grandfather and (she her).

13. The counsellors talked patiently with the last two students, Tiffany and (I me).

14. (It's Its) beautiful view of the lake attracted Kevin and (she her) to the

cabin.

15. After Easter, his family and (he him) always forget where they hid at

least two of the eggs.

EXERCISE

Exercise 2B

Correct any pronoun errors in the following sentences. Some sentences may not contain errors.

1. Alice likes mushrooms and white rabbits more than ~~me.~~ I

2. Is Mr. Matheson or she going to sign the petition?

3. Wasn't that Kevin whom helped you with your trigonometry last night?

4. A bear scared Mario and I as we were walking home last night.

5. They gave the second and third place winners, Catherine and he, bouquets of roses.

6. The old house had obviously lost it's zest for life because the paint was peeling and the windows were all broken.

7. The pit bull barked at Mustafa and I when we walked into the yard.

8. By this time next year, our neighbours and we will have moved to another town.

9. The people who our club visited at the convalescent home gave us fresh bread that they had made.

10. Helga did better on the dexterity test than us.

11. Between him and me was a serious misunderstanding.

12. Give Mark and them these apples.

13. The orang-utan looked as though it was planning it's escape.

14. The referee whom charged the coach and her with a penalty was unfair.

15. The constable and me tried to explain the situation to the judge.

EXERCISE

Exercise 2C

Correct any errors in pronoun case in the following paragraph.

1. Over the past several years, as my wife and ~~me~~ ^I^ have taught our children at home, we have met many people who have confirmed our own experience that home teaching can result in a number of benefits for children. 2. For instance, our friends Art and Renae say that their son's interest in learning has been rekindled since they started teaching his sister and he at home.

3. They say that by the fourth grade their son had decided that school was a bore and that most people were just smarter than him. 4. However, after twelve months of home schooling, he had completed the entire fourth- and fifth-grade class materials, and his sister and him both scored in the upper ten percent on provincial tests. 5. Renae says that once learning was not something "required" by an institution, it became valuable to her son in a way that her and Art still don't fully understand. 6. Another result of home schooling was pointed out to my wife and I by my sister Martha.

7. Martha's children, Jack and Emily, who she teaches at home, often learn in two hours what thirty students in a traditional classroom might need an entire day to learn. 8. As a result, they have the extra time and energy to participate in many extracurricular activities. 9. Emily, for instance, is enrolled in children's theatre and gymnastics, and Jack is just as active as her. 10. The experiences of my wife and I have been similar to those of the parents described above. 11. When we pulled our children out of school, Kelly and her sister, Dana, had already lost the excitement that comes from learning new things. 12. However, within just a few months that excitement

had returned, and Dana was asking what her and her sister could read next.

13. Obviously, home schooling is not for everyone, but for those parents whom have the time and desire to teach their own children, it can produce dramatic results.

Section Three

Pronoun Agreement and Reference

Pronoun–Antecedent Agreement

Because pronouns stand for or take the place of nouns, it is important that you make it clear in your writing which pronouns stand for which nouns. The noun that the pronoun takes the place of is called the **antecedent**.

Pronoun–antecedent agreement refers to the idea that a pronoun must match or "agree with" the noun that it stands for in **person** and **number**.

Person

Person in pronouns refers to the relationship of the speaker (or writer) to the pronoun. There are three persons: **first person, second person,** and **third person.**

1. **First person** pronouns refer to the person speaking or writing:

Singular	Plural
I	we
me	us
my, mine	our, ours

2. **Second person** pronouns refer to the person spoken or written to:

Singular	Plural
you	you
your	your
yours	yours

3. **Third person** pronouns refer to the person or thing spoken or written about:

Singular	Plural
he, she, it	they
him, her, it	them
his, her, hers, its	their, theirs

Because nouns are always in the third person, pronouns that refer to nouns should also be in the third person. Usually this rule poses no problem, but sometimes writers mistakenly shift from third to second person when they are referring to a noun.

E X A M P L E   When a new **student** first enters the large and crowded registration area, **you might** feel confused and intimidated.

In this sentence, *you* has mistakenly been used to refer to *student*. The mistake occurs because the noun *student* is in the third person, but the pronoun *you* is in the second person. There are two ways to correct the sentence:

1. You can change the second person pronoun *you* to a third person pronoun.

E X A M P L E   When a new **student** first enters the large and crowded registration area, **he** or **she** might feel confused and intimidated.

2. You can change the noun *student* to the second person pronoun *you*.

E X A M P L E   When **you** first enter the large and crowded registration area, **you** might feel confused and intimidated.

Here's another incorrect sentence.

E X A M P L E   Most **people** can stay reasonably healthy if **you** watch **your** diet and exercise several times a week.

One way to correct this sentence is to change *you* to *they* and *your* to *their* so that they agree with *people*.

E X A M P L E   Most **people** can stay reasonably healthy if **they** watch **their** diets and exercise several times a week.

Correct any errors in pronoun person in the following sentences. When you correct the pronoun, you also may need to change the verb.

1. When a person wants to get a driver's licence, ~~you~~ *he or she* really need*s* to take

   a test at the Motor Vehicles Branch.

2. Most people can pass a driver's test if you study the rules.

3. A driver will just be wasting time if you don't study for the test.

4. When I watched my cousin take her driving test, you could see that she

   wasn't nervous at all.

5. Finally, I passed the driving test. A person wouldn't want to go through

   that ordeal again.

Number

Errors in number are the most common pronoun–antecedent errors. To make pronouns agree with their antecedents in **number,** use singular pronouns to refer to singular nouns and plural pronouns to refer to plural nouns. The following guidelines will help you avoid errors in number.

1. *When you use a pronoun to refer to words joined by* **and,** *you should use a plural pronoun unless the words are modified by* **each** *or* **every.**

EXAMPLE   **Alberta** and **Saskatchewan** have wheat boards to represent the interests of **their** farmers.

2. *Because the following indefinite pronouns are singular, you should use singular pronouns to refer to them.*

anybody	either	neither	one
anyone	everybody	nobody	somebody
anything	everyone	no one	someone
each	everything	nothing	something

EXAMPLES   **Everything** was in **its** place.

Neither of the girls wanted to give up **her** place in line.

One of the fathers was yelling loudly at **his** son throughout the game.

NOTE: In spoken English, the plural pronouns they, them, *and* their *are often used to refer to the antecedents* everyone *or* everybody. *However, in written English the singular pronoun is preferred:* everyone ... he, *or* everyone ... she, *but not* everyone ... they. *The use of* everyone ... he or she, *or* everyone ... he/she *can become very awkward in writing, and the writer can avoid sexism by using plural antecedents. [See page 242 for a full discussion.]*

EXAMPLES   **Everybody** at the game cheered for **his** favourite team.

The **fans** at the game cheered for **their** favourite team.

3. *You should use singular pronouns to refer to collective nouns.*

EXAMPLES   The tire **factory** outside of town gave **its** workers a large raise last June.

The **troop** of soldiers had almost reached **its** camp when the blizzard started.

4. *When antecedents are joined by the following words, you should use a pronoun that agrees with the closer antecedent.*

either/or

neither/nor

nor

or

not only/but also

EXAMPLE   Not only **Angela** but also the **Johnstons** wanted to complete **their** plan for opening a day care centre.

The plural pronoun *their* agrees with the plural noun *Johnstons* because *Johnstons* is the closer noun.

EXAMPLE   Neither his **brothers** nor **Kirpal** expected **him** to see **his** wallet again.

His and *him* agree with *Kirpal*, not with *brothers.*

PRACTICE

Correct any pronoun–antecedent errors in the following sentences. When you correct a pronoun, you may also need to change the verb.

1. If accountants want to do a good job, ~~you~~ *they* need to be careful and precise.

2. The crowd at Maple Leaf Gardens got to their feet and sang when "O Canada!" was played.

3. When people have spent over eight hours waiting on customers at a restaurant, you sometimes do not feel like cooking and serving another meal at home.

4. One team from Barrie has won all of its games for the past five years.

5. Neither Dr. Jekyll nor Mr. Hyde could explain their recent mood swings.

6. Not only the Nelsons but also Mr. Finch will be bringing their movie camera on the bird-watching trip.

7. No one could find out how the ocelot was escaping from its enclosure.

8. After one eats raw fish a few times, you might actually start to like it.

9. Someone left their books on the desk.

10. Patients at that hospital will sometimes see a military band practising outside their window.

Sexist Language

In the past it has been traditional to use masculine pronouns when referring to singular nouns whose gender could be either masculine or feminine. A good example is the sentence *A **person** should stop delivery of **his** newspaper before **he** leaves on a trip of more than a few days*. Although the noun *person* could be either masculine or feminine, traditionally only masculine pronouns like *he* or *his* have been used in a case like this one.

Because females make up over 50 percent of the English-speaking population, they have been justifiably dissatisfied with this tradition. The problem is that the English language does not contain a singular personal pronoun that can refer to either sex at the same time in the way that the forms of *they* can.

The solutions to this problem can prove awkward. One of the solutions is to use feminine pronouns as freely as masculine ones to refer to singular nouns whose gender could be masculine or feminine. Either of the following sentences using this solution is acceptable.

A **person** should stop delivery on **her** newspaper before **she** leaves on a trip of more than a few days.

A **person** should stop delivery on **his** newspaper before **he** leaves on a trip of more than a few days.

Another solution is to change the *his* to *his or her* and the *he* to *he or she*. Then the sentence would look like this:

> A **person** should stop delivery on **his or her** newspaper before **he or she** leaves on a trip of more than a few days.

As you can see, this solution does not result in a very graceful sentence. Still another alternative is to use *her/his* and *she/he*, but the result would be about the same as the one above. The best solution is to change a singular antecedent to a plural one and use the forms of *they*, which can refer to either gender. That would result in a sentence like this:

> **People** should stop delivery of **their** newspapers before **they** leave on a trip of more than a few days.

This sentence is less awkward and just as fair. Finally, in some situations, the masculine pronoun alone will be appropriate, and in others the feminine pronoun alone will be. Here are two such sentences:

> Each of the hockey players threw **his** false teeth into the air after the victory. (The hockey team is known to be all male.)

> The last runner on the relay team passed **her** opponent ten metres before the finish line. (All members of the relay team are female.)

Whatever your solutions to this problem, it is important that you be logical and correct in your subject–verb agreement in addition to being fair.

Unclear Pronoun Reference

Sometimes, even though a pronoun appears to agree with an antecedent, it is not clear exactly which noun in the sentence is the antecedent. And sometimes a writer will use a pronoun that does not clearly refer to any antecedent at all. The following two points will help you to use pronouns correctly.

1. *A pronoun should refer to a specific antecedent.*

EXAMPLE **Mr. Mellon** told **Larry** that he could take a vacation in late August.

> In this sentence, he could refer either to *Mr. Mellon* or to *Larry*. To correct this problem, you can eliminate the pronoun.

EXAMPLE Mr. Mellon told Larry that **Larry** could take his vacation in late August.

> The meaning is clear now, but the sentence is awkward. Preferably, you can revise the whole sentence so that the pronoun clearly refers to only one antecedent.

EXAMPLES   Mr. Mellon told **Larry** to consider taking his vacation in late August.

OR

Mr. Mellon told Larry, "You can take your vacation in late August."

Here is another example:

EXAMPLE   Every time **Patricia** looked at the cat, she whined.

Who whined, Patricia or the cat? The antecedent is unclear. The pronoun reference needs, therefore, to be clarified.

EXAMPLES   Patricia whined every time **she** looked at the cat.

OR

The cat whined every time Patricia looked at **her**.

PRACTICE

Revise the following sentences so that each pronoun refers to a specific antecedent.

1. John told his roommate that his new contact lenses were at the optometrist's office.

   John said to his roommate, "Your new contact lenses are at the optometrist's office."

2. Once Marvin and the doctor had discussed the illness, he began to worry.

3. I kept misplacing the key to my motorcycle, and then it was stolen.

4. Later, when Mrs. Massey took her children and their test results to the clinic, she discussed them with her doctor.

_____

_____

5. When my cat refused to eat its dinner, I threw it into the garbage compactor.

_____

_____

2. *Pronouns should not refer to **implied** or **unstated** antecedents.* Be especially careful with the pronouns *this, that, which,* and *it.*

EXAMPLE   My baseball coach made us go without dinner if we lost a game; **this** was unfair.

Was it unfair that he made us go without dinner? Was losing the game unfair? The following sentence clarifies the pronoun **reference.**

EXAMPLE   My baseball coach made us go without dinner if we lost a game; this **punishment** was unfair.

Sometimes a pronoun refers to a noun that is missing or only implied in the first part of the sentence.

EXAMPLE   Mrs. Brovelli is a poet, **which** she does some of every day.

In this sentence, the *which* apparently stands for "writing poetry," but "writing poetry" is only implied by the noun *poet.* There is no specific noun for the pronoun *which* to refer to. The faulty pronoun reference can be cleared up in several ways.

EXAMPLES   Mrs. Brovelli is a poet, and **she writes** poetry every day.

Mrs. Brovelli is a poet **who writes** poetry every day.

Mrs. Brovelli writes poetry every day.

PRACTICE

Revise the following sentences so that each pronoun refers to a specific, not an implied or unstated, antecedent. To correct the sentence, you may have to eliminate the pronoun altogether.

1. I have always resisted learning how to serve oysters, which annoys my roommate.

   My resistance to learning how to serve oysters annoys my roommate.

2. We were supposed to leave early, but this was impossible because we overslept.

   _____

   _____

3. The broken pieces of glass were all over the floor, but Robert said that he had fixed it.

   _____

   _____

4. I love to eat jellyfish, which is rather unusual.

   _____

   _____

5. The sound system at the theatre was too loud, and the musicians were eating goldfish, which caused me to leave.

   _____

   _____

Reflexive and Intensive Pronouns

The reflexive and intensive pronouns are those that end in *self* or *selves*. The singular pronouns end in *self*, and the plural ones end in *selves*.

Singular	**Plural**
myself	ourselves
yourself	yourselves
himself	themselves
herself	
itself	
oneself	

These are the only reflexive and intensive forms. Avoid nonstandard forms like *hisself, ourselfs, theirselves,* or *themselfs*.

The **reflexive pronouns** are used to reflect the action of a verb back to the subject.

EXAMPLE   Amos gave himself a bloody nose when he tried to slap a mosquito.

The **intensive pronouns** emphasize or intensify a noun or another pronoun in the sentence.

EXAMPLE   Let's have **Zhang Ming herself** show us how to cross-examine a witness in court.

To help you use intensive and reflexive pronouns correctly, remember these three points.

1. *Do not use a reflexive pronoun unless it is reflecting the action of a verb back to a subject.*

2. *Do not use an intensive pronoun unless the sentence contains a noun or pronoun for it to emphasize or intensify.*

3. *In general, do not use a reflexive or intensive pronoun where a personal pronoun is called for. For example, reflexive and intensive pronouns are never used as subjects.*

EXAMPLES   (incorrect)   Tim's mother and **myself** often go shopping together on Saturdays.

(correct)   Tim's mother and **I** often go shopping together on Saturdays.

(incorrect)   The other employees at the restaurant gave Rachel and **myself** large bouquets of flowers on the anniversary of our first year there.

(correct)   The other employees of the restaurant gave Rachel and **me** large bouquets of flowers on the anniversary of our first year there.

PRACTICE

Correct any errors in the use of reflexive or intensive pronouns in the following sentences.

1. We decided to redecorate the den ~~ourself.~~ *ourselves*

2. Hue and myself decided to go skiing next weekend.

3. I heard that Mr. Wren and hisself had taken the train to Edmonton.

4. We did not deserve it, but Mr. Abernathy gave Mike and myself a raise anyway.

5. They tried to solve the problem by theirself.

PRACTICE

Correct any errors in pronoun reference or in the use of reflexive and intensive pronouns in the following sentences.

1. I used to paint landscapes, but I do not like ~~it~~ anymore. *painting them*

2. The Karupski family and ourselves will take a trip to the zoo next weekend.

3. In the back of the room sat ten people with shaved heads, tattoos, leather jackets, and black boots; this worried me.

4. James told his father that he was concerned about his car.

5. The school gave financial aid to my wife and myself.

6. I would love to go cycling along the coast with you, but I don't have one.

7. The fan yelled at the umpire, which made us angry.

8. He had been wanting to treat hisself to a week by the seashore as a reward for finishing the remodelling project.

9. Byron dropped the vase on his foot and broke it.

10. The salesman told Ramon that he would have to ride the motorcycle around to the front.

Section Three Review

1. The **antecedent** is the word a pronoun stands for.

2. A pronoun must agree with its **antecedent** in **person** and **number**.

3. Use a plural pronoun to refer to antecedents joined by *and*.

4. Use a singular pronoun to refer to an **indefinite pronoun**.

5. Use a singular pronoun to refer to a **collective noun**.

6. When you refer to two antecedents that are joined by *either/or, neither/nor, or, nor,* or *not only/but also,* your pronoun usually should agree with the closer word.

7. Make sure a pronoun refers to a specific antecedent in its sentence or in the previous sentence.

8. Be sure that your pronoun does not refer to an implied or unstated antecedent.

9. A **reflexive pronoun** reflects the action of a verb back to the subject.

10. An **intensive pronoun** emphasizes or intensifies a noun or pronoun in the sentence.

11. Do not use a reflexive or intensive pronoun when a personal pronoun is called for.

EXERCISE

Exercise 3A

Underline the correct pronouns in parentheses.

1. Robin likes to watch the *CBC Primetime News,* but her husband doesn't consider (it them) interesting.

2. Almost everyone at one time or another has problems with (his or her their) car.

3. After the herd had eaten all of the grass, (it they) migrated to other pastures.

4. The family found that there were many hidden expenses that had to be considered in (its their) budget for the trip.

5. When anyone breaks even the smallest rule, Mansour tells (him or her them) about it.

6. As we rounded the corner, we found (ourself ourselves) face-to-face with a man-eating Siberian tiger.

7. If a person intends to jump out of an airplane, (you she they) should have a parachute.

8. After pulling the sled all day, the lead dog was eagerly gobbling (its it's) supper.

9. Each handler at the auction led (her their) horse around the ring.

10. When we had tried every method we knew, we asked (ourself ourselves) if we would ever find a way to serve spinach and beets.

11. Once a teenager is eighteen, (he or she they you) should be able to make responsible decisions.

To avoid sexist language, change singular to plural in sentences 2, 5, 7, and 11 in spaces provided below.

#2.

_____

_____

_____

#5.

_____

_____

_____

#7.

_____

_____

_____

#11.

_____

_____

_____

#5.

EXERCISE

Exercise 3B

Correct all errors in pronoun usage in the following sentences. Do nothing if the sentence is correct.

1. When players have lost three games in a row, ~~you~~ *they* can become rather frustrated.

2. The golf team and its coach Mr. Pilar celebrated after the tournament.

3. Anybody who criticized the leader found a single piece of asparagus on their plate for breakfast.

4. As soon as the door opened, the tour group filed quickly onto their bus.

5. Neither his friends nor Dimitri could find their keys.

6. They wear spikes and ball bearings around their necks, which astounds me.

7. My brother and myself are amazed at the way they dress.

8. My friend Jacques wanted to meet George, but he had to leave town suddenly.

9. One time, at a restaurant, Chad and his friends were refused service, and this made them angry.

10. Whenever a friend of mine sees me with Sharon, they assume I am an eccentric person.

11. Silvie and myself feel that he should dress in any way that pleases him.

To avoid sexist language, practise changing singular to plural in sentences 3 and 11 in spaces provided below.

#3.

_____

_____

_____

#10.

_____

_____

_____

Exercise 3C

Correct any errors in pronoun agreement or reference in the following paragraph.

1. Until recent years, a common practice of a newly married man was to lift his bride over the threshold of their new home. 2. Few people know that this results from a number of ancient traditions. 3. Perhaps the most ancient of them all is the tradition of marriage-by-capture. 4. In many primitive societies, when a man wanted a woman from another tribe, you would seize them if they wandered too far from the protection of home. 5. He would then force her to accompany himself back to his own tribe, and you would do battle with members of her tribe who tried to stop you. 6. In this case, the connection to the bridegroom who picks up their bride and carries her into a new home is clear. 7. This also comes from Roman times, when people believed that the threshold was guarded by both a good spirit and an evil spirit. 8. The Romans believed that it would try to trip the bride as she stepped across the threshold, thus bringing bad luck to the groom and herself. 9. To prevent this, each newly married man would carry their bride over the threshold. 10. Finally, the practice of lifting your bride over the threshold was influenced by one other Roman tradition. 11. Many Romans believed that evil would result if the bride placed their left foot across the threshold first. 12. Neither the bride nor the groom wanted that to happen, so the groom would lift the bride over the threshold.

Section Four

Sentence Practice: Using Transitions

Writers use certain words and phrases to indicate the relationships among the ideas in their sentences and paragraphs. These words and phrases provide links between ideas, leading a reader from one idea to another smoothly. They show relationships like time, addition, or contrast.

Consider this paragraph from Rachel Carson's *Edge of the Sea*:

When the tide is rising the shore is a place of unrest, with the surge leaping high over jutting rocks **and** running in lacy cascades of foam over the landward side of massive boulders. But on the ebb it is more peaceful, **for then** the waves do not have behind them the push of the inward pressing tides. There is no particular drama about the turn of the tide, **but presently** a zone of wetness shows on the gray rock slopes, **and** offshore the incoming swells begin to swirl **and** break over hidden ledges. **Soon** the rocks that the high tide had concealed rise into view and glisten with the wetness left on them by the receding water.

Because she is writing about a process, most of Rachel Carson's transitional words indicate a relationship in time *(when, then, presently, soon)*. But she also uses transitional words that indicate contrast *(but)*, cause *(for)*, and addition *(and)*. As you can see, she uses these expressions to lead her readers smoothly from one idea to another.

The sentence combining exercises in this chapter are designed to give you practice in using transitional words and phrases to link your ideas. Try to use as many different ones as you can. For your convenience, here is a list of commonly used transitional words and phrases.

Be careful because often these words and phrases are *not* interchangeable; you must learn from both reading and experience how subtly different each is from all the others in the list.

Time: *then, soon, first, second, finally, meanwhile, next, at first, in the beginning*

Contrast: *yet, but, however, instead, otherwise, on the other hand, on the contrary*

Addition:	*and, also, besides, furthermore, in addition, likewise, moreover, similarly*
Cause-effect:	*for, because, consequently, so, therefore, hence, thus, as a result*
Example:	*for example, for instance, that is, such as*
Conclusion:	*thus, hence, finally, generally, as a result, in conclusion*

PRACTICE   Add transitions to the following sentences.

1. Sometimes I am indecisive about the most trivial things.

   _____ , this morning I spent fifteen minutes trying to

   decide whether to buy a cinnamon roll or a jelly doughnut.

2. Vancouver Island is known for its beaches. _____ , it

   has many excellent ski resorts.

3. Barbara and Greg have been very successful in their real estate careers.

   _____ , they have raised five well-adjusted, happy

   children.

4. Only seven of our team members showed up for our weekend softball

   game. _____ , we had to forfeit the game to the

   other team.

5. This afternoon I will probably jog for thirty minutes.

   _____ , perhaps I will stay home and eat the last of

   my jelly doughnuts.

EXERCISE

Sentence Combining Exercises

Combine the following sentences, using transitions as indicated in the directions.

EXAMPLE   Combine these sentences into two sentences. Use transitions that indicate contrast, example, and addition. Underline your transitions.

a. Herman knows he needs to lose weight.

b. He is unable to resist the urge to eat ice cream.

c. Yesterday he drank a low-fat fibre shake for lunch.

d. After work he stopped at a 31 Flavors ice cream store.

e. He ate a large chocolate sundae.

<u>Herman knows he needs to lose weight, but he is unable to resist the urge to eat ice cream. For example, yesterday he drank a low-fat fibre shake for lunch, but after work he stopped at a 31 Flavors ice cream store and ate a large chocolate sundae.</u>

1. Combine the following sentences into two sentences. Use transitions that indicate addition. Underline your transitions.
   a. In the fall and winter, Rita watches pro football on television every Sunday.
   b. In the fall and winter, Rita watches college football on television every Saturday.
   c. In the spring and summer, she attends every baseball game played by her local team.
   d. She attends every tennis match hosted by her city.

   _____

   _____

   _____

   _____

   _____

2. Combine the following sentences into two sentences. Use transitions that indicate cause–effect and addition. Underline your transitions.

    a. The crocodile is an Egyptian symbol of evil and fury.
    b. The crocodile is vicious and destructive.
    c. The crocodile lives in a realm between water and earth.
    d. The crocodile is a symbol of fertility and power.

_____

_____

_____

_____

3. Combine the following sentences into two sentences. Use transitions that indicate cause–effect. Underline your transitions.

    a. The most common form of saying farewell is "Good-bye."
    b. The word "good-bye" is a shortened form of "God be with you."
    c. Today we seem to prefer an even shorter form.
    d. We often choose the word "Bye."

_____

_____

_____

_____

3. Combine the following sentences into three sentences, using transitions that show time relationships. Underline your transitions.

    a. Brenda finished reading *Romeo and Juliet*.
    b. Brenda folded her laundry.
    c. Brenda made a list of tasks she had to complete by Monday.
    d. Brenda worked on her poem.
    e. It was very late.
    f. Brenda watched *The Late Late Show.*

_____

_____

_____

_____

_____

5. Combine the following sentences into two sentences. Use transitions that indicate cause–effect and example. Underline your transitions.

   a. Simon avoids his family.
   b. Whenever he visits his family, someone insults him.
   c. Last Christmas his mother said that she ought to serve him for dinner.
   d. He had gained ten kilograms.

_____

_____

_____

_____

6. Combine the following sentences into three or four sentences, using transitions that show time relationships. Underline your transitions.

   a. The holes in bread are made by bubbles of gas.
   b. Flour and water are mixed to form dough.
   c. A small amount of yeast is added.
   d. The yeast grows.
   e. The yeast gives off a gas.
   f. The gas bubbles up through the dough.
   g. The dough expands.

_____

_____

_____

_____

_____

7. Combine the following sentences into two sentences. Use transitions that indicate cause–effect and contrast. Underline your transitions.

   a. In ancient times, wedding guests threw wheat at a new bride.
   b. Wheat was a symbol of fertility and prosperity.
   c. In the first century B.C., Roman bakers began to cook the wheat into small cakes.
   d. Wedding guests did not want to give up the custom of throwing wheat.
   e. They threw the wedding cakes instead.

   _____

   _____

   _____

   _____

   _____

8. Combine the following sentences into two sentences. Join the two sentences with a transition that indicates cause-effect. Underline your transitions.

   a. Periodically the weather in Scandinavia may be too hot for the lemmings.
   b. Periodically the lemmings' food supply may change.
   c. Periodically the lemmings may feel overcrowded.
   d. Thousands of Scandinavian lemmings travel for miles.
   e. They throw themselves into the sea.
   f. They swim until they are exhausted and drown.

   _____

   _____

   _____

   _____

9. Combine the following sentences into two sentences. Use transitions that indicate contrast and cause–effect. Underline your transitions.

   a. Today the paper or plastic kite is a popular child's toy.
   b. It was originally designed by the Chinese in 1200 B.C.
   c. It was designed to send coded military messages.
   d. Each kite's unique shape, colour, and movements were ideal for sending coded messages.
   e. Only someone who knew the code could "read" it.

   _____

   _____

   _____

   _____

10. Combine the following sentences into three sentences. Use transitions that indicate example, cause–effect, and addition. Underline your transitions.

   a. Many superstitions have unusual origins.
   b. It is considered bad luck to walk under a ladder.
   c. A ladder leaning against a wall forms a triangle.
   d. Many ancient societies believed that a triangle was a place sacred to the gods.
   e. Walking through a triangle defiled that space.

   _____

   _____

   _____

   _____

Section Five

Moving from Paragraph to Essay: Part 1

Comparing Paragraphs and Essays

In the last chapter we asked you to write a paragraph using three examples to support your topic sentence. (See page 194.) At the time you were encouraged to write several sentences of specific detail and to add introductory words, phrases, or clauses called transitions. However, when you did that, you may have noticed that your paragraph seemed a trifle long. In fact, you may have felt now it was *much* too long and could easily have been made over into two or three paragraphs.

Of course, you were right. Most college writing consists of essays composed of three or more paragraphs. The very word *paragraph* comes from two Greek words that indicate that this paragraph is meant to be considered in relation to all the other paragraphs. *Para* means "beside," and *graphos* means "writing," so a paragraph is writing that is meant to be written with other paragraphs.

Many paragraphs in this text could be expanded into brief essays with a little work and imagination. In fact, the paragraph in Exercise 2C in Chapter Three (reproduced on the next page) is somewhat too long. It consists of 253 words. If one considers the average size of a paragraph to be around 100 to 150 words, then this paragraph is indeed too long. Let us see how we can expand it into an essay of five separate paragraphs.

The Original Paragraph

Topic sentence

First support

Examples

Second support

Examples

Third support

Examples

Conclusion

Many English-speaking people are surprised when they discover the number of everyday words that are drawn from different mythologies. <u>For example, the names of several of our weekdays—Tuesday, Wednesday, Thursday, and Friday—derive from Norse mythology</u>. Tuesday and Thursday refer to Tiu, the Norse god of war, and Thor, the Norse god of thunder. Wednesday refers to Woden, who was the king of the Norse gods, and Friday refers to Frigga, the Norse goddess of love. <u>Other common words are derived from Greek mythology</u>. For instance, the word *tantalize* refers to Tantalus, who was a king condemned to Hades as a punishment for his crimes. In Hades, he was forced to stand below fruit that was just beyond his reach and in water that he could not drink. Another common Greek word in our language is *atlas*, which refers to a map of the world. The mythological figure Atlas was a Titan who was condemned to support the heavens on his shoulders. <u>Finally, Roman mythology, which in many ways parallels Greek mythology, is another source of many English words</u>. For example, the month of January is named after Janus, the Roman god with two faces. Janus, whose two faces allowed him to watch two directions at once, was the Roman god of doorways. June, another of the many months that refer to Roman mythology, is named after Juno, the goddess of marriage and childbirth. <u>These examples are just a few of the hundreds of English words that reflect the many mythologies of the world</u>.

Converting the Paragraph into an Essay

Introduction
Thesis Statement

Topic sentence of
first body paragraph

Examples

Many English-speaking people are surprised when they discover the number of everyday words that are drawn from different mythologies.

    <u>For example, the names of several of our weekdays—Tuesday, Wednesday, Thursday, and Friday—derive from Norse mythology</u>. Tuesday and Thursday refer to Tiu, the Norse god of war, and Thor, the Norse god of thunder. Wednesday refers to Woden, who was the king of the Norse gods, and Friday refers to Frigga, the Norse goddess of love.

Topic sentence of second body paragraph

Examples

Topic sentence of third body paragraph

Examples

Conclusion

<u>Other common words are derived from Greek mythology</u>. For instance, the word *tantalize* refers to Tantalus, who was a king condemned to Hades as a punishment for his crimes. In Hades, he was forced to stand below fruit that was just beyond his reach and in water that he could not drink. Another common Greek word in our language is *atlas*, which refers to a map of the world. The mythological figure Atlas was a Titan who was condemned to support the heavens on his shoulders.

<u>Finally, Roman mythology, which in many ways parallels Greek mythology, is another source of many English words</u>. For example, the month of January is named after Janus, the Roman god with two faces. Janus, whose two faces allowed him to watch two directions at once, was the Roman god of doorways. June, another of the many months that refer to Roman mythology, is named after Juno, the goddess of marriage and childbirth.

<u>These examples are just a few of the hundreds of English words that reflect the many mythologies of the world</u>.

As you can see, the original paragraph can be expanded into an essay with three major sections: introduction, body, and conclusion. Of course, the paragraphs are now too small and will need more sentences of development. Two of the paragraphs are only one sentence long, and the longest, the third paragraph, consists of only five sentences and is only 86 words long.

Later, we will consider various ways to develop these paragraphs. For now, let's look at the *structure* of this new essay. It looks something like this:

First paragraph:	**Introduction and thesis statement**
Second paragraph:	**First topic sentence** to support the thesis **Examples** to support the topic sentence
Third paragraph:	**Second topic sentence** to support the thesis **Examples** to support the topic sentences
Fourth paragraph:	**Third topic sentence** to support the thesis **Examples** to support the topic sentence
Fifth paragraph:	**Conclusion**

You should note *three fundamental changes* that have occurred in expanding the paragraph into the essay:

1. The topic sentence becomes the THESIS.

2. The support sentences become the TOPIC SENTENCES.

3. The paragraph now has a three-part structure:
   a. thesis paragraph
   b. middle, or supporting, paragraphs
   c. concluding paragraph.

Each of these types of paragraphs is constructed differently. In the next chapters we will look at their differences and also practise writing them. For now, all you need to do is note the three-part structure of an academic essay.

PRACTICE

In the paragraph practice of Chapter Three you composed a paragraph using examples. Take your paragraph now and convert it into an essay, following the structure we just examined.

Make sure each of the three examples of your original paragraph contains more than one sentence. If not, your instructor may ask you to invent more supporting sentences to each **middle paragraph** so that you can practise developing your paragraphs. Pattern your new essay on the model provided in this text.

PRACTICE TEST

Chapter Four Practice Test

I. Review of Chapters One, Two, and Three

A. Underline all subjects once and complete verbs twice. Place all prepositional phrases in parentheses.

   1. Neither the rhubarb cake nor the eggplant pie were big hits at last

      night's party.

   2. When the rains finally ended, the mosquitoes began to bite.

   3. Before he leaves for work, Jason always sets his security alarm.

   4. Lise put the night crawler into a large jar and then hurried to tell

      Claude about it.

   5. The aroma of wet, rotting things drifted across the swamp and into

      Claude and Lisa's house.

B. Correct any fragments, fused sentences, or comma splices in the following sentences. Do nothing if the sentence is correct.

   6. Hundreds of salmon, swimming upstream to spawn.

      _____

      _____

   7. A bear stared into the stream soon it saw the salmon.

      _____

      _____

   8. The salmon, swimming swiftly upstream, did not see the bear, which
      flicked many of them out of the water with its huge paw.

      _____

      _____

9. The stream was icy cold from the melting snows, however, the bear did not seem to mind.

_____

_____

10. The bear, after wading in the stream for an hour and catching many salmon, which it then ate.

_____

_____

C. At the places indicated by (^), add adjective clauses, appositives, infinitive phrases, or participial phrases to the following sentences as directed in the parentheses. Use commas where they are needed.

11. The German shepherd attacked the thief ∧ . (adjective clause)

_____

_____

12. Abdul sold his favorite car ∧ to his sister. (appositive)

_____

_____

13. ∧ Roseanne fell asleep in her theatre seat. (participial phrase)

_____

_____

14. Because he did not have enough cash on hand, Mario asked his brother ∧ . (infinitive phrase)

_____

_____

15. The wind ʌ nearly caused our fire to go out. (participial phrase)

_____

_____

D. Correct any dangling or misplaced modifiers in the following sentences. Do nothing if the sentence is correct.

16. The firefighters found five kittens near the fire station that had been left in a box.

_____

_____

17. John was so hungry that he almost ate the entire cake.

_____

_____

18. Searching frantically through her briefcase, the loan documents could not be found.

_____

_____

19. The alligator swam slowly toward the duck with a hungry look in its eyes.

_____

_____

20. Determined to find a job, Lindsey's eyes searched the "Help Wanted" section.

_____

_____

II. Review of Chapter Four

A. Underline the correct verb form in the parentheses.

   21. Every dog and cat in the yard (has have) to be taken to the pound.

   22. Mathematics (is are) more difficult for some people to learn than for others.

   23. There (was were) a new Mercedes and a restored 1966 Shelby Cobra parked next to my rusty Volkswagen.

   24. A committee of concerned neighbours (decide decides) which landscaping company we use.

   25. Neither the student nor the professor (has have) read the book.

B. Correct any subject–verb agreement errors in the following sentences. Do nothing if the sentence is correct.

   26. A broken tractor and an empty cart with only one wheel sits in my driveway.

   27. Everything that you need to make tasty cookies and cakes are included in these recipes.

   28. One hundred dollars seems like a fair price for my collection of broken roof tiles.

   29. Do Claude or Lisa know who has been poaching alligators?

   30. A coyote with its three pups sleep in our garage every night.

C. Underline the correct pronoun in the parentheses.

   31. The pizza was delivered to Bill and (I me).

   32. Arsenio returned to work after his brother and (he him) had eaten lunch.

33. Dalia said that the two survivors, her father and (she her), should receive all of the insurance money.

34. Last semester our history instructor gave Monica a higher grade than (I me).

35. The man (who whom) Mrs. Maples saw in the bank looked like her deceased husband.

D. Correct any pronoun errors in the following sentences. Do nothing if the sentence is correct.

36. Ahmed drove his car to the side of the freeway, where he changed it's flat tire.

37. Vanessa studied more than Otis, yet he received better grades than her.

38. Do you want Sheila and him to leave now?

39. Between Franco and I, we knew we could raise enough money to buy the house.

40. The lady next door asked Alice and I to join her in a game of croquet.

E. Underline the correct pronouns in the parentheses.

41. Someone in this room has not paid for (her their) ticket.

42. Before a person buys a used car, (you he or she they) should have an independent mechanic check it out.

43. The inheritance was a complete surprise to Jean and (him himself hisself).

44. The jury returned to the courtroom because (it they) had finally reached a verdict.

45. Neither of the finalists was willing to discuss (his their) spiritual beliefs.

F. Correct any pronoun errors in the following sentences. Do nothing if the sentence is correct.

46. Mr. Poseidon recently purchased a new swim suit, which is his favourite sport.

47. Whenever An-Mei visited her mother, she complained about the neighbourhood.

48. Early white settlers thought Chinese immigrants would take their jobs away, but this did not materialize.

49. Everyone who visits the cave is shocked when they see the graffiti on the wall.

50. When we were told how much it would cost to repair our roof, we decided to fix it ourself.

ANSWERS

Answers to Practices in Chapter Four

Pages 210–211:

2. The balloons from the picnic have not popped yet.
3. Sometimes, my brother calls me late at night.
4. A commercial airliner passes over my house every day.
5. Rain showers always make the highways slick and dangerous.

Pages 212–213:

                         S
2. A grilled cheese sandwich with potato chips (<u>does</u> do) sound good right now.

               S   S
3. Every kangaroo and koala (<u>wants</u> want) to escape from the zoo.

                         S   S
4. In the morning, a hot shower and a cup of strong tea (helps <u>help</u>) Sam wake up.

        S
5. Most of the pasta in the pots on the stove (<u>was</u> were) overcooked.

                                      S   S
6. Because of the extreme heat, every window and door in the barracks (<u>was</u> were) open.

        S
7. Somebody high in the mountains (<u>plays</u> play) a horn each evening.

             S   S
8. The car's upholstery and paint job (<u>make</u> makes) it look almost new.

        S
9. Half of the people at the concert (was <u>were</u>) crying.

           S
10. A large bear with its two cubs (<u>is</u> are) eating the dog food.

Pages 214–215:

              S
2. A whole society of aphids (<u>has</u> have) taken up residence in my garden.

        S   S
3. Hampton is one of the rats that quickly (runs <u>run</u>) through the maze.

                 S   S
4. Neither the gorillas nor the tiger at the zoo (<u>was</u> were) very happy with the living quarters.

           S   S
5. A cold shower or two glasses of lemonade (refreshes <u>refresh</u>) Amanda after her run.

                S

6. Tomorrow the committee on foreign affairs (<u>decides</u> decide) whether or not to ban travel to other countries.

              S   S

7. The only one of the laughs that (<u>counts</u> count) is the last one.

                    S   S

8. (<u>Has</u> Have) your mother or your brother arrived yet?

                    S   S

9. The softball team that my sister plays for on weekends (<u>was</u> were) in last place.

                 S   S

10. My younger sister is one of the girls who (has <u>have</u>) qualified for the tournament.

Page 216:

               S

2. Three hundred hectares of grain (<u>produces</u> produce) a good income for some farmers.

      S

3. One of Malvina's favourite recordings (<u>is</u> are) a David Foster album.

                      S

4. According to Robert Louis Stevenson, politics (<u>is</u> are) perhaps the only profession for which no preparation is necessary.

        S

5. (<u>Is</u> Are) measles still a problem in some parts of the world?

        S

6. Eighty kilometres in two days (<u>does</u> do) sound like a long, hard hike.

         S

7. (<u>Does</u> Do) Charles always bring his bloody cleaver to work?

            S

8. There still (<u>are</u> is) people who believe that the earth is flat.

        S

9. The main problem of this neighbourhood (<u>is</u> are) the planes flying over every half hour.

        S   S

10. Here (<u>is</u> are) the $525 that I owe you.

Pages 225–226:

2. obj	7. sub
3. sub	8. obj
4. obj	9. sub
5. obj	10. obj
6. sub	

Pages 227–228:

2. me
3. her, me
4. he
5. me
6. me

7. me
8. she
9. she
10. they

Page 229:

2. who
3. who

4. whomever
5. whoever

Pages 229–230:

2. him
3. he

4. he
5. me

Page 230:

2. me
3. she

4. him
5. I

Page 231:

2. I
3. I
4. she
5. whomever
6. him

7. her
8. me
9. whom
10. she

Page 240:

2. Most people can pass a driver's test if **they** study the rules.
3. A driver will just be wasting time if **he doesn't** study for the test.
4. When I watched my cousin take her driving test, I could see that she wasn't nervous at all.
5. Finally, I passed the driving test. I wouldn't want to go through that ordeal again.

Pages 241–242:

2. The crowd at Maple Leaf Gardens got to **its** feet and sang when "O Canada!" was played.
3. When people have spent over eight hours waiting on people at a restaurant, **they** sometimes do not feel like cooking and serving another meal at home.
4. correct
5. Neither Dr. Jekyll nor Mr. Hyde could explain **his** recent mood swings.
6. Not only the Nelsons but also Mr. Finch will be bringing **his** movie camera on the bird-watching trip.
7. correct
8. After one eats raw fish a few times, **one** might actually start to like it.
9. Someone left **her** books on the desk.
10. correct

Pages 244–245:

Answers will vary. Here are some possible ones.

2. Once Marvin and the doctor had discussed the illness, Marvin began to worry.
3. I kept misplacing the key to my motorcycle, and then the motorcycle was stolen.
4. Later, when Mrs. Massey took her children and their test results to the clinic, she discussed the test results with the doctor.
5. When my cat refused to eat its dinner, I threw the food into the garbage compactor.

Page 246:

Answers will vary. Here are some possible ones.

2. We could not leave early because we overslept.
3. The broken pieces of glass were all over the floor, but Robert said that he had fixed the window.
4. It is rather unusual that I love to eat jellyfish.
5. The sound system at the theatre was too loud, but I didn't leave until the musicians started to eat goldfish.

Page 248:

2. Hue and I decided to go skiing next weekend.
3. I heard that Mr. Wren and **he** had taken the train to Edmonton.
4. We did not deserve it, but Mr. Abernathy gave Mike and **me** a raise anyway.
5. They tried to solve the problem by **themselves**.

Page 248:

2. The Karupski family and **we** will take a trip to the zoo next weekend.
3. In the back of the room sat ten people with shaved heads, tattoos, leather jackets, and black boots; **these people** worried me. (Other correct answers are possible.)
4. James told his father that he was concerned about **his father's** car. (Other correct answers are possible.)
5. The school gave financial aid to my wife and **me**.
6. I would love to go cycling along the coast with you, but I don't have a **bicycle**.
7. The fan's yelling at the umpire made us angry. (Other correct answers are possible.)
8. He had been wanting to treat **himself** to a week by the seashore as a reward for finishing the remodelling project.
9. Byron broke his foot when he dropped the vase on it. (Other correct answers are possible.)
10. The salesman told Ramon to ride the motorcycle around to the front. (Other correct answers are possible.)

Page 256:

Answers will vary. Here are some possible ones.

1. Sometimes I am indecisive about the most trivial things. <u>For example</u>, this morning I spent fifteen minutes trying to decide whether to buy a cinnamon roll or a jelly doughnut.
2. Vancouver Island is known for its beaches. <u>In addition</u>, it has many excellent ski resorts.

3. Barbara and Greg have been very successful in their real estate careers. <u>Furthermore,</u> they have raised five well-adjusted, happy children.

4. Only seven of our team members showed up for our weekend softball game. <u>Therefore</u>, we had to forfeit the game to the other team.

5. This afternoon I will probably jog for thirty minutes. <u>On the other hand</u>, perhaps I will stay at home and eat the last of my jelly doughnuts.

Chapter Five

Using Punctuation and Capitalization

When we speak to people face-to-face, we have a number of signals, aside from the words we choose, to let them know how we feel. Facial expressions—smiles, frowns, grimaces—convey our emotions and attitudes. Tone of voice can tell a listener whether we feel sad or lighthearted or sarcastic about what we are saying. Hand gestures and other body language add further refinements. In fact, experts tell us that these nonverbal communications make up over 80 percent of the messages in a conversation.

So, when we communicate with a reader, we must make up for that 80 percent of lost, nonverbal communication by using the writing signals that we all know. Our most important writing signals are punctuation marks. They signal whether we are making a statement or asking a question. They indicate the boundaries of our sentences. They determine much of the rhythm and emotion of our writing.

If you are able to use punctuation effectively, you have a powerful tool to control how your writing affects your readers. If you do not know the basic rules of punctuation, you run the risk of being misunderstood or of confusing your readers. In this chapter we will discuss the essential rules of punctuation, not just so that your writing will be correct but, more important, so that you will be able to express your ideas exactly the way you want them to be expressed.

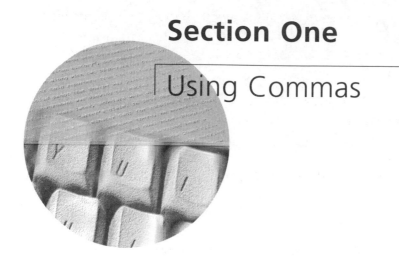

Section One

Using Commas

The comma gives writers more trouble than any of the other punctuation marks. Before printing was developed, commas came into use to tell readers when to put in a slight pause while reading aloud. Now, although the placement of the comma does affect the rhythm of sentences, it also conveys many messages that are more important than when to pause. Because the comma is such an important punctuation mark and because it can be troublesome to you if you don't know how to use it correctly, we take it up first. You are probably already familiar with some of its uses.

The rules for comma use are quite simple:

1. *Use commas before coordinating conjunctions that join main clauses to form a compound sentence.*

2. *Use commas between elements in a series.*

3. *Use commas after introductory elements.*

4. *Use commas before and after interrupters.*

Commas in Compound Sentences

1. *When you join two main clauses with one of the coordinating conjunctions to form a compound sentence, use a comma before the conjunction.*

EXAMPLES   I don't know her, **but** I like her already.

The tableware in the restaurant was exquisite, **and** the food was sublime.

2. *When conjunctions join other parts of a sentence, such as two words, two phrases, or two subordinate clauses, do **not** put commas before the conjunctions.*

E X A M P L E   Every morning that scoundrel **has** a drink <u>and</u> then thoroughly **beats** his dog.

> No comma is needed before *and* because it does not join two main clauses. Instead, it joins the verbs *has* and *beats*.

E X A M P L E   I decided to visit France because I had never had a chance to see that country <u>and</u> because my travel agent was able to offer me a special discount on the trip.

> No comma is needed before *and* because it joins two subordinate clauses, not two main clauses.

PRACTICE

Add commas to the following sentences where necessary.

1. Joan steamed broccoli for supper but her son Jamey wouldn't touch it.

2. She told him it was good for him and he made a funny face.

3. He ate his meat and potatoes and then pushed away his plate.

4. She said, "Eat your broccoli or you won't get any dessert."

5. He thought about it and decided against both broccoli and dessert.

Commas with Elements in a Series

1. *When you list three or more elements (words, phrases, clauses) in a series, separate them by commas.* When the last two elements are joined by a coordinating conjunction, a comma before the conjunction is optional.

E X A M P L E S   (words)   The gazpacho was **cold, spicy, and fresh.**

(phrases)   In the mountains, he had been **thrown by his horse, bitten by a snake, and chased by a bear.**

(clauses)   To rescue the koala, **the firefighters brought a ladder, the police brought a rope, and the mayor brought a speech.**

2. *When you use two or more adjectives to modify the same noun, separate them with commas if you can put* and *between the adjectives without changing the meaning or if you can easily reverse the order of the adjectives.*

EXAMPLES   She eagerly stepped into the **comforting, cool water**.

A **stubborn, obnoxious** boll weevil is ruining my cotton patch.

Note that you could easily use *and* between the above adjectives. (The water is *comforting* and *cool*; the boll weevil is *stubborn* and *obnoxious*.) You could also reverse the adjectives (the *cool, comforting water* or the *obnoxious, stubborn* boll weevil).

3. *On the other hand, if the adjectives cannot be joined by* and *or are not easily reversed, no comma is necessary.*

EXAMPLE   A bureaucrat wearing **a black leather jacket** and a smirk strode into the auditorium.

Notice how awkward the sentence would sound if you placed *and* between the adjectives (*a black and leather jacket*) or if you reversed them (*a leather black jacket*).

PRACTICE

Insert commas between main clauses joined by a coordinating conjunction and between items in a series.

1. The bill was only $10.50 so Vera paid it in cash.

2. The film was scary hilarious and insipid at the same time.

3. Jamey doesn't know that broccoli is inexpensive tastes good and fights cancer.

4. The elves could be seen traipsing across the untidy overgrown lawn.

5. Julian wanted to buy an assortment of flowers for his mother had invited him to dinner.

Commas with Introductory Elements

When you begin a sentence with certain introductory words, phrases, or clauses, place a comma after the introductory element.

1. *Use a comma after the following introductory words and transitional expressions.*

Introductory Words		Transitional Expressions
next	similarly	on the other hand
first	nevertheless	in a similar manner
second	therefore	in other words
third	indeed	for example
moreover	yes	for instance
however	no	in fact
		in addition
		as a result

EXAMPLES   **First,** we will strike at the heart of the matter and then pursue other cliches.

For example, let's all stand up and be counted.

2. *Use a comma after introductory prepositional phrases of five or more words. However, you may need to use a comma after a shorter introductory prepositional phrase if not doing so would cause confusion.*

EXAMPLES   **After a long and thrilling nap,** Buster went looking for a cat to chase.

After dinner we all went for a walk around the lake.

In spring, time seems to catch up with small furry animals.

Without the comma, this last sentence might look as if it begins in *springtime.*

3. *Use a comma after all introductory infinitive and participial phrases.*

EXAMPLES   **Blackened with soot,** the little boy toddled out of the smoldering house.

Begging for her forgiveness, Jamie decided to eat his broccoli.

To break in your new car properly, drive at varying speeds for the first one thousand kilometres.

4. *Use a comma after introductory adverb subordinate clauses.*

EXAMPLES   **Because Amy Wu played the tuba so well,** she was awarded a music scholarship.

As soon as he arrived on shore, Columbus claimed the land for Spain.

Although it was raining furiously, Yoko ran six kilometres anyway.

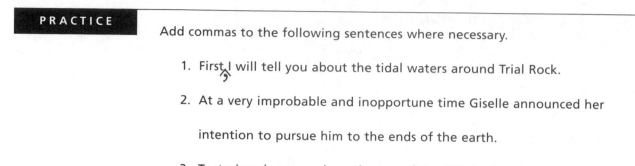

PRACTICE   Add commas to the following sentences where necessary.

1. First, I will tell you about the tidal waters around Trial Rock.

2. At a very improbable and inopportune time Giselle announced her intention to pursue him to the ends of the earth.

3. Teetering dangerously at the top of the hill the large stone might have rolled down and crushed Sisyphus.

4. When you see her the next time she will have removed that load from her shoulders.

5. No I would prefer not to copy the manuscript at this time.

6. To determine the accuracy of her instruments Paula Halim ran some tests.

Commas with Interrupters

Sometimes certain words, phrases, or clauses will interrupt the flow of thought in a sentence to add emphasis or additional information. These interrupters are enclosed by commas.

1. *Use commas to set off parenthetical expressions.* Common parenthetical expressions include *however, indeed, consequently, as a result, moreover, of course, for example, for instance, that is, in fact, after all, I think,* and *therefore.*

EXAMPLES   The answer, **after all,** lay right under his left big toe.

That big blue bird by the feeder is, **I think,** one of those unruly Steller's jays.

She is, **moreover,** a notorious misspeller of the word **deceitful**.

PUNCTUATION NOTE: Whenever a parenthetical expression introduces a second main clause after a semicolon, the semicolon takes the place of the comma in front of it. The parenthetical expression is now called a **conjunctive adverb.**

EXAMPLE   Yes, you may eat your snails in front of me; **after all,** we are old friends.

| PRACTICE | Use commas to set off any parenthetical elements in the following sentences. |

1. The red Mustang after all did signal before turning left.

2. The professor of philosophy for example always polished his shoes with cotton balls and kerosene.

3. Loggers are moving into that area of the forest; therefore protesters will have to leave Nanaimo early tomorrow morning.

4. He has a cup of tea I think every time that he has a difficult decision to make.

5. Harry had been shocked by his electric train transformer; consequently he mistrusted all electronic technology.

---

2. *Use commas to set off nonrestrictive elements.* Nonrestrictive elements are modifying words, phrases, or clauses that are not restricted to the words they modify and, hence, are not necessary to identify them. They include adjective subordinate clauses, appositives, and participial phrases.

Adjective Clauses

(See pages 159–160 if you need to review adjective clauses.) If the information in an adjective clause *is not necessary to identify the word it modifies*, it is called a **nonrestrictive clause**, and *it is enclosed in commas*.

EXAMPLE   Ms. Nancy Wong, **who is chair of the board of that company,** began twenty years ago as a secretary.

Because the name of the person is used, the adjective clause is not necessary to identify which woman began twenty years ago as a secretary, so the commas are needed.

However, if her name is not used, the adjective clause is a **restrictive** one *because the woman is not already identified*—hence the clause is *restricted* to it. In this case, the commas are not necessary.

EXAMPLE   The woman **who is chair of the board of that company** began twenty years ago as a secretary.

The following are additional examples of **nonrestrictive clauses.**

E X A M P L E   My oldest brother, **who is a park ranger,** showed me his collection of arrowheads

Because a person can have only one oldest brother, the brother is already identified, and the adjective clause is not needed to identify him, making it nonrestrictive.

E X A M P L E   His home town, **which is somewhere in northeastern Indiana,** wants him to return for its centennial celebration.

A person can have only one home town, so the adjective clause is nonrestrictive.

PRACTICE

In the following sentences, set off all nonrestrictive clauses with commas.

1. La Paloma which is an old theater near my house is my favourite place to see films.

2. *Front Page Challenge* which was a very popular television show in the 1980s often dealt with people's prejudices.

3. My oldest daughter who is a painter often uses *Alice in Wonderland* characters in her work.

4. The man who stole Dee's car was finally caught.

5. This airplane which has electric motors will ultimately replace those using kerosene.

Appositives

(See pages 161–162 if you need to review appositives.)

As with adjective clauses, appositives that contain information *not necessary to identify the words they modify* are nonrestrictive and are set off by commas. Appositives that contain information *necessary to identify the words they modify* are restrictive and do not require commas.

E X A M P L E   (nonrestrictive)   Natalie's mother, **a lawyer in North Bay,** will be coming to visit her soon.

Because Natalie's mother is already specifically identified, the appositive *a lawyer in North Bay* is nonrestrictive and the commas are necessary.

EXAMPLE   (restrictive)   The word ***pedigree*** comes from two French words meaning "crane's foot."

Here *pedigree* is an appositive that renames *word*. Commas are not necessary because the appositive identifies which word the sentence is about.

EXAMPLES   Kleenex**, a household necessity,** was invented as a substitute for bandages during World War I because of a cotton shortage.

Parker took his stamp collection to Mr. Poindexter**, a noted stamp expert.**

Note that in each of these examples the specific names *Kleenex* and *Mr. Poindexter* make the appositive nonrestrictive, so commas are used.

PRACTICE   In the following sentences, set off all nonrestrictive appositives with commas.

1. The Tickled Trout a nearby seafood restaurant attracts many

   customers.

2. Every Christmas he sends his mother twelve pounds of broccoli her

   favourite food.

3. Perry's father a retired librarian swore that he never wanted to see

   another book.

4. The television program *W5* sometimes exposes corruption in

   government.

5. The orca a member of the dolphin family is usually called a killer whale.

Participial Phrases

(See pages 150–151 if you need to review participial phrases.)

   Participial phrases that *do not contain information necessary to identify the words they modify* are nonrestrictive and are therefore set off by commas. Restrictive participial phrases do not require commas.

EXAMPLE   (nonrestrictive)   The prime minister, **seeking to be reelected,** travelled throughout the country making speeches and kissing babies.

Because we have only one prime minister, the participial phrase *seeking to be reelected* is nonrestrictive. It is not necessary to identify who is meant by *prime minister*.

EXAMPLE   (restrictive)   The woman **sitting by the door** is a famous surgeon.

Sitting by the door is a restrictive participial phrase because it is necessary to identify which woman is the famous surgeon.

EXAMPLE   Foxworth, **not discouraged by a smart slap to the side of his head,** continued to tease his pet chimpanzee.

PRACTICE

In the following sentences, set off nonrestrictive participial phrases with commas.

1. Paul Groves worrying about his friend's mental state offered to build a deck for him.

2. Sergeant Owens finally showing his impatience made the recruits do one hundred situps.

3. Leonard Cohen trying not to show his despair kept singing in front of the three beautiful women in black.

4. The concert was about to begin, and Troy hoping to play well closed his eyes in concentration.

5. Charlie raised in a polite household courteously told me that his favourite singer was Barry Manilow.

3. *Use commas to set off words of direct address.* If a writer addresses someone directly in a sentence, the words that stand for that person or persons are set off by commas. If the words in direct address begin the sentence, they are followed by a comma.

EXAMPLES   And now, **my good friends,** I think it is time to end this conversation.

Mr. Chairman, I rise to a point of order.

I would like to present my proposal, **my esteemed colleagues.**

4. *Use commas to set off dates and addresses.* If your sentence contains two, three, or more elements of the date or address, use commas to set off these elements. The following sentences contain two or more elements.

EXAMPLES   We visited my uncle on **Monday, July 1,** to avoid the weekend rush.

We visited my uncle on **Monday, July 1, 1985,** to avoid the weekend rush.

Celia has lived at **225 Oliver Street, Victoria,** for five years.

Celia has lived at **225 Oliver Street, Victoria, British Columbia,** for five years.

The following sentences contain only one element.

EXAMPLES   We visited my uncle on **Monday** in order to avoid the weekend rush.

Celia has lived at **225 Oliver Street** for five years.

PRACTICE

In the following sentences, use commas to set off words in direct address or dates and addresses that have two or more elements.

1. Hester, have you lived at 4590 Burdette Street, Toronto, Ontario, for the

    past two years?

2. On June 24 1981 my youngest daughter was born.

3. Find out Charles if you can visit us in 1993.

4. Send this order of salmon to Harbour House 334 Oak Street Saint John

    New Brunswick.

5. Emily where is my handkerchief?

PRACTICE

Use commas to set off parenthetical expressions, nonrestrictive elements, words in direct address, and dates and addresses that have two or more elements.

1. Caffeine Brown, for instance, is rarely seen without a coffee cup.

2. The first man on the moon who was an American astronaut made a

    clever statement as he stepped down from the spacecraft.

3. *Frankenstein* a novel by Mary Shelley has been the subject of several films and many articles.

4. Will you help me with my letter of apology Maria?

5. Michelle was born in a hospital in Winnipeg Manitoba in 1981 on a sunny afternoon.

6. On July 20 1969 the first man landed on the moon.

7. Kenneth suddenly remembered his pet iguana forgotten in his car two hours ago.

8. The road that leads to White River the next town is closed.

9. The first part of the rafting trip however is smooth.

10. Gordon will you tell John who is working out back that it is time to quit?

Rules for the Use of the Comma

REVIEW

1. *Use a comma before a coordinating conjunction that joins two main clauses.*

2. *Use commas to separate elements in a series.*
   a. Elements in a series may be words, phrases, or clauses.
   b. Two or more adjectives that modify the same noun may need to be separated by commas.

3. *Use a comma after an introductory element.* Introductory elements include
   a. Introductory words
   b. Transitional expressions
   c. Prepositional phrases
   d. Verbal phrases
   e. Adverb clauses

4. *Use commas to separate interrupters from the rest of the sentence.* Interrupters include
   a. Parenthetical expressions
   b. Nonrestrictive clauses
   c. Nonrestrictive appositives
   d. Nonrestrictive participial phrases
   e. Words in direct address
   f. Dates and addresses with two or more elements

EXERCISE

Exercise 1A

Add commas to the following sentences where necessary.

1. Masami Teraoka is Japanese and he is a satirical painter.

2. Spider Lee had long thin arms and legs but never considered herself unattractive.

3. She was of course very proud of her figure.

4. The band played a reggae version of "Eleanor Rigby" a Beatles song.

5. Yes we will be glad to bring a dessert to the party.

6. My dentist who is also a lepidopterist has pictures of butterflies on his walls.

7. At the end of the tedious boring film the main character smokes a last cigar and mercifully walks away forever.

8. Jimmy Smith sitting thoughtfully by the fire decided to compose a poem that would gain him the love of Narcissa.

9. Heartened by the audience's enthusiasm Hominy Grits a rap band decided to do an encore.

10. Shawn stop unravelling and listen to me.

11. After he took a deep breath Pin Tien took a sip of milk and started on his third cherry pie.

12. On March 15 1988 the expedition was to begin but predictions of wet cold weather prevented its departure.

13. Barry Bledhart began his fifth novel about knowledge painfully gained and love irretrievably lost; however he was soon too happy to go on.

14. Yes I also anxiously await the arrival in Berens River of the first McDonald's.

15. Keena Kensington who is known for her sense of humour refuses to laugh at blonde jokes.

EXERCISE

Exercise 1B

Add commas to the following sentences where necessary.

1. Because they are entirely self-consuming candles have burnt up their own history.

2. Their origins of course are based on what early people wrote about them.

3. Appearing in Roman writings of the first century A.D. the earliest description of candles shows that the Romans considered them as an inferior substitute for oil lamps.

4. Made from animal or vegetable fat candles were also edible and many accounts tell of starving Roman soldiers eating their candle rations.

5. A few centuries later British lighthouse keepers isolated for months at a time made eating candles almost an acceptable habit.

6. Even the most expensive British candles required regular half-hour "snuffing" the delicate task of snipping off the charred end of the wick without putting out the flame.

7. Not only did an unsnuffed candle provide much less light but also the low-burning flame melted the rest of the candle.

8. In a candle left unattended only five percent of it actually burned and the rest ran off as waste.

9. Without proper and timely snuffing eight candles were consumed in less than half an hour.

10. Burning hundreds of candles weekly the owner of a castle maintained a staff of "snuff servants."

11. Snuffing required great skill judgment and timing.

12. James Boswell the biographer of Samuel Johnson had many occasions to snuff candles and he was not always successful.

13. On one occasion in 1793 he wanted to stay up all night and write but he accidentally snuffed out his candle and couldn't get it relit.

14. Before friction matches were invented relighting a candle when the household fire had gone out could be a time-consuming chore.

15. With the widespread use of beeswax candles in the late seventeenth century the art of snuffing died out and the word snuff came to mean "extinguish."

16. During the late eighteenth century the best candles were white beeswax ones from England yellow tallow ones from China and green bayberry-scented ones from America.

EXERCISE

Exercise 1C

In the following paragraph, add commas wherever they are needed.

1. When my wife and I recently visited the mountain resort where we had spent our honeymoon, we were stunned at how much it had changed. **2.** The main street used to have quaint arts and crafts shops a small mom-and-pop restaurant a bakery and a few other miscellaneous stores. **3.** Now however we found that the arts and crafts shops had been replaced by gift shops full of "souvenirs" made in foreign countries and the small restaurant where we had eaten hot roast beef fresh vegetables and homemade apple pie had been changed into a modern fast-food restaurant complete with "drive-thru" service. **4.** Although we were disappointed by the change in the village we decided to find the remote mountain waterfall where we had spent most of our time. **5.** We parked our car and hiked into the woods. **6.** As we walked we talked about the hours we had spent listening to the roar of the falls or swimming in the clear pool that the falls emptied into. **7.** After hiking for thirty minutes we found the pool and the waterfall but we wished we hadn't. **8.** The lush colourful bushes that used to border the water had been hacked away by campers. **9.** Now the pool was bordered by two or three groups of campers and all around them were scattered used paper plates empty beer and soft drink cans and what looked like the remains of their breakfast. **10.** Even the roar of the falls was drowned out by the screaming of a radio tuned to a hard rock station. **11.** Disappointed my wife and I headed back to the village. **12.** We wanted to visit one other place the cabin we had stayed in on our honeymoon. **13.** We headed for the cabin in a bad mood. **14.** After the changes we had found we would not have been surprised to have discovered a paved parking lot where the cabin had once stood. **15.** However we were greeted by a pleasant sight. **16.** Nestled against the side of the mountain our cabin still stood just as it had ten years earlier. **17.** After getting the key from the owner who lived down the road we unlocked the door to find the cabin unchanged. **18.** Feeling almost as if we had stepped ten years into the past we walked from room to room.

19. Finally we opened the back door and stared into the woods. **20.** Ten years had passed but just beyond the door stood the same trees and across their branches raced what looked to be the same squirrels chased by the same jays that we had seen years earlier. **21.** Yes much had changed but just enough had remained the same to make our trip back a memorable one.

Section Two

Other Punctuation Marks

Punctuation would be simple if we could just include a page of punctuation marks at the end of a piece of writing and invite readers to sprinkle them about anywhere they choose. But if you want to be an effective writer, it helps a great deal to know how to use not only those troublesome commas but also all of the other marks of punctuation. In this section, we will take up end punctuation and the other punctuation marks.

The placement of punctuation marks can affect the meaning of a sentence profoundly. Here are a few examples.

In this sentence, the dog recognizes its owner:

A clever dog knows **its** master.

In this one, the dog is in charge:

A clever dog knows **it's** master.

In this sentence, we find a deliberately rude butler:

The butler stood by the door and called the **guests** names as they entered.

In this sentence, he is more mannerly:

The butler stood by the door and called the **guests'** names as they entered.

And in this sentence, we find a person who doesn't trust his friends:

Everyone **I know** has secret ambitions.

Add two commas, and you change the meaning:

Everyone**,** **I know,** has secret ambitions.

As you can see, punctuation marks are potent tools.

End Punctuation

The Period

1. *The period is used at the end of a sentence that makes a statement or gives a command.*

EXAMPLES   This rule is probably the easiest of all.

Circle the subject in the above sentence.

2. *The period is used with most abbreviations.*

EXAMPLES   Mr., Mrs., Dr., A.D., Ph.D., B.C., N.D.P., min., sec., tsp.

NOTE: The period is not used with metric abbreviations.

The Question Mark

1. *The question mark is used at the end of sentences that ask questions.*

EXAMPLES   Where have all the flowers gone?

Is the water hot yet?

2. *A question mark is not used at the end of an indirect question.*

EXAMPLES   (direct question)   Why is Emile going to the dance?

(indirect question)   I wonder why Emile is going to the dance.

The Exclamation Point

1. *The exclamation point is used after words, phrases, and short sentences that show strong emotion.*

EXAMPLES   Rats!

Not on your life!

Watch it, Buster!

Ouch! That hurt!

2. *The exclamation point is not often used in college writing. For the most part, the words themselves should express the excitement.*

EXAMPLE   Chased by a ravenous pack of ocelots, Cedric raced through the forest to his condo, bolted up his stairs, swiftly locked the door, and threw himself, quivering and exhausted, onto his beanbag chair.

PRACTICE   Use periods, question marks, and exclamation points in the following sentences.

1. Robinson Crusoe wondered whether he would ever leave the island

2. Is the condor still an endangered species

3. Help, I'm drowning

4. Ask Melanie if her jaw still hurts

5. Weren't those two herons we just saw fly by

6. What a brilliant idea

7. The play was first performed around 450 BC

8. Forsyth asked where the nearest taxidermist was

Internal Punctuation

The Semicolon

1. *A semicolon is used to join two main clauses that are not joined by a coordinating conjunction.* Sometimes a transitional word or phrase follows the semicolon.

EXAMPLES   Thirteen people saw the incident; each one described it differently.

All tragedies end in death; on the other hand, all comedies end in marriage.

2. *A semicolon can be used to join elements in a series when the elements require further internal punctuation.*

EXAMPLE   Before making his decision, David consulted his banker, who abused him; his lawyer, who ignored him; his minister, who consoled him; and his mother, who scolded him.

3. *Do not use a semicolon to separate two phrases or two subordinate clauses.*

EXAMPLE (incorrect) I will pay you for the work when you return the tape deck that was stolen from our car; and when you repair the dented left fender.

The Colon

1. *A colon is used to join two main clauses when the second clause is an example, an explanation, or a restatement of the first clause.*

EXAMPLES The past fifty years had been a time of turmoil: war, drought, and famine had plagued the small country.

The garden was a delight to all insects: aphids abounded in it, ladybugs exulted in it, and praying mantises cavorted in it.

2. *A colon is used when a complete sentence introduces an example, a series, or a list.* Often a colon will come after the words *follows* or *following.*

EXAMPLES The student wrote about three Canadian novelists: Margaret Atwood, Alice Munro, and Marie-Claire Blais.

The list of complaints included the following items: leaky faucets, peeling wallpaper, and a nauseous green love seat.

3. *A colon is generally **not used** after a verb.*

EXAMPLES (incorrect) At the store I bought: bread, eggs, and bacon.

(correct) At the store I bought bread, eggs, and bacon.

PRACTICE

In the following sentences, add semicolons and colons where necessary.

1. Crack three eggs into the pan then stir them slowly.

2. The following people will form the research team Esmeralda, Kurt, Sonia, and Aki.

3. At last our prime minister was a woman however, she was not in office very long.

4. Here is a list of ingredients olive oil, flour, salt, garlic, and chicken.

5. Hockey became increasingly violent in the 1980s however, Guy Lafleur refused to wear a helmet.

Quotation Marks

1. *Quotation marks are used to enclose direct quotations and dialogue.*

EXAMPLES   "When a stupid man is doing something he is ashamed of, he always declares that it is his duty."—George Bernard Shaw

Woody Allen said, "If my film makes one more person miserable, I've done my job."

2. *Quotation marks are **not** used with indirect quotations.*

EXAMPLES   (direct quotation)   Fernando said, "I will be at the airfield before dawn."

(indirect quotation)   Fernando said that he would be at the airfield before dawn.

3. *Place periods and commas inside quotation marks.*

EXAMPLES   Rohinton Mistry wrote the short story "Auspicious Occasion."

"Always forgive your enemies—nothing annoys them so much," quipped Oscar Wilde.

4. *Place colons and semicolons outside quotation marks.*

EXAMPLES   Priscilla was disgusted by the story "The Great Toad Massacre": it was grossly unfair to toads and contained too much gratuitous violence.

Rachel read Margaret Laurence's "To Set Our House in Order"; then she went to her room to reconsider the rest of her life.

5. *Place the question mark inside the quotation marks if the quotation is a question. Place the question mark outside the quotation marks if the quotation is not a question but the whole sentence is.*

EXAMPLES   The poem asks, "What are patterns for?"

Did Lester Pearson say, "We have not suffered two defeats, but only one in two places"?

6. *Place the exclamation point inside the quotation marks if the quotation is an exclamation. Place it outside the quotation marks if the quotation is not an exclamation but the whole sentence is.*

EXAMPLES   "An earwig in my ointment!" the disgusted pharmacist proclaimed.

Please stop saying "It's time to leave"!

PRACTICE

Add semicolons, colons, and quotation marks to the following sentences.

1. Dante said, I like this place, but I would like to leave now however,

   Virgil told him that no one was allowed to leave.

2. The first sentence of Hugh MacLennan's novel *The Watch That Ends the*

   Night is, There are some stories into which the reader should be led

   gently, and I think this may be one of them.

3. Hong looked into the mailbox inside he found two tax refund cheques.

4. Evanne laid her essay on her teacher's desk and said, Have a good summer.

5. Ms. Frontiere replied, Your work has been good all semester, Kendall.

6. How much does it cost to place a want ad? Willis asked the operator.

7. When he got to the top of the hill and watched the stone roll back to

   the bottom, Sisyphus shouted, Not again!

8. Was it Bette Davis who said, Fasten your seatbelt, we're in for a rough

   ride?

9. Tina's team must have won she was smiling broadly as she entered the

   locker room.

10. When President Charles de Gaulle visited Quebec, he said, Vive Quebec

    Libre!

The Apostrophe

Apostrophes are too often misunderstood. This is Jack. This is a pen. The pen belongs to Jack. How do we express this relationship more simply?

This is Jacks pen? This is Jacks' pen? This is Jack's pen?

Which is right? You probably chose the third example because the sentence is very simple. But what about this?

In todays society we think only about ourselves.

The relationship between *today* and *society* is more difficult to conceive, so many writers forget to use an apostrophe to show that society belongs to today:

In **today's** society we think only about ourselves.

Here are a few rules on the use of the apostrophe.

1. *Use an apostrophe to form a contraction.* A *contraction* is a word in which one or more letters have been omitted and replaced by an apostrophe.

it is = it's	cannot = can't
I am = I'm	were not = weren't
they are = they're	is not = isn't
you are = you're	does not = doesn't

2. *Add 's to show possession in all singular nouns and indefinite pronouns that do **not** end in* s.

   The **girl's** hair was shiny.

   Setsuko's car is rolling down the hill!

   It is **anybody's** ball game now.

   Is this **somebody's** raincoat?

3. *Add 's to show possession in all singular nouns that end in* s.

   I love **Chris's** carrot cake.

4. *Add **only** an apostrophe to show possession in plural nouns that end in* s. However, add *'s to form the possessive of plural nouns that do **not** end in* s.

(plural nouns that end in *s*)	The **boys'** stories do not agree.
	We could hear the three **friends'** conversation all the way down the hall.
(plural nouns that do not end in *s*)	During the storm the parents were concerned do about their **children's** safety.

5. *Add 's to the last word in a singular compound of words or phrases.*

Mr. Bird left on Monday to attend his **son-in-law's** graduation.

6. *Add 's to only the last noun in a joint possession.*

Vladimir and Natasha's wedding was long and elaborate.

7. *Do **not** use an apostrophe with the possessive forms of personal pronouns.*

Incorrect	Correct
her's	hers
our's	ours
their's	theirs
it's	its

NOTE: It's *means "it is." The possessive form of* it *is* its. *This is one of most irksome mistakes student writers make. You probably will need to make a conscious effort to avoid this error.*

(incorrect) The police car had **it's** siren on as it raced down the street.

(correct)   The police car had **its** siren on as it raced down the street.

8. *Do **not** use an apostrophe with present tense verbs.*

(incorrect) The river **run's** through it.

(correct)   The river **runs** through it.

9. *Do **not** use an apostrophe to form a nonpossessive plural.*

(incorrect) The **politician's** can no longer fly to the Caribbean for conferences.

(correct)   The **politicians** can no longer fly to the Caribbean for conferences.

PRACTICE

Add apostrophes (or 's) to the following sentences where necessary.

1. Everyone was looking for Alices rabbit; he wouldnt come when we called him.

2. Are these Louis keys on the table?

3. Did you like Ben Kingsleys acting in the movie about Gandhi?

4. The police officer was awarded an extra months salary for bravery in the line of duty.

5. Karas mother wasnt amused when she saw what had happened to her husbands car.

6. Its a wonder that my cat can find its way home.

7. As he rode in the back of his managers car, the boxer said, "I couldve been a contender!"

8. My sister-in-laws father was given a years salary when he left his company.

9. Right in the middle of Billys concert, everyones watch alarm and beeper went off.

10. The five travellers luggage was lost somewhere in Nova Scotia.

PRACTICE   Write sentences of your own according to the instructions.

1. Write a complete sentence in which you use the possessive form of *women.*

   <u>The women's basketball team is now playing in the semifinals.</u>

2. Write a complete sentence in which you use the possessive form of *Charles.*

   _____

   _____

3. Write a complete sentence in which you use the possessive form of *brother-in-law.*

   _____

   _____

4. Write a complete sentence in which you use the possessive form of *children*.

_____

_____

5. Write a complete sentence in which you use the possessive form of *Mr. Norman Jones* and the contraction for *has not*.

_____

_____

REVIEW

Section Two Review

1. Use a **period** at the end of sentences that make statements or commands.

2. Use a **period** to indicate most abbreviations.

3. Use a **question mark** at the end of sentences that ask questions.

4. Do not use a **question mark** at the end of an indirect question.

5. Use an **exclamation point** after exclamatory words, phrases, and short sentences.

6. Use the **exclamation point** sparingly in college writing.

7. Use a **semicolon** to join two main clauses that are not joined by a coordinating conjunction.

8. Use a **semicolon** to separate elements in a series when the elements require further internal punctuation.

9. Do not use a **semicolon** to separate two phrases or two subordinate clauses.

10. Use a **colon** to join two main clauses when the second main clause is an example, an explanation, or a restatement.

11. Use a **colon** to introduce an example, a series, or a list.

12. Do not use a **colon** to introduce a series of items that follows a verb.

13. Use **quotation marks** to enclose direct quotations and dialogue.

14. Do not use **quotation marks** with indirect quotations.

15. Place periods and commas inside **quotation marks.**

16. Place colons and semicolons outside **quotation marks.**

17. If a quotation is a question, place the question mark inside the **quotation marks.** If the quotation is not a question, but the whole sentence is, place the question mark outside the quotation marks.

18. If the quotation is an exclamation, place the exclamation mark inside the quotation marks. If the quotation is not an exclamation, but the whole sentence is, place the exclamation point outside the quotation marks.

19. Use **apostrophes** to form the possessives of nouns and indefinite pronouns.

20. Use **apostrophes** to form contractions.

EXERCISE

Exercise 2A

Add periods, question marks, exclamation points, semicolons, colons, quotation marks, and apostrophes (or 's) to the following sentences as necessary.

1. The fireman shouted, "Watch out!"

2. Henri wondered where all the money had gone

3. Isnt Dad ever coming home asked Telemachus

4. To play racketball, you need the following equipment a racket non-skid court shoes white clothing some balls and lots of energy

5. The constable directing traffic pointed at my cars tires and laughed

6. Lily Tomlin said, The trouble with the rat race is that, even if you win, youre still a rat

7. Olaf asked Erika, How do you like the new Germany

8. It rained throughout the country yesterday therefore, all games but those in domed stadiums were postponed

9. Did Joseph Campbell say, Follow your bliss

10. The notice stated that Corinne Sandoval, Ph D, a noted anthropologist, would present a lecture on underwater excavations on Wednesday

11. The ski patrol came as fast as its skimobile would go then the paramedic examined Rebeccas leg.

12. Boyds mother brought asparagus wine to the reception however, no one would drink it because of its olive green tint

13. Couldnt we stop arguing about the future of the Canada Council

14. The cavalry captain raised his sword and bellowed, Charge

15. On June 1, 1992, Serafina Maldonado received her BA degree.

Exercise 2B

Add periods, question marks, exclamation points, semicolons, colons, quotation marks, apostrophes (or 's), and commas to the following sentences where necessary.

1. The lobsters were bound for Rudys Fish House 591 Front Street Regina Saskatchewan

2. Quiet shouted the irritated librarian

3. Are you still planning to build a pyramid or have you changed your mind

4. I didnt care for the appetizers however the soup certainly deserved a round of applause

5. Everyone enjoyed the Morriss housewarming party in fact we stayed later than wed planned to stay

6. Television is a device that permits people who havent anything to do to watch people who cant do anything said Fred Allen

7. Oscar Wilde said To love oneself is the beginning of a lifelong romance unfortunately there were a number of powerful people who didnt love Oscar

8. Did Aaron really ask to borrow your plaid cummerbund for the dance at the country club

9. The little boy asked his mother Is there really a Santa Claus

10. Take that you old curmudgeon hooted Jessica while brandishing her umbrella

11. The groups agent said Youll need the following to succeed in this business tattoos on both forearms a scar on one cheek tight leather pants ear plugs and little sensitivity to music.

12. The minister wondered whether anyones attention was on him that morning

13. What happened to your ear asked Theo

14. The childrens trip to the park was interrupted when the vans right front tire blew out

15. The pilot intended to land the airliner no matter what the conditions of the runway were moreover he intended to land it safely.

Exercise 2C

In the following paragraph, correct any errors in the use of periods, exclamation points, question marks, semicolons, colons, quotation marks, or apostrophes.

1. We have many sayings that refer in one way or another to food, but their meaning's today are quite different from what they used to be. **2.** For example, to make a point today, someone might say, "If I'm wrong, I'll eat my hat". **3.** Sometimes in slapstick comedies a person who has made such a statement actually end's up taking a bite out of his hat. **4.** However, the original expression did not refer to eating something worn on the head, rather, it referred to an early European food called hatte. **5.** This dish was made of: eggs, veal, dates, saffron, tongue, kidney, fat, cinnamon, and other ingredients. **6.** According to a European cookbook, its nearly inedible if not prepared correctly. **7.** Hence, if someone backed a bet by offering to "eat hatte", he or she either had a strong stomach or was quite confident of winning. **8.** Another expression that has a meaning today different from it's meaning in the past is: "to bring home the bacon". **9.** Today, this expression refers to earning a living; to bringing home the money with which one can buy food ("bacon"). **10.** In the fifteenth century; however, this same expression referred to winning a side of cured and salted bacon in a contest involving couple's who had just completed their first year of marriage. **11.** In England, such a "bacon award" was presented annually to the Essex County couple who judges decided lived in greater harmony and fidelity than any of the other competing couples'. **12.** Finally, havent most people at one time or another given someone "a cold shoulder?" **13.** Today, this expression refers to ignoring or slighting someone who isn't welcome or liked. **14.** In the Middle Ages; however, it referred to an actual "cold shoulder" of beef that was served as a meal to guests who had overstayed their welcome. **15.** After a few such meal's, even the most insensitive guest should have been able to take the hint. **16.** Hundreds of other saying's and slogan's exist in our language, and most of these expressions have evolved in a variety of ways from their original meanings.

Section Three

Titles, Capitalization, and Numbers

Learning the rules regarding titles, capitalization, and numbers may seem less important than, say, learning how to use commas. After all, you can probably forget to capitalize a word or two in a sentence or write "38" when it should be "thirty-eight," and you will still be understood. Yet, without knowing these rules you cannot express your thoughts clearly. You might write, for instance, "it was kind of blue, and I saw joe and the kids in the hall." Your reader might think you were talking about Miles Davis, coffee, and your neighbours, whereas you probably meant to say you were feeling blue and so you went to see your friend Joe and together watched the TV series *The Kids in the Hall.*

Here are a few good reasons to learn these three rules. Capitalization, for instance, tells your reader that you are talking about something or someone in particular, rather than generalizing. Learning how to indicate titles of books and articles is vital since most academic papers often cite from these sources, and knowing when to use arabic numerals rather than spelling numbers out will simplify your expression.

Titles

1. *Underline or place in italics the titles of works that are published separately, such as books, periodicals, and plays.*

   - Books: *The Manticore, Gage Canadian Dictionary*
   - Plays: *Hamlet, The Ecstasy of Rita Joe*
   - Pamphlets: *How to Paint Your House, Worms for Profit*
   - Long musical works: Beethoven's *Egmont Overture,* Miles Davis's *Kind of Blue*
   - Long poems: *Paradise Lost, Beowulf*
   - Periodicals: *The Globe and Mail, Saturday Night*
   - Feature-length films: *The Last Emperor, The Adjuster*
   - Television and radio programs: *The Kids in the Hall, CBC Morning Edition*
   - Works of art: Rembrandt's *Nightwatch,* Tom Tomson's *Northern River*

EXAMPLES   Meredith has subscriptions to *Chatelaine* and *Equinox*.

The Vancouver Symphony Orchestra played Bach's *Brandenburg Concerto Number Five*.

2. *Use quotation marks to enclose the titles of works that are parts of other works, such as articles, songs, poems, and short stories.*

- Songs: "Honeysuckle Rose," "Suzanne"
- Poems: "Stopping by Woods on a Snowy Evening," "The Cariboo Horses"
- Articles in periodicals: "Canada's Role in NATO," "The Quebec Question"
- Short stories: "Royal Beatings," "The Age of Lead"
- Essays: "A Modest Proposal," "Why I Love Opera and Find It Irresistibly Funny"
- Episodes of radio and television programs: "Tolstoy: From Rags to Riches," "Lord Mountbatten: The Last Viceroy"
- Subdivisions of books: "Why I Went to Zurich" (Part 1 of *The Manticore*)

EXAMPLES   The professor played a recording of Dylan Thomas reading his poem "After the Funeral."

Many writing textbooks include Jonathan Swift's essay "A Modest Proposal."

PRACTICE

In the following sentences, correct any errors in the use of titles.

1. At the beach I sat next to a woman who was reading Carol Shield's <u>The Stone Diaries.</u>

2. He always begins the first day of his literature class with a discussion of Alice Munro's short story, White Dump.

3. On the table in the dentist's office was a stack of Maclean's and Modern Mouth magazines.

4. Celeste presented a dramatic reading of Robert Browning's poem My Last Duchess.

5. I have seen two David Cronenberg films, The Fly and Scanners.

Capitalization

1. *Capitalize the personal pronoun I.*

EXAMPLE   In fact, **I** am not sure I like the way you said that.

2. *Capitalize the first letter of every sentence.*

EXAMPLE   The road through the desert was endlessly straight and boring.

3. *Capitalize the first letter of each word in a title except for* a, an, *and* the, *coordinating conjunctions, and prepositions.*

NOTE: The first letter of the first word of a title is always capitalized.

- Titles of books: *My Father Took a Cake to France, The Watch That Ends the Night*
- Titles of newspapers and magazines: *Maclean's, Edmonton Journal*
- Titles of stories, poems, plays, and films: "Tricks with Mirrors," "Bartok and the Geranium," *Jesus of Montreal*

4. *Capitalize the first letter of all proper nouns and adjectives derived from proper nouns.*
   - Names and titles of people: George Woodcock, Mayor Golding, Prime Minister Chrétien, Cousin Jack, Aunt Bea
   - Names of specific places: Banff National Park, Saskatoon, Ontario, Saudi Arabia, Skydome, Lion's Gate Bridge, Yonge Street, Earth, the Red River, the Rocky Mountains, the Far North, the Prairies

NOTE: Do not capitalize the first letter of words that refer to a direction (like "north," "south," "east," or "west"). Do capitalize such words when they refer to a specific region.

EXAMPLES   The police officer told us to drive east along the gravel road and turn north at the big pine tree.

Nova Scotia and Prince Edward Island are on the East Coast.

   - Names of national, ethnic, or racial groups: Canadian, Iranian, Chinese, Caucasian, Mohawk, First Peoples, or First Nations people
   - Names of groups or organizations: Anglicans, Moslems, Liberals, New Democrats, Progressive Conservatives, the Opposition, the Mounties, Winnipeg Jets, Better Business Bureau
   - Names of companies: Canadian Pacific, Air Canada, Scott Paper, Cominco Bank of Montreal

- Names of the days of the week and months of the year, but not the seasons: Thursday, August, spring, fall
- Names of holidays and historical events: Canada Day, Easter, the French Revolution, Confederation
- Names of specific gods and religious writings: God, Allah, Buddha, Confucius, Talmud, the Bible

5. *The names of academic subjects are not capitalized unless they refer to an ethnic or national origin or are the names of specific courses.* Examples include mathematics, political science, English, French, but Mathematics 10, Political Science 105.

PRACTICE

Correct any errors in the use of titles or capitalization.

1. In february, the vancouver symphony will present a series of concerts featuring mozart's piano concerti.

2. sinclair ross' novel as for me and my house is set in the prairies.

3. each summer i look forward to catching up on reading my old harrowsmith magazines.

4. uncle seymour always enjoys hearing ella fitzgerald sing his favourite song, my funny valentine.

5. on friday premier bob rae said none of the premiers wanted to discuss the issue.

6. every year kingston, ontario, sponsors an easter egg hunt on the saturday before easter sunday.

7. heirs of the living body is the title of a short story in alice munro's book lives of girls and women.

8. every actor wants a chance to play the leading role in william shakespeare's play hamlet.

9. when professor hope took her seat in the first-class cabin, a steward offered her copies of saturday night, chatelaine, and time magazines.

10. the catholic church on laurier avenue held a peace vigil one night last spring.

Numbers

The following rules about numbers apply to general writing rather than to technical or scientific writing.

1. *Spell out numbers that can be expressed in one or two words. Do not forget to use the hyphen in these words if they are adjectives. Use numerals for numbers that require more than two words.*

EXAMPLES   Last summer it rained for thirty-four days straight.

In 1986 it rained on more than 120 days.

2. *Always spell out a number at the beginning of a sentence.*

EXAMPLE   **Six hundred and ninety** kilometres in one day is a long way to drive.

3. *In general, use numerals in the following situations:*
   - Dates: August 9, 1995   1715–1869   1166 A.D.
   - Sections of books and plays: Chapter 5, page 22
   - Act 1, scene 3, lines 30–41
   - Addresses: 1756 Grand Avenue
                Winnipeg, Manitoba
   - Decimals, percents, and fractions: 75.8   30% or 30 percent   1/5
   - Exact amounts of money: $7.95 $1,378,000
   - Scores and statistics: Blue Jays 8   Yankees 2   a ratio of 6 to 1
   - Time of day: 3:05 a.m.   8:15 p.m. *but* six o'clock, not 6 o'clock
   - Temperatures 24°C –5°C

NOTE: *Round amounts of money that can be expressed in a few words can be written out:* twenty cents, fifty dollars, one hundred dollars. *Also, when the word* o'clock *is used with the time of day, the time of day can be written out:* seven o'clock.

4. *When numbers are compared, are joined by conjunctions, or occur in a series, either consistently use numerals or consistently spell them out.*

EXAMPLE   For the company picnic we need twenty-five pounds of fried chicken, fifteen pounds of potato salad, one hundred twenty-five cans of soda, eighty-five paper plates, two hundred thirty napkins, and eighty-five sets of plastic utensils.

OR

For the company picnic we need 25 pounds of fried chicken, 15 pounds of potato salad, 125 cans of soda, 85 paper plates, 230 napkins, and 85 sets of plastic utensils.

PRACTICE

Correct any errors in the use of numbers in the following sentences.

1. *Twenty thousand* ~~20,000~~ fans attended the Metallica concert at the stadium, and ~~20~~ *twenty* of them were ejected for various offenses.

2. The manager wants me to start at five o'clock, but I prefer to begin at 7:30.

3. For the class party, Suzette bought 10 boxes of plastic knives and forks, one hundred forty-five paper plates of various sizes, 55 plastic cups, one hundred ten paper coffee cups, and three hundred fifty paper napkins.

4. On April second, 1968, the war was not going well.

5. Professor Zacharias had to make twenty more copies of the assignment.

Section Three Review

REVIEW

1. Underline or place in italics the **titles** of works that are published separately, such as books, plays, and films.

2. Use quotation marks to enclose the **titles** of works that are parts of other works, such as songs, poems, and short stories.

3. **Capitalize** the personal pronoun I.

4. **Capitalize** the first letter of every sentence.

5. **Capitalize** the first letter of each word in a title except *a, an, the*, coordinating conjunctions, and prepositions.

6. **Capitalize** all proper nouns and adjectives derived from proper nouns.

7. **Do not capitalize** names of academic subjects unless they refer to an ethnic or national origin or are the names of specific courses.

8. Spell out **numbers** that require no more than two words. Use numerals for numbers that require more than two words.

9. Always spell out a **number** at the beginning of a sentence.

10. In general, use **numerals** for dates, sections of books and plays, addresses, decimals, percents, fractions, exact amounts of money, scores, statistics, and time of day.

11. When **numbers** are compared, are joined by conjunctions, or occur in a series, either consistently use numerals or consistently spell them out.

EXERCISE

Exercise 3A

The following sentences contain errors in the use of titles, capitalization, and numbers. Correct any errors you find.

1. The movie *f̲a̲t̲a̲l̲ a̲ttraction* caused much discussion about how men treat women and women treat men.

2. Director john huston's last film was an adaptation of james joyce's short story the dead.

3. The united nations forces tried to restore order in bosnia last winter.

4. once the temperature reached 33 degrees, i decided to take off my sweater and loosen my brooks brothers tie.

5. Last night the expos beat the mets by a score of four to two.

6. When sharon mispronounced mr. dearie's name 3 times, he told her that she had made a freudian slip.

7. Before he could graduate, paul had to pay a fine to the university of regina library of fifty-five dollars and seventy cents.

8. After he typed the memorandum on his apple computer, the secretary ordered three reams of copy paper, 250 file folders, four boxes of pencils, and 150 filters for the coffee machine.

9. The msg computer company donated two thousand three hundred forty dollars to langara college for computer programs to study the effect of a coffee diet on discontented students.

10. Erin likes to hear composer antonio vivaldi's the four seasons played by the berlin philharmonic orchestra.

11. after the ctv news jeremy went to bed and read an article in maclean's called why you can't go to sleep after watching the evening news on television.

12. i read an article that said that 10% of the people who shop at supermarkets buy one of those gossip newspapers like national enquirer, but i'm not sure which newspaper the article was in.

13. radmila yawned as professor williams told the class how important the missing father is in the play the glass menagerie.

14. Over 2500 people view rembrandt's painting nightwatch every day.

15. Only 20 sailors had read captain clark's essay entitled the importance of being seaworthy.

EXERCISE

Exercise 3B

Compose sentences of your own according to the instructions.

1. Write a sentence that includes the author and title of a book.

   During his vacation, Jamey read Carol Shield's novel The Stone Diaries.

2. Write a sentence that describes a song you like and the musician who wrote it or performs it.

   _____

   _____

3. Tell what movie you last saw in a theatre and how much you paid to see it.

   _____

   _____

4. Write a sentence that tells what school you attend and what classes you are taking.

   _____

   _____

5. Write a sentence that tells the number of people in your family, the number of years you have gone to school, the number of classes you are taking, and the approximate number of students at your school.

   _____

   _____

6. Write a sentence that mentions a magazine you have read lately. If possible, include the title of an article.

   _____

   _____

7. In a sentence, describe your favourite television program.

_____

_____

8. Tell where you would go on your ideal vacation. Be specific about the name of the place and its geographical location.

_____

_____

9. Write a sentence that includes your age and address. (Feel free to lie about either one.)

_____

_____

10. Write a sentence that names a musician or musical group that you like and an album, tape, or compact disc that you like.

_____

_____

EXERCISE

Exercise 3C

In the following paragraph, correct any errors in the use of capitalization, numbers, or titles.

1. The books and magazines displayed at checkout stands in most grocery stores are as different from each other as the people who buy them. 2. For readers of science fiction, Isaac Asimov's Science Fiction Magazine provides stories of what could be waiting for humankind in Space or on other worlds. 3. Each edition of his Magazine carries as many as 10 excellent short stories. 4. On the other hand, for readers who want their Science Fiction now rather than in the future, "National Enquirer" makes perfect reading. 5. In this journal, readers will find all their imaginative fantasies fulfilled. 6. They might read articles entitled UFO over bermuda triangle or "Venusians land in Vermont." 7. Of course, the checkout stand also features books for those people who prefer more substantial reading material. 8. For example, the romance-starved might try The Passionate Flower of Love or "Madness in Malaysia." 9. Novels like these require little thought while providing fast-paced action in Exotic places. 10. In fact, for as little as three dollars and ninety-five cents, these novels allow the readers to experience adventures that they would never experience otherwise. 11. In contrast to these popular romance novels, books by american authors whose works are taught in College literature classes also grace the aisles of many checkout stands. 12. Amy Tan's novel "The Kitchen God's Wife" or Anne Tyler's "Saint Maybe" were 2 recent favourites. 13. Finally, for those readers in search of self-help material, there are many contrasting choices. 14. A person who wants some light reading might page through a cosmopolitan

magazine to find articles such as "How to become the person you want to be." **15.** On the other hand, the more studious readers can pick up Psychology Today to examine an article called Jung's archetypes at work in your life. **16.** Truly, the reading materials presented at most grocery checkout stands reflect the varied reading interests of today's Public.

Section Four

Sentence Practice: Sentence Variety

Writing is challenging. It is a process that requires constant and countless choices. You can structure your sentences any way you like. Each structure changes subtly or dramatically the relationships among your ideas.

Sometimes a short sentence is best. Look at the one that begins this paragraph and the one that begins the paragraph above. At other times you will need longer sentences to get just the right meaning and feeling. Sentence combining exercises give you an opportunity to practise how to express ideas in various ways by encouraging you to move words, phrases, and clauses around to achieve different effects.

When you construct a sentence, you should be aware not only of how it expresses your ideas but also of how it affects the other sentences in the paragraph. Consider the following paragraph as an example. It is the opening paragraph of Rachel Carson's book *The Edge of the Sea*.

> The edge of the sea is a strange and beautiful place. All through the long history of the earth it has been an area of unrest where waves have broken heavily against the land, where the tides have pressed forward over the continents, receded, and then returned. For no two successive days is the shoreline precisely the same. Not only do the tides advance and retreat in their eternal rhythms, but the level of the sea itself is never at rest. It rises or falls as the glaciers melt or grow, as the floor of the deep ocean basins shifts under its increasing load of sediments, or as the earth's crust along the continental margins warps up or down in adjustment to strain and tension. Today a little more land may belong to the sea, tomorrow a little less. Always the edge of the sea remains an elusive and indefinable boundary.

Rachel Carson opens her paragraph with a short, simple sentence. Then she writes a longer and more complicated sentence because she wants to specify the general ideas in the first one. It even seems to capture the rhythm of the sea against the land. She follows that one with another short, simple sentence. As the paragraph continues, she varies the length and complexity of her sentences according to what she needs to say. Notice how she ends the paragraph with another simple statement that matches her opening sentence.

Sentence Combining Exercises

In the following sentence combining exercises, you will practise writing sentences so that some are short and concise and others are longer and more complicated.

EXAMPLE   Combine the following sentences into either two or three sentences. Experiment with whichever sounds best.

a. There was a feud.
b. It began simply enough.
c. The Smiths' youngest son refused to marry the Millers' favourite daughter.
d. Mrs. Miller fed Grandfather Smith some potato salad.
e. The potato salad was tainted.
f. They were at the annual curling club picnic.
g. Nothing was the same after that.

The feud began simply enough. When the Smiths' youngest son refused to marry the Millers' favourite daughter, Mrs. Miller fed Grandfather Smith some tainted potato salad at the annual curling club picnic. Nothing was the same after that.

1. Combine the following sentences into three sentences. Add a transition to the last sentence.

   a. There was a choice.
   b. It was not difficult to make.
   c. Jake was not the one who had robbed the stage.
   d. Jake knew that the townspeople were convinced he was guilty.
   e. The townspeople planned to lynch him if they caught him.
   f. Jake had to steal a horse.
   g. Jake had to leave town now.

   _____

   _____

   _____

   _____

   _____

2. Combine the following sentences into three sentences.

    a. The male stickleback fish must be quite shy.
    b. He usually has a silver-coloured belly.
    c. He is brown to green everywhere else.
    d. During mating season, his belly turns bright red.
    e. Perhaps he is trying to attract a mate.
    f. Perhaps he is blushing.

_____

_____

_____

_____

_____

_____

3. Combine the following sentences into two sentences.

    a. Mr. Darian told Harrison the bad news.
    b. The roof was leaky.
    c. The hot water heater wasn't working.
    d. Its heating element was broken.
    e. Mr. Darian said that between them they would have to raise money.
    f. The money was to fix the roof.
    g. The money was to get a new water heater.

_____

_____

_____

_____

_____

_____

4. Combine the following sentences into three sentences.

    a. The expression "going over the top" is curious.
    b. It derives from trench warfare.
    c. It is a type of combat in which vast armies swarmed out of deep-cut ditches.
    d. They engaged one another in hand-to-hand combat.
    e. Never was this more true than in the Battle of Vimy Ridge.
    f. On Easter Sunday, 1917, there were one hundred thousand Canadians.
    g. They were prepared to attack a seemingly impregnable German fortress.
    h. It would occur at dawn of the following day.

_____

_____

_____

_____

5. Combine the following into four sentences.

    a. During the night it began to snow.
    b. At 5:30 a.m. one thousand cannons opened fire.
    c. The Canadian troops "went over the top."
    d. They stumbled through the blinding storm.
    e. They overwhelmed the Germans.
    f. They surprised the Germans.
    g. A fierce hand-to-hand combat raged for three days.
    h. In the end the Canadians were victorious.
    i. Headlines around the world proclaimed the victory of the Canadian troops.
    j. They proclaimed the emergence of Canada.
    k. The proclaimed the emergence from its colonial status into nationhood.

_____

_____

_____

_____

6. Combine the following sentences into two or three sentences.

    a. Some dictators are called benevolent.
    b. They do good things for the people.
    c. Napoleon Bonaparte was considered benevolent.
    d. Under Napoleon, industry expanded.
    e. Universities flourished.
    f. The civil law system was improved.
    g. The judicial system was reorganized.
    h. The Bank of France was established.
    i. Most dictators, however, are not benevolent.

_____

_____

_____

_____

_____

_____

7. Combine the following sentences into three sentences.

    a. The crow is despised by some people.
    b. The crow is respected by other people.
    c. The crow has a larger brain than most other birds.
    d. The crow can quickly learn that a "scarecrow" is nothing to fear.
    e. Hunters have discovered something about the crow.
    f. Crows can distinguish between a farmer and a hunter.
    g. The farmer is going about his business.
    h. The hunter has a rifle and plans to shoot the crow.

_____

_____

_____

_____

8. Combine the following sentences into two or three sentences.

   a. One of the legends about the discovery of coffee involves an Arab goat herd.
   b. His name was Kaldi.
   c. It was about 850 A.D.
   d. He was puzzled by the strange behaviour of his goats.
   e. He sampled some berries.
   f. His goats had been feeding on the berries.
   g. He felt a strong sense of exhilaration.
   h. He announced his discovery to the world.

   _____

   _____

   _____

   _____

9. Combine the following sentences into three sentences.

   a. The house was almost silent.
   b. A couple sat at a table.
   c. The table was in the kitchen.
   d. They were talking softly.
   e. They were talking about their children.
   f. The children were sleeping.
   g. The children were in their rooms upstairs.
   h. A clock was on a wall.
   i. The wall was filled with brightly coloured crayon drawings.
   j. The clock had looked down on almost twenty years of family meals.
   k. The clock ticked quietly.

   _____

   _____

   _____

   _____

10. Combine the following sentences into three or four sentences.

   a. Today's "hot dog" really is named after a dog.
   b. The popular sausage was first developed in the 1850s.
   c. It was developed in Frankfurt, Germany.
   d. Some people called it a "frankfurter," after the city.
   e. Others called it a "dachshund sausage."
   f. It had a dachshund-like shape.
   g. In 1906 a New York cartoonist was drawing a vendor.
   h. The vendor was selling "hot dachshund sausages."
   i. The vendor was at a baseball game.
   j. The cartoonist abbreviated the term to "hot dog."
   k. The name stuck.

   _____

   _____

   _____

   _____

   _____

Section Five

Moving from Paragraph to Essay: Part 2

Introduction and Concluding Paragraphs

In Chapter Four you learned that an academic essay has three parts: an introduction, several middle or supporting paragraphs, and a conclusion. Some writers compose the middle paragraphs before attempting the more difficult introduction and conclusion paragraphs. You might consider doing this yourself.

However, for now, let us learn how to write **good openings** and **good conclusions**. A good opening makes readers want to, even *need to*, read your essay. Without an interesting opening, your readers may turn to other writers. A good conclusion brings your essay to a satisfactory completion. Without a sense of completion, your essay appears merely to end, and your readers are left hanging, feeling dazed and confused, wondering what they are to make of your essay.

Beginnings and endings are *that* important!

The Introduction, or Thesis, Paragraph

Do you remember our original topic sentence from the essay we developed in Chapter Four?

> Many English-speaking people are surprised when they discover the number of everyday words that are drawn from different mythologies.

Because this sentence now introduces an entire essay, not just one paragraph, we call it the **thesis statement**. A thesis statement states the topic of the essay and tells readers what you intend to say about the topic.

DEFINITION | **thesis statement** | The thesis statement of an essay is the sentence that states the topic and the central point of the essay.

Of course, this thesis statement is not a paragraph. You know now that a paragraph is more than one sentence long. Here is one way you could develop the thesis statement into a paragraph:

Only recently has English become *the* international language. People around the globe are now required to learn it as a second language to their own. Yet, ironically, English is a language that has borrowed freely from all the other languages of the world. English speakers themselves know that many of the words they consider to be everyday English come from other languages. They know, for example, that the word *patio* comes from Spanish, *reservoir* from French, *recognize* from Latin, and *psychology* from Greek. They know, too, that the name for their most intimate apparel, *pajamas,* derives from Hindi. **However, many English-speaking people are surprised when they discover the number of everyday words that are drawn from different mythologies.**

Notice where we put the thesis statement: *at the bottom of the introductory paragraph*. This may come as a surprise to you. You may be accustomed to placing it first, but that is actually a rare placement.

How is the introductory paragraph developed? Notice that the paragraph begins with a broad, general statement: "Only recently has English become *the* international language." The sentence tells readers your starting point, not your concluding point. The purpose of all the other sentences in the first paragraph is to lead to and introduce the thesis sentence.

This background statement is only one way to introduce a thesis. There are many others. You might, for instance, relate an interesting anecdote or brief story, use a few relevant quotations or questions, provide startling and provocative information, or perhaps stack up statistics and numbers. Make each sentence count. Think of each sentence as one step closer to the thesis. Integrate your lead-in material with the thesis. Work toward making a smooth transition from your introduction to your thesis.

PRACTICE

In Chapter Four you converted your paragraphs into an essay. Now take your first "paragraph"—it is, of course, at this point only a sentence—and convert it into an introductory paragraph. To do this, first create a new and interesting opening sentence and then a series of sentences that narrow, and anticipate the topic sentence, which will now become your thesis statement.

The Conclusion

Look once again at our original conclusion from page 263:

These examples are just a few of the hundreds of English words that reflect the many mythologies of the world.

Note that the conclusion of an essay *rewords* the thesis statement. It does not merely repeat it word for word. Compare it to the thesis:

> Many English-speaking people are surprised when they discover the number of everyday words that are drawn from different mythologies.

The *reworded* thesis sentence that introduces the concluding paragraph of the essay reflects the content of the essay and expresses a sense of completion in the words, *"These examples are just a few ..."*

Of course, you should expand the concluding paragraph just as you did your introductory paragraph. To do so, first reword the thesis statement, and then add a few sentences in conclusion. Here is one way to do it:

> **These examples are just a few of the hundreds of English words that reflect the many mythologies of the world.** They give evidence not merely of the capacity of the English language to absorb other cultures, but also of the viability and energy of the mythology of the ancient world. We simply cannot avoid this mythology. In fact, we find it quite impossible to communicate with one another in the simplest of everyday terms without using words that refer to mythological figures or events. To try to do so would truly be a Herculean task.

The structure of the concluding paragraph is the reverse of the thesis paragraph. In the thesis paragraph, we begin generally and **narrow** toward the thesis statement; in the conclusion, we begin with a reconstruction of the thesis statement and then **broaden** toward a more general statement.

This is just one way to do it. Good writers know as many ways to conclude an essay as to start one. What you must remember is that the introduction serves up the thesis, and the conclusion reminds readers what you have told them. One could say that the writer has three tasks in writing an essay: first, to tell readers what you will say; second, to say it; and third, to tell them what you have said. In this way, we can envision the structure of the three-part academic essay.

PRACTICE

Just as you took your original topic sentence and recreated an introductory paragraph, now take your final sentence and create a satisfactory conclusion to your essay. Follow the example above in creating your concluding paragraph.

PRACTICE TEST

Chapter Five Practice Test

I. Review of Chapters Two, Three, and Four

A. Correct any fragments, fused sentences, or comma splices in the following sentences. Do nothing if the sentence is correct.

1. Two cashiers working overtime to help handle the unexpected crowd.

   _____

   _____

2. The play was only half over, however, nearly all of the audience had already left.

   _____

   _____

3. When she saw the two mountain climbers who had been lost for fourteen days.

   _____

   _____

4. Ignoring the red light, the truck raced through the intersection it nearly hit a pedestrian.

   _____

   _____

5. Jack had not eaten all day, as a result, his stomach started to growl during his afternoon meeting with the astrologer.

   _____

   _____

B. Correct any dangling or misplaced modifiers in the following sentences. Do nothing if the sentence is correct.

6. After eating the entire container of ice cream, Hassan's depression was worse than ever.

    _____

    _____

7. To arrive at the meeting on time, breakfast was skipped.

    _____

    _____

8. The girl who was riding the horse with red tennis shoes waved at her brother.

    _____

    _____

9. It was almost time to drive home, so Omar only decided to order a Coke.

    _____

    _____

10. Trying to find a little peace and quiet, the television was unplugged for a month.

    _____

    _____

C. Correct any subject–verb agreement errors in the following sentences. Do nothing if the sentence is correct.

11. Each of the members of the two motorcycle clubs wants to win the cross-country race.

12. Do your daughter or the children next door plan to attend the birth-day party?

13. The audience have finally stopped clapping, so we can continue with the performance.

14. There is a clown and a masked man waiting to see the dentist.

15. Fifteen years was as long as Kyoko was willing to wait.

D. Correct any pronoun use errors in the following sentences. Do nothing if the sentence is correct.

16. Everyone who attended the lecture agreed it was the best she had ever heard.

17. The bicyclist crashed into the man carrying a bag of groceries, but he was not injured.

18. The police officer asked Igor and I to step out of the car.

19. Karen wanted to know if the winners of the lottery were Keiko and her.

20. Most people know that you should drive slowly through a school zone.

II. Review of Chapter Five

A. Add commas to the following sentences where necessary. Make no changes if the sentence is correct.

21. The damp dense fog made it difficult to see but Nick decided to leave anyway.

22. After living in Red Deer Alberta for two years Omar decided to return to Paris France.

23. Diane did you notice the full moon last night or were you too busy preparing today's lecture?

24. Simon's true love had no idea what she would do with four calling birds three French hens two turtle doves and a partridge in a pear tree.

25. When March 18 1992 finally arrived François loaded his car with supplies and headed for British Columbia.

26. He ran quickly to the end of the alley and climbed over the fence.

27. Chantal's dog a large English mastiff followed her into the house; however it was not allowed to stay inside.

28. Dan Leonard who won last week's golf tournament was surprised when he received his award a new Mazda Miata.

29. Unfortunately the storm has caused a major traffic jam and has knocked out the electricity to half of the city.

30. Yes Jane is still at her riding lesson so she will be late for dinner.

B. Add periods, exclamation points, question marks, quotation marks, semi-colons, colons, and apostrophes (or *'s*) where necessary. Do not add or delete any commas.

31. Farzad wondered whether he should buy the Honda or the Buick

32. Humpty Dumpty asked, Do you think you can put me back together

33. Alain knew that he needed a needle, a spool of black thread, a thimble, and a box of bandages

34. The people chained to the gate screamed, No clear cut No clear cut

35. The tin man wasnt able to move however, a little oil soon solved that problem

36. The volcano rumbled ominously all night long soon it would explode

37. Garth we really shouldnt go any farther, advised Shane

38. Willys sons were neither as successful nor as well-liked as Howards son

39. James asked, Are you sure you know how to get out of here

40. Dr Steinbach didnt want to miss the childrens play therefore, she left the office early

C. In the following sentences correct any errors in the use of titles, capitalization, and numbers. Do not add or delete any commas. Make no changes if the sentence is correct.

41. Last night I read joseph conrad's short story the secret sharer 2 times.

42. In nineteen ninety-two michael ondaatje published his novel the english patient.

43. More than 300 people were standing in line to see the movie silence of the lambs.

44. 785 cars pass through this intersection every thursday.

45. Everyone was surprised when the old beatles' album sergeant pepper's lonely heart's club band was played at forest lawn cemetery.

46. April and may were more like winter, but june promised to be more like spring.

47. At the end of the second world war all the villages along the alaska highway became boom towns.

48. After Satoshi finished preparing for his math test, he started to write his english paper on gary geddes' poem letter of the master of horse.

49. After 16 weeks of teaching, professor chou still did not know the names of all the students in her class.

50. At seven-fifteen in the morning, we already had seen 5 african elephants, 102 flamingos, and 1 white rhinoceros.

ANSWERS

Answers to Practices in Chapter Five

Page 279:

2. She told him it was good for him, and he made a funny face.
3. correct
4. She said, "Eat your broccoli, or you won't get any dessert."
5. correct

Page 280:

2. The film was scary, hilarious, and insipid at the same time.
3. Jamey doesn't know that broccoli is inexpensive, tastes good, and fights cancer.
4. The elves could be seen traipsing across the untidy, overgrown lawn.
5. Julian wanted to buy an assortment of flowers, for his mother had invited him to dinner.

Page 282:

2. At a very improbable and inopportune time, Giselle announced her intention to pursue him to the ends of the earth.
3. Teetering dangerously at the top of the hill, the large stone might have rolled down and crushed Sisyphus.
4. When you see her next time, she will have removed that load from her shoulders.
5. No, I would prefer not to copy the manuscript at this time.
6. To determine the accuracy of her instruments, Paula Halim ran some tests.

Page 283:

2. The professor of philosophy, for example, always polished his shoes with cotton balls and kerosene.
3. Loggers are moving into that area of the forest; therefore, protesters will have to leave Nanaimo early tomorrow morning.
4. He has a cup of tea, I think, every time that he has a difficult decision to make.
5. Harry had been shocked by his electric train transformer; consequently, he mistrusted all electronic technology.

Page 284:

2. *Front Page Challenge*, which was a very popular television show in the 1980s, often dealt with people's prejudices.
3. My oldest daughter, who is a painter, often uses *Alice in Wonderland* characters in her work.
4. correct
5. This airplane, which has electric motors, will ultimately replace those using kerosene.

Page 285:

2. Every Christmas he sends his mother twelve pounds of broccoli, her favourite food.
3. Perry's father, a retired librarian, swore that he never wanted to see another book.
4. correct
5. The orca, a member of the dolphin family, is usually called a killer whale.

Page 286:

2. Sergeant Owens, finally showing his impatience, made the recruits do one hundred situps.
3. Leonard Cohen, trying not to show his despair, kept singing in front of the three beautiful women in black.
4. The concert was about to begin, and Troy, hoping to play well, closed his eyes in concentration.
5. Charlie, raised in a polite household, courteously told me that his favourite singer was Barry Manilow.

Page 287:

2. On June 24, 1981, my youngest daughter was born.
3. Find out, Charles, if you can visit us in 1993.
4. Send this order of salmon to Harbour House, 334 Oak Street, Saint John, New Brunswick.
5. Emily, where is my handkerchief?

Pages 287–288:

2. The first man on the moon, who was an American astronaut, made a clever statement as he stepped down from the spacecraft.
3. *Frankenstein*, a novel by Mary Shelley, has been the subject of several films and many articles.
4. Will you help me with my letter of apology, Maria?
5. Michelle was born in a hospital in Winnipeg, Manitoba, in 1981 on a sunny afternoon.
6. On July 20, 1969, the first man landed on the moon.
7. Kenneth suddenly remembered his pet iguana, forgotten in his car two hours ago.
8. The road that leads to White River, the next town, is closed.
9. The first part of the rafting trip, however, is smooth.
10. Gordon, will you tell John, who is working out back, that it is time to quit?

Page 297:

2. Is the condor still an endangered species?
3. Help, I'm drowning!
4. Ask Melanie if her jaw still hurts.
5. Weren't those two herons we just saw fly by?
6. What a brilliant idea!
7. The play was first performed around 450 B.C.
8. Forsyth asked where the nearest taxidermist was.

Page 298:

2. The following people will form the research team: Esmeralda, Kurt, Sonia, and Aki.
3. At last our prime minister was a woman; however, she wasn't in office very long.
4. Here is a list of ingredients: olive oil, flour, salt, garlic, and chicken.
5. Hockey became increasingly violent in the 1980s; however, Guy Lafleur refused to wear a helmet.

Page 300:

2. The first sentence of Hugh MacLennan's novel *The Watch that Ends the Night* is, "There are some stories into which the reader should be led gently, and I think this may be one of them."

3. Hong looked into the mailbox; inside he found two tax refund cheques.

4. Evanne laid her essay on her teacher's desk and said, "Have a good summer."

5. Ms. Frontiere replied, "Your work has been good all semester, Kendall."

6. "How much does it cost to place a want ad?" Willis asked the operator.

7. When he got to the top of the hill and watched the stone roll back to the bottom, Sisyphus shouted, "Not again!"

8. Was it Bette Davis who said, "Fasten your seatbelt, it's going to be a rough ride"?

9. Tina's team must have won; she was smiling broadly as she entered the locker room.

10. When President Charles de Gaulle visited Quebec, he said, "Vive Quebec Libre!"

Pages 302–303:

2. Are these Louis's keys on the table?

3. Did you like Ben Kingsley's acting in the movie about Gandhi?

4. The police officer was awarded an extra month's salary for bravery in the line of duty.

5. Kara's mother wasn't amused when she saw what had happened to her husband's car.

6. It's a wonder that my cat can find its way home.

7. As he rode in the back of his manager's car, the boxer said, "I could've been a contender!"

8. My sister-in-law's father was given a year's salary when he left his company.

9. Right in the middle of Billy's concert, everyone's watch alarm and beeper went off.

10. The five travellers' luggage was lost somewhere in Nova Scotia.

Pages 303–304:

Answers will vary. Here are some possible ones.

2. Charles's new car certainly looks expensive.

3. My brother-in-law's house was robbed last night.

4. Do you think the children's room should be cleaned?

5. Mr. Norman Jones's order hasn't arrived yet.

Page 312:

2. He always begins the first day of his literature class with a discussion of Alice Munro's short story "White Dump."

3. On the table in the dentist's office was a stack of <u>Maclean's</u> and <u>Modern Mouth</u> magazines.

4. Celeste presented a dramatic reading of Robert Browning's poem "My Last Duchess."

5. I have seen two David Cronenberg films, <u>The Fly</u> and <u>Scanners</u>.

Page 314:

2. Sinclair Ross' novel <u>As for Me and My House</u> is set in the Prairies.
3. Each summer I look forward to catching up on reading my old <u>Harrowsmith</u> magazines.
4. Uncle Seymour always enjoys hearing Ella Fitzgerald sing his favourite song, "My Funny Valentine."
5. On Friday Premier Bob Rae said none of the premiers wanted to discuss the issue.
6. Every year Kingston, Ontario, sponsors an Easter egg hunt on the Saturday before Easter Sunday.
7. "Heirs of the Living Body" is the title of a short story in Alice Munro's book <u>Lives of Girls and Women</u>.
8. Every actor wants a chance to play the leading role in William Shakespeare's play <u>Hamlet</u>.
9. When Professor Hope took her seat in the first-class cabin, a steward offered her copies of <u>Saturday Night</u>, <u>Chatelaine</u>, and <u>Time</u> magazines.
10. The Catholic church on Laurier Avenue held a peace vigil one night last spring.

Page 316:

2. The manager wants me to start at 5:00, but I prefer to begin at 7:30.
3. For the class party, Suzette bought 10 boxes of plastic knives and forks, 145 paper plates of various sizes, 55 plastic cups, 110 paper coffee cups, and 350 paper napkins.

or

For the class party, Suzette bought ten boxes of plastic knives and forks, one hundred forty-five paper plates of various sizes, fifty-five plastic cups, one hundred ten paper coffee cups, and three hundred fifty paper napkins.
4. On April 2, 1968, the war was not going well.
5. correct

Chapter Six
Choosing the Right Words

English is a diverse language. It has borrowed words from hundreds of different sources. *Moccasin*, for instance, is Native American in origin; *patio* comes from Spanish; *colonel* and *lieutenant* entered English from Norman French; and *thermonuclear* is both Greek and Latin. All of this diversity makes English a complex and interesting language, but it also makes it quite difficult sometimes.

As you know, we have three words that sound just like *to* and three words that sound just like *there*. In fact, English is full of words that sound alike or that have such similar meanings that they are often mistaken for one another. A careful writer learns to make distinctions among these words.

Failing to make correct word choices can cause a number of problems. Most importantly, you may fail to make your ideas clear, or you may confuse your reader if you make an incorrect word choice. Also, you may lose the confidence of your reader if your writing contains misspelled or poorly chosen words. Sometimes, you can even embarrass yourself.

For instance, here is a fellow who wants to meet either a fish or the bottom of a shoe:

When I went to college, I did not know a **sole**.

This person has writing mixed up with the building trade:

I began to take my talent for writing for **granite**, but I lacked the ability to organize my thoughts in a coherent **manor**.

And here the early settlers enjoy a means of transportation that hadn't yet been invented:

The pioneers appeared to prefer the open **planes** to the dense forests.

Most incorrect word choices, however, are not as humorous or embarrassing as these. Instead, they are simple errors in word choice that are usually caused by carelessness and a lack of attention to detail.

Use Your Dictionary

This chapter will cover common problems in word choice—irregular verbs, confusing sets of words, and levels of diction (jargon, slang, and so on). If you are not sure of a word choice (the difference between *effect* and *affect*, for instance), consult your dictionary. A dictionary shows how to spell, pronounce, and use words. Dictionaries give you the definitions of words, show you the principal parts of verbs, and tell you whether or not a word is appropriate for formal writing. In addition, most dictionaries contain other useful information, such as biographical and geographical data.

Section One

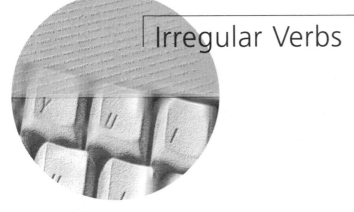

Irregular Verbs

In order to form the various tenses of verbs, you need to know the basic verb forms. These basic forms are known as the **three principal parts of the verb:** the **present,** the **past,** and the **past participle.**

You use the present to form both the present and future tenses, the past to form the past tense, and the past participle (with *have, has,* and *had*) to form the perfect tenses.

Most verbs, the **regular verbs,** form the past and past participle by adding "d" or "ed" to the present. For example, the three principal parts of *create* are *create* (present), *created* (past), and *created* (past participle). The three principal parts of *talk* are *talk, talked,* and *talked.*

However, about two hundred verbs form the past and past participle in different ways. These verbs are called the **irregular verbs.** They are some of the oldest and most important verbs in English, like *eat* or *fight* or *buy*—basic human actions. Because these words are so common, you should know their principal parts. Here is a list of the principal parts of most irregular verbs.

Present	Past	Past Participle
am, are, is	was, were	been
beat	beat	beaten
become	became	become
begin	began	begun
bend	bent	bent
bet	bet	bet
bite	bit	bitten
bleed	bled	bled
blow	blew	blown
break	broke	broken
bring	brought	brought
build	built	built
burst	burst	burst
buy	bought	bought
catch	caught	caught
choose	chose	chosen
come	came	come

Present	Past	Past Participle
cost	cost	cost
cut	cut	cut
dig	dug	dug
do, does	did	done
draw	drew	drawn
drink	drank	drunk
drive	drove	driven
eat	ate	eaten
fall	fell	fallen
feed	fed	fed
feel	felt	felt
fight	fought	fought
find	found	found
fly	flew	flown
forget	forgot	forgotten or forgot
freeze	froze	frozen
get	got	got or gotten
give	gave	given
go, goes	went	gone
grow	grew	grown
hang	hung	hung
hang (to execute)	hanged	hanged
have, has	had	had
hear	heard	heard
hide	hid	hidden
hit	hit	hit
hold	held	held
hurt	hurt	hurt
keep	kept	kept
know	knew	known
lay (to place or put)	laid	laid
lead	led	led
leave	left	left
lend	lent	lent
let	let	let
lie (to recline)	lay	lain
light	lit	lit
lose	lost	lost
make	made	made
mean	meant	meant
meet	met	met
pay	paid	paid
prove	proved	proved or proven
put	put	put
quit	quit	quit
read	read	read
ride	rode	ridden
ring	rang	rung

Present	**Past**	**Past Participle**
rise	rose	risen
run	ran	run
say	said	said
see	saw	seen
sell	sold	sold
send	sent	sent
set	set	set
shake	shook	shaken
shine	shone	shone
shoot	shot	shot
show	showed	shown
shrink	shrank	shrunk
shut	shut	shut
sing	sang	sung
sink	sank	sunk
sit	sat	sat
sleep	slept	slept
slide	slid	slid
speak	spoke	spoken
speed	sped	sped
spend	spent	spent
spin	spun	spun
stand	stood	stood
steal	stole	stolen
stick	stuck	stuck
sting	stung	stung
strike	struck	struck
swear	swore	sworn
sweep	swept	swept
swim	swam	swum
swing	swung	swung
take	took	taken
teach	taught	taught
tear	tore	torn
tell	told	told
think	thought	thought
throw	threw	thrown
wake	woke or waked	woke or waked
wear	wore	worn
weave	wove	woven
weep	wept	wept
win	won	won
wind	wound	wound
wring	wrung	wrung
write	wrote	written

Special Problems with Irregular Verbs

lie–lay

1. The irregular verb *lie* means "to recline." It never takes a direct object. The principal parts of this verb are *lie*, *lay*, and *lain*.

EXAMPLES   On Saturdays, **I lie** in bed until at least eleven o'clock.

Last Saturday **I lay** in bed until almost one o'clock.

Today, **I have lain** in bed too long.

2. The verb *lay* means "to place or put." It takes a direct object. Its principal parts are *lay*, *laid*, and *laid*.

EXAMPLES   As Paul enters the house, he always **lays** his keys on the table.

Yesterday Paul **laid** his keys on the television set.

After he **had laid** the flowers on the kitchen table, Mr. Best kissed his wife.

sit–set

1. The verb *sit* means "to be seated." It never takes a direct object. Its principal parts are *sit*, *sat*, and *sat*.

EXAMPLES   At the movies, Juan usually **sits** in the back row.

Last week Juan **sat** in the middle of the theatre.

2. The verb *set* means "to place or put." It takes a direct object. Its principal parts are *set*, *set*, and *set*.

EXAMPLES   At night Nizar always **sets** a glass of water by his bed.

Lynn **set** her books on the librarian's desk.

rise–raise

1. The verb *rise* means "to stand" or "to attain a greater height." It never takes a direct object. Its principal parts are *rise*, *rose*, and *risen*.

EXAMPLES   I like it when the sun **rises** over the mountains on a clear day.

All of the people **rose** every time the queen entered the room.

2. The verb *raise* is a regular verb. It means "to elevate." It takes a direct object. Its principal parts are *raise*, *raised*, and *raised*.

EXAMPLES   Every morning a Boy Scout **raises** the flag in front of the school.

Christopher always politely **raised** his hand whenever he had a question.

Verbs with "U" in the Past Participle

Because these verbs sound odd, some people tend to use the past form when they should be using the past participle. Here are the ones that are most often confused.

drink	drank	drunk:	So far I **have drunk** eight glasses of water today.
swim	swam	swum:	Lynn **has swum** thirty-five laps today.
shrink	shrank	shrunk:	The grocer wondered why his profits **had shrunk**.
sing	sang	sung:	Often Carmine **has sung** "O Canada!" before hockey games.

PRACTICE   Underline the correct verb form in the parentheses.

1. In the daytime, Michelle's pet rat just (lays lies) in the corner of his cage and sleeps.

2. After three hours, Andrew decided he had (drank drunk) enough coffee, so he switched to water.

3. When we looked back, we could not believe that we had (swam swum) all the way across the river.

4. The collie trotted up and (lay laid) the newspaper at its master's feet.

5. Virginia walked up the spiral staircase of her lighthouse, and then she (set sat) down to read a novel.

6. My pen is (lying laying) on the table.

7. The man who owns the cleaners called to tell me that my coat had (shrank shrunk).

8. This morning my cat (drank drunk) some milk that was (sitting setting) on the table.

9. Although Emmy had (sang sung) well on the Hominy Grits' latest album, she could not (rise raise) enough money to accompany them on their concert tour.

10. Nancy told her son to (lie lay) down and take a nap, but he told her that he had already (laid lain) down earlier.

REVIEW

Section One Review

1. The **three principal parts of a verb** are **present, past,** and **past participle.**

2. **Regular verbs** form the past and past participle by adding "d" or "ed" to the present.

3. **Irregular** verbs form the past and past participle in a variety of other ways. See the lists on pages 347–349.

4. Irregular verbs that often cause confusion are **lie/lay, sit/set, rise/raise,** and **verbs with "u" in the past participle.**

EXERCISE

Exercise 1A

Underline the correct form of the verb in the parentheses.

1. Participating on the swim team, Naomi figures she has (swam <u>swum</u>) thousands of kilometres.

2. Last week Victor (saw seen) Carol buying a case of his favourite food at the grocery.

3. The watermelon fell out of the bag and (busted burst) all over my shoes.

4. The party for his girlfriend (costed cost) Victor a week's wages.

5. The detective knew that no one had been to the house for several weeks because dozens of newspapers (lay laid) unopened in the driveway.

6. We must have (set sat) in the train station for at least three hours.

7. Within seconds after the alarm had (rang rung) the fire squad was on its way.

8. It was a beautiful sight as the sun (raised rose) above the fir trees.

9. When Yuan checked with the bank, he found that his savings had (shrank shrunk) to only a dollar.

10. When did the admiral get the news that the battleship had (sank sunk)?

11. Mr. Peterson thought that he had (lain laid) his key on the desk in his office.

12. My mother must have (threw thrown) her purse at the robber as he ran from the store.

13. Before Superman (hanged hung) up his cape, he (wringed wrung) it out.

14. Most mornings Lester (sat set) and read the newspaper after breakfast.

15. Selena told us that once the ordeal was over, she had (shook shaken) for two hours.

EXERCISE

Exercise 1B

In the blanks, write the correct form of the verb indicated.

1. Mark looked down and saw that a ten dollar bill _____lay_____ by his right shoe. (lie)

2. Every day last week Kiansa _____ in the front row of her women's studies class. (sit)

3. Each of the past five years, my grandmother has _____ my brother and me money to go to the fair. (give)

4. I have gone to Europe three times, but I have never _____ on the Concorde. (fly)

5. Toni was so worried about the test that she _____ six cups of coffee. (drink)

6. In Indonesia the sun _____ around six in the morning all year. (rise)

7. Galileo _____ down his instrument and pondered over what he had just seen. (lay)

8. Mrs. Chen told the doctor that she had _____ seven glasses of water each day. (drink)

9. Jimmy felt that he had _____ enough anti-logging demonstrations for one day. (see)

10. We could have _____ earlier if we hadn't gotten caught in a traffic jam. (come)

11. Have you _____ the bell for exercise class yet? (ring)

12. The tourists watched in awe as the grey whales _____ out of the water. (rise)

13. Victor was sure that he _____ in the hammock for only ten minutes before he went to sleep. (lie)

14. Cecilia had _____ only two laps when her knee began to ache. (swim)

15. He tried to tell his wife that by mistake he had _____ his own kids! (shrink)

Exercise 1C

Check the following paragraph for correct verb forms. Underline any incorrect verb forms and write the correct forms above them.

1. Although many people lead their lives by following the proverb "Look before you leap," I have always thought that life is much more entertaining and exciting if I leaped first and looked later. **2.** For example, just last month, on the day before spring break, my phone rung. **3.** It was a friend asking me if I'd like to spend the week laying on a cruise ship while it sailed to Cabo San Lucas, Mexico. **4.** I suppose I should have took a moment or two to think about it. **5.** I should have sat the phone down and opened my chequebook. **6.** After counting up my money, I should have began to think about the consequences of taking a week off from my part-time job. **7.** And then I should have decided to stay home. **8.** But I didn't do any of those things. **9.** Instead, I said, "Count me in!" **10.** By the end of that spring break, I had laid in the sun for hours, swam in the clear, cool ocean, and drank my fill of tropical cocktails. **11.** I had spent a wonderful week enjoying the party atmosphere of the Carnivale Cruise Lines, and I had brung home with me memories that I will never lose. **12.** Another time when I leaped before I looked happened last year when I was in my last year at high school. **13.** Just before the school year begun, the principal called and asked if I would like to participate in an exchange program with a student from France. **14.** If I had stopped to think about it, I probably would have shrank from the opportunity, but I didn't think about it. **15.** Instead, I just said "Yes, I'll go," and am I ever glad I did. **16.** In France I met people who taught me how to look at the world in ways different from my own limited point of view, and I seen sights there that I'll never forget. **17.** I suppose sometimes it's safer to look before you leap, but living a safe, careful life is just not for me.

Section Two

Commonly Confused Words

Most word choice errors are made either because two words sound alike or look alike or because their meanings are so similar that they are mistakenly used in place of each other. Here are some of the most commonly confused sets of words.

a/an/and

A is used before words that begin with consonant sounds. It is an article, a type of adjective.

EXAMPLE   **a** porcupine, **a** bat, **a** sword, **a** good boy

An is used before words that begin with vowel sounds. It is also an article.

EXAMPLE   **an** apple, **an** honour, **an** unusual cloud formation

And is a coordinating conjunction used to join words, phrases, or clauses.

accept/except

Accept means "to take or receive what is offered or given." It is a verb.

EXAMPLE   George gladly **accepted** the reward for the money he had returned.

Except means "excluded" or "but." It is a preposition.

EXAMPLE   Flowers were in everyone's room **except** Sonia's.

advice/advise

Advice means "an opinion about what to do or how to handle a situation." It is a noun.

EXAMPLE   The counsellor gave Andrea **advice** about how to apply for graduate school.

Advise means "to give advice" or "to counsel." It is a verb.

EXAMPLE   The magistrate **advised** the crown attorney to control his temper.

affect/effect

Affect means "to influence" or "to produce a change in." It is a verb.

EXAMPLE   The continued destruction of the ozone layer will **affect** future weather patterns drastically.

Effect is "a result" or "something brought about by a cause." It is a noun.

EXAMPLE   The decorator liked the **effect** of the newly painted room.

NOTE: Effect can be used as a verb when it means "to bring about" or "to cause."

EXAMPLE   The reward **effected** a change in the lion's behaviour.

all ready/already

All ready means "everyone or everything is prepared or ready."

EXAMPLE   After a strenuous game of softball, we were **all ready** for a cold root beer.

Already means "by or before a specific or implied time."

EXAMPLE   By the time he had climbed the first flight of stairs, Bob was **already** out of breath.

all right/"alright"

All right means "satisfactory" or "unhurt."

EXAMPLE   After she fell from her horse, Hannah smiled and said she was **all right.**

Alright is a misspelling. Do not use it.

"alot"/allot

Alot is not a word. Use "many" instead.

EXAMPLE   (incorrect)   There are **alot** of reasons for taking public transport.

(correct)   There are **many** reasons for taking public transport.

Allot means "to assign a share or portion of" something to someone.

EXAMPLE   The steering committee **allotted** twelve seats to the delegation from British Columbia.

among/between

Use *among* when discussing three or more things or ideas. It is a preposition.

EXAMPLE   **Among** the demands of the workers was drinkable coffee.

Use *between* when you are discussing only two things or ideas. It is a preposition.

EXAMPLE   Betty could not choose **between** Sid and Slim.

amount/number

Use *amount* to refer to things that are uncountable, such as milk, oil, salt, or flour.

EXAMPLE   The **amount** of sugar the recipe calls for is two cups.

Use *number* to refer to things that can be counted, such as people, books, cats, or apples.

EXAMPLE   The large **number** of people in the small room made the air stuffy.

anxious/eager

Anxious means "apprehensive, uneasy, worried." It is an adjective.

EXAMPLE   The lawyer was **anxious** about the jury's verdict.

Eager means "keen desire or enthusiasm in pursuit of something." It is also an adjective.

EXAMPLE   The children were **eager** for summer vacation to begin.

are/our

Are is a linking verb or a helping verb.

EXAMPLES   We **are** late for dinner.

We **are** leaving soon.

Our is a possessive pronoun.

EXAMPLE   **Our** dinner was delicious.

brake/break

Brake is the device that stops or slows a vehicle. It may be used as a noun or a verb.

EXAMPLES   The service station attendant told Molly that her **brakes** were dangerously worn.

Arlo **braked** just in time to avoid going over the cliff.

Break can also be used as a noun or verb. As a verb it means "to cause to come apart by force."

EXAMPLE   Every time Humphrey walks through a room, he **breaks** something.

As a noun, *break* means "an interruption of an action or a thing."

EXAMPLES   When there was a **break** in the storm, we continued the game.

The worker fixed the **break** in the water pipe.

choose/chose

Choose means "select." It is a present tense verb.

EXAMPLE   Every Friday afternoon, the children **choose** a movie to watch in the evening.

Chose means "selected." It is the past tense of "choose." Its principle parts are *choose, chose, chosen.*

EXAMPLE   Last Friday, the children **chose** *E.T.*

complement/compliment

A *complement* is "that which completes or brings to perfection." It is a noun or a verb.

EXAMPLES   The bright yellow tie was a handsome **complement** to Pierre's new suit.

The bright yellow tie **complemented** Pierre's new suit.

A *compliment* is "an expression of praise, respect, or courtesy." It is a noun or a verb.

EXAMPLES   Whenever Mr. Fraser receives a **compliment** for his beautiful sculptures, he smiles and blushes.

Whenever his wife **compliments** Mr. Fraser for his beautiful sculpture, he smiles and blushes.

conscience/conscious

Conscience is "a knowledge or sense of right and wrong." It is a noun.

EXAMPLE   Garth said that his **conscience** kept him from looking at Lucy's paper during the physics examination.

Conscious can mean either "aware" or "awake." It is an adjective.

EXAMPLE   As he walked through the forest, Garth was **conscious** of this precious heritage.

disinterested/uninterested

Disinterested means "neutral" or "impartial." It is an adjective.

EXAMPLE   A judge must remain **disinterested** as he considers a case before him.

Uninterested means "not interested." It is an adjective. Follow it with the preposition "in."

EXAMPLE   Wayne was profoundly **uninterested** in professional sports.

Underline the correct word in the parentheses.

1. The hikers were so (<u>eager</u> anxious) to get to the trail that they forgot to get (<u>advice</u> advise) about the local weather.

2. Mr. Chen's (conscience conscious) told him to leave his fortune to charity because he did not have (a an) heir.

3. There was a disagreement (between among) the three mechanics about who would fix the (brakes breaks) on the truck.

4. The television antismoking campaign had no (affect effect) upon the habits of teenage smokers.

5. The television antismoking campaign did not (affect effect) the habits of teenage smokers.

6. We dashed to the theatre, but the doors were closed because the concert had (already all ready) begun.

7. I felt (alright all right) even though I had a temperature of 39°.

8. The (number amount) of traffic accidents in Brampton set a new record this year.

9. We knew that (are our) chances of winning were small if they did not give Wayne Gretzky a longer (break brake) between shifts.

10. At their last convention the Liberals (choose chose) a new leader.

fewer/less

Use *fewer* to discuss items that are countable, such as trees, automobiles, or pencils. It is an adjective.

EXAMPLE   When the "arborists" had finished, there were many **fewer** trees in our neighbourhood.

Use *less* to refer to amounts that are uncountable, such as water, dirt, sand, or gasoline. It is an adjective.

EXAMPLE   Because we waste water, there is **less** of it in the reservoirs this year.

lead/led

As a noun, *lead* is a heavy metal or a part of a pencil. As a verb, it is the present tense of the verb "to lead," meaning "to guide" or "to show the way."

EXAMPLES   The diver used weights made of **lead** to keep him from floating to the surface.

Every summer Mr. Archer **leads** his scout troop on a long backpacking trip.

Led is the past or past participle form of the verb "to lead."

EXAMPLE   Last summer, Mr. Archer **led** his scout troop on a backpacking trip.

loose/lose

Loose means "not confined or restrained, free, unbound." It is an adjective.

EXAMPLE   Mr. Wang was chasing a cow that had gotten **loose** and was trampling his garden.

Lose means "to become unable to find" or "to mislay." It is a verb.

EXAMPLE   I was afraid I would **lose** my contact lenses if I went swimming with them.

nauseous/nauseated

If something is *nauseous* it causes nausea or is sickening or disgusting. Nauseous is an adjective.

EXAMPLE   A **nauseous** odour filled the room.

To be *nauseated* is to be sick or to feel nausea. *Nauseated* is the past or past participle form of the verb *nauseate* and is often used as an adjective.

EXAMPLE   The bad news made Alice feel **nauseated**.

passed/past

Passed is the past or past participle form of the verb "to pass," which means "to go or move forward, through, or out."

EXAMPLE   As I drove to school, I **passed** a serious traffic accident.

Past as an adjective means "gone by, ended, over." As a noun it means "the time that has gone by." As a preposition it means "beyond."

EXAMPLES   His **past** mistakes will not bar him from further indiscretions.

In the **past**, I have always been in favour of opening doors for women.

Horst waved as he drove **past** Jill's house.

personal/personnel

Personal means "private" or "individual." It is an adjective.

EXAMPLE   Helen feels her political ideas are her **personal** business.

Personnel means "persons employed in any work or enterprise." It is a noun.

EXAMPLE   The sign on the bulletin board directed all **personnel** to report to the auditorium for a meeting.

precede/proceed

Precede means "to go before." It is a verb.

EXAMPLE   The Great Depression **preceded** World War II.

Proceed means "to advance or go on." It is a verb.

EXAMPLE   After a short pause, the clerk **proceeded** with her inventory.

principal/principle

As an adjective, *principal* means "first in rank or importance." As a noun, it usually means "the head of a school."

EXAMPLES   Kevin's **principal** concern was the safety of his children.

At the assembly the **principal** discussed drug abuse with the students and teachers.

A *principle* is a "fundamental truth, law, or doctrine." It is a noun.

EXAMPLE   One of my **principles** is that you never get something for nothing.

quit/quite/quiet

Quit means "to stop doing something." It is a verb.

EXAMPLE   George **quit** smoking a year ago.

Quite means "completely" or "really." It is an adverb.

EXAMPLE   It was **quite** hot during the whole month of August.

Quiet means "silent." It is usually used as an adjective, but it can be used as a noun.

EXAMPLES   The **quiet** student in the third row rarely said a word.

In the **quiet** of the evening, Hank strummed his guitar.

than/then

Use *than* to make comparisons. It is a conjunction.

EXAMPLE   It is cloudier today **than** it was yesterday.

Then means "at that time" or "soon afterwards" or "next." It is an adverb.

EXAMPLE   Audrey mowed the backyard, and **then** she drank a large iced tea.

their/there/they're

Their is a possessive pronoun meaning "belonging to them."

EXAMPLE   All of the people in the room suddenly started clinking the ice in **their** drinks.

There is an adverb meaning "in that place."

EXAMPLE   "Let's park the car over **there**," proclaimed Fern.

They're is a contraction for "they are."

EXAMPLE   "**They're** back," said the girl as the little monsters crawled out of the cracks.

threw/through

Threw is the past tense form of the verb "to throw."

EXAMPLE   Hector **threw** the spear with godlike accuracy.

Through is a preposition meaning "in one side and out the other side of."

EXAMPLE   The ship sailed **through** the Bermuda Triangle without incident.

to/too/two

To is a preposition meaning "in the direction of."

EXAMPLE   Jeremy went **to** his rustic cabin by the babbling brook for a poetic weekend.

Too is an adverb meaning "also" or "more than enough."

EXAMPLES   Cecily was at the game, **too**.

Wayne Gretzky finds the burden of public adulation is **too** heavy.

Two is the number after one.

EXAMPLE   Bill has **two** daughters and one cat and too many televisions, so he wants to go to Jeremy's rustic cabin, too.

we're/were/where

We're is a contraction for "we are."

EXAMPLE   Relax, **we're** almost there.

Were is a linking verb or a helping verb in the past tense.

EXAMPLES   We **were** late for dinner again.

Our hosts **were** eating dessert when we arrived.

Where indicates place.

EXAMPLES   **Where** is the key to the cellar?

He showed them **where** he had buried the money.

your/you're

Your is a possessive pronoun meaning "belonging to you."

EXAMPLE   "**Your** insights have contributed greatly to my sense of well-being," said the corporation president.

You're is a contraction for "you are."

EXAMPLE   "**You're** just saying that because you're so nice," replied John.

PRACTICE

Underline the correct words in the parentheses.

1. The (<u>number</u> amount) of players on the team is decreasing because of (to <u>too</u> two) many injuries, so the managers announced that (there <u>they're</u> their) probably going to cancel the next game.

2. There are (fewer less) reasons to rent a house (than then) there are to buy one.

3. Did you say that (your you're) (principal principle) problem is that there is not enough light?

4. The truck emitted (nauseous nauseated) fumes as it went (passed past) the playground.

5. As the professor (led lead) his students (through threw) an explanation of the Milky Way, he worried that he would (loose lose) (they're their there) attention.

6. Rachel always goes by the (principle principal) that honesty is the best policy.

7. (To Too Two) hours is not (to too two) long (to too two) study for an exam.

8. The (number amount) of fuel in the gas tank is (less fewer) (then than) it was last time I checked.

9. It was (quiet quit quite) early when I woke up, so I was (quiet quit quite) as I made the coffee.

10. The skunks (we're were where) too friendly (we're were where) we camped last June.

Exercise 2A

Underline the correct word in the parentheses.

1. The prospects for victory are much greater now (then <u>than</u>) they were just five minutes ago.

2. The movers promised not to (brake break) any of Mrs. Robinson's fragile china hearts.

3. The sailors were (eager anxious) to get off of the ship and be with (there they're their) families and friends.

4. The grandfather divided the shares of corporate stock (between among) his ten grandchildren.

5. Conrad was embarrassed about (accepting excepting) his award as employee of the year.

6. What you have for breakfast can (affect effect) your whole day.

7. Yi Ping was (conscience conscious) that everyone was looking at him.

8. Karl wanted to talk about the last game of the World Series, but his girlfriend was completely (disinterested uninterested) in baseball.

9. The huge (number amount) of people at the concert for the homeless raised more money than was expected.

10. If (your you're) going to eat that raw fish in front of me, I'm going to eat my stewed broccoli in front of you.

11. When we got to the bookstore the famous author had (all ready already) left.

12. Helga received many (complements compliments) about the way she sang the role of Pamina in the opera.

13. The bass player was afraid that if he stayed away (to too two) long, he would (lose loose) his wife and home.

14. The canoeists lost (their there they're) nerve when they saw the rapids they (we're were where) approaching.

15. We are going (to too two) the museum, and you can go (to too two) if you are not (to too two) busy.

EXERCISE

Exercise 2B

Correct any word choice errors in the following sentences.

1. Mr. Clark felt honoured as he ~~excepted~~ *accepted* his award for heroism.

2. Has the mail come all ready?

3. My conscious told me that I was partially at fault to.

4. Everything will be alright if your here with me.

5. Satoshi gave me advise about how to escape hamburger deprivation.

6. Jennifer lead her business associates threw her new condominium.

7. Farzad hoped he would not loose his head over Ms. Lafarge.

8. The Greenbergs lost there confidence in the salesman because he seemed so anxious to sell them a Volkswagen.

9. Icarus was more careless then his father.

10. William Tell received a large amount of complements for his accuracy.

11. I was in love with Ke Shan until I discovered she was completely disinterested in jazz.

12. The principal of our high school persuaded Cher to give the commencement address.

13. I became nauseous when I saw the colours that the decorator had chosen for you're office.

14. The three of us could not agree between ourselves about which type of breaks we should put on the van.

15. The driver of the second car was still conscience when the police arrived.

EXERCISE

Exercise 2C

Edit the following paragraph for word use. Underline any incorrect words, and write the correct words above them.

1. Beach City College gets many <u>complements</u> [*compliments*] for its academic and sports programs, but its cafeteria is worse <u>then</u> [*than*] any I have ever been in. **2.** The person in charge of food services needs to visit other college cafeterias and get some advise on how to prepare good, inexpensive food, how to design a pleasant, efficient serving area, and how to chose and train the people who work in a cafeteria. **3.** The personal who cook seem disinterested in giving us tasty, nutritious food. **4.** For instance, if you walk passed the food line in the morning, your likely to see a huge vat of soupy scrambled eggs next to a tray of barely cooked, greasy bacon next to a plate of cold toast. **5.** Then, if you precede to the salad bar, hoping that at least things their will be alright, you will see wilted lettuce, a few green tomatoes, some listless cucumber slices, and only one dressing—Thousand Island. **6.** The college needs to be more conscience of the needs of students because there paying high prices for nauseated food. **7.** The food is bad enough, but the place were it is served is almost worse. **8.** It is a poorly designed maze where your constantly bumping into other people. **9.** The floor is often so slippery with spilled food that your constantly in danger of falling and braking something. **10.** In addition, the room is cheerless and to dark. **11.** I know of students who risk starvation because they fear that they will loose they're way and never get out. **12.** The personal who serve the food and take you're money are another problem. **13.** You can usually find at least three of them arguing between themselves. **14.** Most of them are less friendly then a led weight.

15. There main principal seems to be if we decrease the amount of students who come to the cafeteria, we won't have to work as much. **16.** They act as if it is a honour for you to give them you're money. **17.** All of these problems make it unpleasant just to walk threw the cafeteria. **18.** In fact, it often makes you nauseous. **19.** Having a good, nutritious meal or snack should be a pleasant brake between classes. **20.** We should not except this situation. **21.** If we students complain to the business manager enough, we can have an affect on the conditions in the cafeteria.

Section Three

Formal Written Canadian English

In the previous two sections, you studied errors in word choice caused by the misuse of irregular verbs or by confusing words that look or sound alike. Now we will consider errors caused when you use *inappropriate words,* even though they may convey what you want to say. You may have already noticed that people use different kinds of words in different situations. In fact, you probably change your own vocabulary depending on whether you are talking to your close friends, your parents, your banker, or your teacher. For example, if you were applying for a job as a computer technician, you probably would not write on the application that you have had "awesome" experience or that you think you would be a "totally rad" technician. Obviously, such words would sound ridiculous—not because they express the wrong ideas, but because they are not *appropriate* to the situation.

Writing in college is a special situation. It requires a certain set of words; in fact, in a number of ways it requires words different from the ones you use when you are talking informally. These words we describe as **formal written Canadian English**. They are used not only by college writers but also by newspaper and magazine writers, essayists, business journalists, and professional writers of all kinds.

Formal written Canadian English is an agreed-upon set of signals that educated people use when they write. It conforms to the rules of grammar and usage you have studied in this textbook. In addition, it is free of *obscenity* or *vulgarity, slang,* many of the terms of *informal spoken English, jargon,* and *pretentious language,* such as *bureaucratese* and *doublespeak.*

Obscenity and Vulgarity

These two categories are inappropriate in almost any situation, although you may need to use them if you are quoting someone. You should not use obscenity or vulgarity in college-level writing because you most certainly will lose your audience.

Slang

Slang is an informal language spoken within a particular group of people at a certain time, often containing vivid and unusual *coinings,* or invented meanings. Like poetry, slang uses imaginative metaphor and simile, such as *righteous, rad, awesome,* and *dude.* The problem with slang is that it quickly comes into style and quickly goes again. As well, it does not serve the purposes of writers who try to communicate with precision and clarity. "This place is Ripoffsville, man!" may contain real energy of expression, but for the purposes of college writing, you can be more precise by writing: "This business is motivated solely by profits." This may not have the energy of the first statement, but it is more precise and will be understood long after *Ripoffsville* has slid into the dust bin of dead words. List here some slang terms you use or have used—either recently or in the past:

_____

_____

_____

_____

Informal Spoken English

Informal spoken English, also called "colloquial" English, consists of casual, everyday words and expressions that we all use in our speech. Often these words slip into our writing unconsciously. Here are some examples of informal expressions:

a lot	hang out with	pretty good
a bunch	out of it	super
sort of	lousy	you know
kind of	weird	I mean like

When we speak informally, we say that we have *a lot* of friends, rather than *many* friends. Or we say we are *sort of* worried rather than *somewhat* worried. And we *hang out* with friends rather than *associate with* them.

Such casual words and expressions are acceptable when we are talking with friends and acquaintances. However, in written English these terms are too casual and imprecise. In college writing, you should try to be as precise as possible.

NOTE: *Contractions are also considered to be too informal for formal written Canadian English. However, many writers do use contractions when avoiding them would result in unusually stiff or awkward expressions. Check with your instructors as to their policy before using contractions.*

Here are some examples of informal expressions and contractions and their alternatives. At the end of the list, add examples of your own.

Informal	More Formal
cop	constable
cruisin' for a brusin'	looking for a fight
busted	had no money; arrested
loaded	intoxicated, drugged
a cinch	easy
ripped off	stolen, cheated
I'm	I am
he'd	he had

_____

_____

_____

_____

_____

NOTE: Your dictionary will tell you whether a word is appropriate for formal written Canadian English. If you look up a word and it is labelled "colloquial" (informal English), "slang," "obsolete," or "dialect," it is inappropriate.

PRACTICE

Identify the slang or informal words in the following sentences, replacing these words with their more formal equivalents.

1. I was floored when I heard what you had said.

   <u>I was surprised when I heard what you had said.</u>

2. That dude's got a real problem.

   _____

3. An awful lot of his friends think that Paul messes up too much when he tries to impress people.

   _____

   _____

4. Sandy's boss thought it was neat that she always showed up on time, but he wasn't too crazy about the quality of her work.

_____

_____

5. The gross smell made the speaker clam up for a minute.

_____

_____

6. After the cop busted Bill, he took out after Steve.

_____

_____

7. I really get a kick out of, like, goofing off on Saturdays.

_____

_____

8. Sometimes I'm in the dumps, but at other times I'm just super.

_____

_____

9. My father'd have a cow if he knew that I was into skydiving.

_____

_____

10. She hits the slopes a lot.

_____

_____

Jargon

Like slang, jargon consists of formal, specialized words and expressions that are unique to a particular group of people or express specific activities. Computer programmers, for example, use terms such as *windows, ram,* and *customize;* sociologists refer to *nuclear families;* and biologists talk about *eutophicates.*

Among the members of a particular group or profession, jargon can be a very effective use of language. However, you should *not* use jargon when writing for a general audience that perhaps does not fully comprehend the specific meaning of these terms.

EXAMPLES	(inappropriate jargon)	Your input is valuable to me. It helps me access my own feelings.
(clear writing)	Your suggestions are valuable to me. They help me understand my own feelings.

Pretentious Language, Euphemisms, Doublespeak, and Bureaucratese

Student writers often believe that they can impress readers by using big words. Such is not the case. Just as jargon confuses readers, pretentious language calls attention to itself with its own polysyllabic fireworks and evasiveness. The purpose of writing is to communicate ideas, not obfuscate or evade them by hiding a lack of content within a maze of words. For example, avoid using *verbal communication* when you mean *talk, utilize* for *use, interdigitation* for *holding hands, in a family way* for *pregnant,* or *a non-renewed contract* for *fired.* Do not use two words when one will do, and do not use a long word when you can use a short one.

Avoid *doublespeak* at all costs. It is an artificial language that hides the truth and, at the same time, insidiously attempts to control people's thoughts. For instance, parliament does not raise taxes, it "seeks new revenues"; military men do not bomb people, they "pacify" them; Chinese students demonstrating for democratic reform are "counterrevolutionary insurrectionists." In this Orwellian nightmare, used cars are "pre-owned," killing off a population with a different political or religious conviction is "cleansing," and clearcutting forests is "maximizing profitability."

Bureaucratese is overblown and complex technical jargon, thought to have originated from bureaucrats. It consists of stiffly formal Latinate expressions, clusters of nouns, passive verbs, and complex language structures that, some feel, are designed to prevent understanding. With a little effort, "Please send three copies of your tax forms" can become "Submission of payment forms pertaining to tax matters should herewith be transmitted to postal collection agencies or regional tax offices in triplicate form only." Eight words can become twenty-four.

You should be suspicious of any heavy use of Latinate noun clusters and technical jargon. Impress readers with the quality of your reasoning, not the number of nouns you know.

PRACTICE

Identify any jargon, pretentious language, doublespeak, euphemism, and bureaucratese. Replace such expressions with words appropriate for college-level writing. You may need to rewrite the whole sentence.

1. After Robin consumed his evening meal, he reclined upon a sofa and partook of a brief sleep period.

   After Robin ate his dinner, he took a nap on the sofa.

2. Shane's input regarding the means whereby I might be able to reconstruct my nuclear family dwelling was most enlightening.

3. Nizar wanted to relieve himself of some excess weight, so he initiated a regime of physical exertion at his local gymnastics facility.

4. In many areas it is unlikely that successful housing renewal programs can be implemented without increasing the viability of housing association rehabilitation, and in recognizing the contributions that housing associations can make.

5. The two business executives utilized the restaurant's menu to determine what monetary outlay would be necessary for their Christmas party.

6. Jack had always been desirous of a thespian career, but he had never succeeded in attaining one.

7. When interfacing with their children, parents should utilize as much positive feedback as possible.

   _____

   _____

8. After commencing the activity of bowling, I became cognizant of the fact that it was not enjoyable to me.

   _____

   _____

9. North Saskatchewan Airlines is currently experiencing some scheduling difficulties with respect to its service between Saskatoon and Regina that is a direct result of inclement weather.

   _____

   _____

10. A stone in the process of periodic revolution does not accrue quantities of lichenous material.

    _____

    _____

EXERCISE

Exercise 3A

In the following sentences, underline the word or expression that would be the most appropriate for college writing or formal written Canadian English.

1. Every evening Jerry spends one hour watching his (boob tube, <u>television</u>, audio-visual entertainment device).

2. We will be able to leave for Hawaii as soon as we (finalize, complete, wrap up) our preparations.

3. Last Friday, Kyoto and her cousin went to see the latest (movie, flick, cinema presentation).

4. When Jenna heard that her toy horse was broken, she began to (cry, lament, bawl).

5. Julie searched the entire parking lot, but she couldn't find her (vehicle, wheels, car).

6. The car that she decided to buy was really very (cost effective, inexpensive, cheap).

7. Diane did not want to be (chastised, chewed out, scolded), so she decided to tell a little lie.

8. After being questioned for five hours, the suspect finally (gave access to his data, told all he knew, spilled his guts).

9. Needing a place to (crash, rest, repose), Denise stopped at her mother-in-law's house.

10. Mr. Egan was chosen for the job because he is (a straight arrow, at the top of the reliability index, honest and hard-working).

11. He opened his lunchbox and stared at the (eats, sustenance, food) in it.

12. After I heard that I had not passed the test, I was (depressed, morose, down in the dumps).

13. After her weeks of study, Marie could hardly believe that her class was finally (finished, terminated, history).

14. As Lynn sped down the freeway, she watched for a (cop, law-enforcement agent, constable).

15. Roberta does not like to talk to people who constantly (put down, insult, verbally affront) others.

Exercise 3B

In the following sentences, revise any use of slang, informal spoken English, overly formal or pretentious language, or jargon into language appropriate for college writing or formal written Canadian English.

1. Fernando was saving his bucks so that he could remodel the food preparation area of his house.

   <u>Fernando was saving his money so that he could remodel his kitchen.</u>

2. I had a difficult time thinking as a result of the high decibel level of the television.

   _____

   _____

3. Sumi's snooty attitude has caused many of her buddies to start avoiding her.

   _____

   _____

4. When Zach realized his program had failed, he was kind of depressed.

   _____

   _____

5. George's maternal parent started to bawl at the funeral.

   _____

   _____

6. Since we haven't had a chance to become acquainted, why don't we have our evening repast together?

   _____

   _____

7. Jeff told me that I'll see a lot of butterflies while I'm cruising through Lethbridge.

_____

_____

8. The birdbrain that answered the telephone couldn't understand what I was trying to tell him.

_____

_____

9. When Martha saw Mansour's face, she knew he'd blown some serious money in Vegas.

_____

_____

10. Most Canadian kids are cognizant of the dangers of cigarette smoke.

_____

_____

11. Although his family had derived pleasure from the flick, Sergio offered a negative assessment of the main character's acting.

_____

_____

12. Although I love the beach, I know that excessive solar exposure can damage my skin.

_____

_____

13. The weather was just super, so Rene and a bunch of her friends made the decision to accompany each other to the beach.

_____

_____

14. Simon's prognostication that the Blue Jays would win the pennant this year blew my mind.

_____

_____

15. James knew it'd be a pain to find a reliable pre-owned motor vehicle, but he didn't have a desire to make the purchase of a new one.

_____

_____

EXERCISE

Exercise 3C

Read the following paragraph to find any errors in word choice. Change any slang, informal language, jargon, or overly formal language into formal written Canadian English.

1. People who refuse to eat in places like McDonald's or Wendy's are *making a mistake* ~~really blowing it~~. **2.** One reason that I am deeply appreciative of having the opportunity to eat in such establishments is that they provide a quick, hot meal for hardly any bucks at all. **3.** At McDonald's I can chow down on a Big Mac, a large order of fries, and a low-calorie cola beverage for under $4.00. **4.** And the McDonald's near my humble abode is now offering free refills, making the monetary expenditure even more acceptable to my wallet. **5.** No kidding—as a full-time student and a part-time sales clerk, I gotta pinch every penny I can. **6.** Another reason I like fast food is that a whole bunch of these places offer an abundance of culinary choices. **7.** It ain't like the old days when all a dude could get were a burger and fries (although I have to admit I do love my burger and fries). **8.** Today, depending on where I go, I can access salads, different kinds of finger food, chicken, fish, stuffed baked potatoes, and even Chinese food. **9.** Just the other day I ordered a "variety pack" at Wendy's and got three miniature chimichangas, three egg rolls, and three pieces of spicy chicken—all for about three bucks.

10. Finally, I think fast-food restaurants are just super because they are totally convenient. **11.** I have to be at my place of gainful employment twenty minutes after my last class ends, so I don't have much time to eat.

12. Luckily, I can pull a "U" into the local White Spot, grab a fast-food dinner, and consume it in my vehicle while I drive the ten miles to work.

13. By the time I get to my job, I've eaten my dinner and am feeling a lot

better. **14.** I know that many people think fast food is just gross, but my

own experience tells me that they are way off base.

Section Four

Sentence Practice: Effective and Meaningful Sentences

These final sentence combining exercises present you with a new challenge. No specific directions are given. Experiment to discover the most effective way to combine the sentences, and remember you must supply transitional markers. You may also want to change the sentences about to create a smooth flow of ideas. Avoid jargon and pretentious language.

Sentence Combining Exercises

EXAMPLE

a. The first marathon was run in 1896.
b. It was run at the Olympic Games in Athens, Greece.
c. The marathon was founded to honour the Greek soldier Pheidippides.
d. He is supposed to have run from the town of Marathon to Athens in 490 B.C.
e. The distance is 22 miles, 1470 yards.
f. He ran to bring the news of the victory of the Greeks over the Persians.
g. In 1924 the distance was standardized to 26 miles, 385 yards.

The first marathon was run at the Olympic Games in Athens, Greece, in 1896. The marathon was founded to honour the Greek soldier Pheidippides, who, in 490 B.C., is supposed to have run from the town of Marathon to Athens, a distance of 22 miles, 1470 yards, to bring the news of the victory of the Greeks over the Persians. In 1924, however, the distance was standardized to 26 miles, 385 yards.

1. Combine the following sentences.

   a. Some people feel boxing should be outlawed.
   b. Boxing is a violent sport.
   c. Two people try to knock each other unconscious.
   d. One boxer hits the other boxer in the face.
   e. The brain of the boxer who is hit slams against the inside of his skull.
   f. He has a concussion.
   g. He is knocked out.

   _____

   _____

   _____

   _____

   _____

2. Combine the following sentences.

   a. It was the first tide of immigration into the Canadian prairies.
   b. It began in the early 1900s.
   c. The great central plateau at last stood peaceful and inviting.
   d. The Laurier government advertised all over Europe.
   e. It advertised for homesteaders.
   f. Soon shiploads of poor, energetic people began arriving.
   g. The ships came to Montreal.

   _____

   _____

   _____

   _____

   _____

3. Combine the following sentences.

    a. Reverend Isaac Barr was a Canadian.
    b. In 1902 he was curate at St. Saviour's Church in London, England.
    c. He advertised and lectured widely.
    d. It was in an effort to form a colony in the Saskatchewan Valley.
    e. On March 31, 1903, two thousand Barr colonists set sail from Liverpool.
    f. Troubles began when they discovered that Barr had lied to them.
    g. He had lied to them about the conditions aboard ship.

_____

_____

_____

_____

_____

4. Combine the following sentences.

    a. They arrived in Saskatoon in winter weather.
    b. They were shocked to find that no arrangements had been made to take care of them.
    c. They had to live in tents.
    d. They had to try on their own to purchase overland materials.
    e. These materials were for their journey to colony lands.
    f. The colony lands were two hundred miles away.
    g. These demands fuelled inflation.
    h. This inflation was caused in part by Barr.
    i. He insisted on a percentage from merchants on all sales to the colonists.

_____

_____

_____

_____

5. Combine the following sentences.

    a. At last the Barr colonists left Saskatoon.
    b. They experienced severe problems along the way.
    c. They faced floods.
    d. They faced prairie fires.
    e. They reached their land grant territory.
    f. They found an empty store.
    g. They found a poor hospital with only three nurses in it.
    h. They found a totally unworkable system of land allocation.
    i. Barr fled back to Battleford with the three nurses.
    j. The settlers were under the new leadership of Reverend George Lloyd.
    k. They erected a notable settlement.
    l. They named it "Lloydminster."

_____

_____

_____

_____

_____

6. Combine the following sentences.

    a. There is a custom of hanging holly in the house at Christmas.
    b. Old Germanic races of Europe used to hang evergreen plants indoors in winter.
    c. The plants were a refuge for the spirits of the forest.
    d. Holly was considered a symbol of survival by pre-Christian Romans.
    e. The Romans used it as a decoration during their Saturnalia festival at the end of December.
    f. Christians began to celebrate Christmas at the end of December.
    g. Many of the old customs like hanging holly were preserved.

_____

_____

_____

_____

_____

7. Combine the following sentences.

    a. The Battle of Hastings took place in 1066.
    b. It is said to be the most important event in the history of the English language.
    c. The Norman French defeated the English.
    d. It is known as the Norman Conquest.
    e. The Normans spoke French.
    f. French became the dominant language in England for a while.

_____

_____

_____

_____

_____

8. Combine the following sentences.

    a. The English commoners tended the animals in the fields.
    b. The words for animals before we eat them are *cow, pig, deer,* and *lamb*.
    c. These are original English words.
    d. The Norman French nobility ate the meat of the animals the English tended in the fields.
    e. The words for animals when we eat them are *steak, pork, venison,* and *mutton*.
    f. These words came from French.

_____

_____

_____

_____

9. Combine the following sentences.

   a. The Normans conquered the English in battle.
   b. Many military terms in English are borrowed from French.
   c. *Lieutenant, sergeant, colonel, peace, war, soldier, army,* and *navy* come from French.
   d. The Normans became the rulers.
   e. Many titles of rule were imposed by the French.
   f. *Crown, prince, princess, realm, royal, palace,* and *nation* are terms that come from French.
   g. The Normans brought a number of political and legal terms into English.
   h. *Parliament* comes from French.
   i. *Judge, jury, verdict, innocent, defendant,* and *sentence* are from French.

   _____

   _____

   _____

   _____

   _____

10. Combine the following sentences.

    a. An optometrist tested 275 major league baseball players.
    b. He found that having cross-dominant eyesight can help a person hit a baseball better.
    c. Cross-dominant eyesight refers to seeing better with the left eye if a person is right-handed and vice versa.
    d. Only about 20 percent of the general population has cross-dominant eyesight.
    e. Over 50 percent of the baseball players that he examined have it.

    _____

    _____

    _____

    _____

    _____

Section Five

Moving from Paragraph to Essay: Part 3

Middle Paragraphs, Proofreading, and Submitting an Essay

Review

We construct the middle paragraphs of an essay differently from introductory and concluding paragraphs. Our first and last paragraphs, you may remember from Chapter 5, *do not* have topic sentences; instead, they state the *thesis* of the essay.

Middle paragraphs, on the other hand, *do have topic sentences.* Each topic sentence states the topic and the central point of the paragraph. It also explains or supports the thesis of the essay. Of course, each topic sentence is followed by other sentences, often examples, which explain or support it. You can visualize the structure of an essay this way:

First paragraph:	**Introduction and thesis statement**
Second paragraph:	**First topic sentence** to support the thesis **Examples** to support the topic sentence
Third paragraph:	**Second topic sentence** to support the thesis **Examples** to support the topic sentences
Fourth paragraph:	**Third topic sentence** to support the thesis **Examples** to support topic sentences
Fifth paragraph:	**Conclusion**

Assignment

1. As your final assignment in the construction of an academic essay, assemble all the parts of your essay—introductory (or thesis) paragraph, middle paragraphs, and concluding paragraph. You should have five complete paragraphs now. If at this stage your paragraphs are too small and undeveloped, you may need to work on them. If you are having trouble, ask your instructor for help.

2. Once you have the entire paper assembled, edit your paper. Correct any spelling, grammar, or punctuation errors that you might find. Watch particularly now for any grammatical errors that you know you regularly make.

3. Then, compose a clean final draft, following the format your instructor has designed for your class. Double-space your work and write on only one side of the page. Keep 2.5-cm (one-inch) margins on all four sides. Number your pages.

4. Last, *proofread* your final draft. This is *crucial*. If you forget to proofread your paper, you miss the final step in the writing process. To proofread properly, read your paper slowly, line by line, perhaps with a ruler in hand. Some writers start at the end of the essay and read backward, thereby not allowing themselves to be distracted by the *content* of the paper. Another method is to read it aloud, either to yourself or to a friend. This last method is excellent, for it also allows you to hear what the paper sounds like to another person. If your paper is handwritten, check at this stage to see that it is legible. Check for letters or words left out. If you find more than, say, one or two errors on a page, you will have to rewrite the entire page. Avoid messy papers. No one, least of all your instructor, wishes to waste time trying to decipher a messy paper.

Chapter Six Practice Test

I. Review of Chapters Three, Four, and Five

A. Correct any misplaced or dangling modifiers. Do nothing if the sentence is correct.

1. Pulling at the stuck door, Jack's face began to turn red.

_____

_____

2. Sara almost fainted when Mr. Kong asked her to dance.

_____

_____

3. Larry found the biology paper tucked between the pages of the encyclopedia that he had written the night before.

_____

_____

4. Trying not to let his feet get too wet, he quickly paddled the canoe across the lake with a leak in it.

_____

_____

5. Wondering what was wrong with the brakes, the car raced down the dangerous mountain road.

_____

_____

B. Correct any subject–verb agreement or pronoun use errors in the following sentences. Do nothing if the sentence is correct.

6. The measles, which are a potentially serious disease, can be avoided with proper vaccines.

7. William was looking forward to playing the new stereo system in his car, but he couldn't get it to start.

8. Each horse and rider were given a number before the show began.

9. Sandy was delighted to hear that the college said it would mail the books to her brother and herself.

10. A person in a car should always wear a seatbelt if you want to be safe.

C. Add commas to the following sentences where necessary.

11. Under the old elm tree in Farzad's backyard a 1976 Ford Pinto is rusting away and a discarded mattress is slowly disintegrating.

12. Sherry glanced at the clock and wondered when all of the bickering gossiping and backbiting would ever end.

13. Mathieu knew that his house at 401 Bates Street was haunted; however he preferred living there to the house he used to own in Sherbrooke, Quebec.

14. When she arrived home Jenna was unable to find Mischief her pet rat.

D. Add periods, question marks, exclamation points, quotation marks, semi-colons, colons, and apostrophes where necessary, and correct any mistakes in the use of capitalization, titles, and numbers. Do not add or delete any commas.

15. Nicole said that she would be late as a result, she would not be able to pick up any of these items for the picnic the volleyball, the volleyball net, the frisbee, the barbecue, or the charcoal

16. When Jims hard disk crashed, he went to his father and said, Now I have a perfect excuse for not turning in an essay I cant write.

17. Did NDP leader David Lewis actually describe huge corporations as corporate welfare bums

18. When 2 copies of chatelaine arrived in the mail, Celeste didnt know what to do

19. According to the newspaper article entitled riots erupt at the skydome, last nights final score was jays five yankees three

20. Bonny enjoyed her psychology class, but her fathers illness last spring forced her to drop it.

II. Review of Chapter Six

A. In the blanks, write in the correct forms of the verbs indicated.

21. As he drove into his driveway, he wondered why two white rhinos were _____ on his front lawn. (lie)

22. By three that afternoon, Marilyn Bell had _____ nearly fifteen kilometres. (swim)

23. First, Claude sang his favourite country song; then, he _____ in the laundry. (bring)

24. Do you really suppose that Simon could have _____ that entire keg of beer? (drink)

25. Hermes had _____ almost the entire race before anyone noticed the wings on his feet. (run)

B.   Correct any verb form errors in the following sentences. Do nothing if the sentence is correct.

26. Colleen had never sang the part of Susanna in Toronto.

27. Every summer all she wants to do is lay in the sun and get a tan.

28. The last time that Robert saw his gold watch, it was setting on top of the coffee table.

29. Because of her migraine headache, Karen lay in bed for three hours yesterday.

30. When his balloon bursted, Jason began to cry.

C.   Underline the correct word in the parentheses.

31. Although Bill had (lead led) the entire race, in the end Cyrano won by a nose.

32. The (principal principle) reason for leaving at three in the morning is to beat the traffic.

33. The mere thought of having a cavity filled has a very disturbing (effect affect) on Irene.

34. Whenever he needs (advise advice), Geraldo writes to Ann Landers.

35. The members of the jury spent five days discussing the evidence (among between) themselves.

D.   Correct any incorrect word choices in the following sentences. Do nothing if the sentence is correct.

36. Ron was pleased to find that his polka-dotted tie perfectly complimented his striped coat.

37. Jeremy's conscious was clear: he knew he had not taken the missing pack of chewing gum.

38. The amount of people who attended the concert surprised even its organizers.

39. Dorothy was already to go, but the Wizard had already started to float away.

40. At last night's party, Albert ate more chocolate mousse then any other guest.

E. Underline the word or expression that would be most appropriate for college writing or formal written Canadian English.

   41. The spider web across his door (frightened, freaked out, scared the hell out of) Herman.

   42. When the lost hiker (cast an eye upon, saw, eyeballed) the water, he knew he would live.

   43. He stepped up to the bar and ordered a glass of (suds, beer, fermented grains and barley).

   44. A bolt of lightning streaked across the (heavens, sky, upper atmosphere) and struck the roof of our house.

   45. After working all night, Sara wanted to go home and (crash, sleep, enter a state of unconsciousness).

F. Revise any use of slang, informal spoken English, overly formal language, or jargon into language appropriate for college writing or formal written Canadian English.

   46. John knew he'd been busted, yet he continued to prevaricate.

   _____

   _____

47. Mustafa had always been desirous of interfacing with the person who had written his computer program, but his wish had yet to come true.

_____

_____

48. Jenny was kind of grossed out when she was offered a plate of tripe.

_____

_____

49. As they watched their solar companion disappear beyond the far horizon, Mac and Tabatha began to feel really weird.

_____

_____

50. Yesterday, Peter got a lot of new stuff at the business establishment that markets wearing apparel for men.

_____

_____

ANSWERS

Answers to Practices in Chapter Six

Pages 351–352:

2. drunk
3. swum
4. laid
5. sat
6. lying

7. shrunk
8. drank, sitting
9. sung, raise
10. lie, lain

Page 362:

2. conscience, an
3. among, brakes
4. effect
5. affect
6. already

7. all right
8. number
9. our, break
10. chose

Page 367:

2. fewer, than
3. your, principal
4. nauseous, past
5. led, through, lose, their
6. principle

7. Two, too, to
8. amount, less, than
9. quite, quiet
10. were, where

Pages 375–376:

Answers other than the following are also possible.

2. That man is in trouble.
3. Many of his friends think that Paul makes too many mistakes when he tries to impress people.
4. Sandy's boss was happy that she always arrived on time, but he did not appreciate the quality of her work.
5. The disgusting smell made the speaker stop talking for a minute.
6. After the officer arrested Bill, he pursued Steve.
7. I really enjoy relaxing on Saturdays.
8. Sometimes I feel depressed, but at other times I am quite happy.
9. My father would be furious if he knew that I had started skydiving.
10. She skis as much as she can.

Page 378:

Answers other than the following are also possible.

2. Shane's suggestions about how to fix my house were helpful.
3. Nizar wanted to lose some weight, so he started working out at his local gym.
4. You can't build houses without also improving housing associations.
5. The two business executives read the restaurant's menu to see how expensive their Christmas party would be.
6. Jack had always wanted to become an actor, but he had not succeeded in becoming one.
7. When talking to their children, parents should praise them as much as possible.
8. After I began bowling, I realized that I did not like it.
9. Because of bad weather, flights on North Saskatchewan Airlines are being delayed.
10. A rolling stone gathers no moss.

FINAL EXAM

Practice Final Examination

I. Chapter One

A. Underline all subjects once and all verbs twice.

  1. Do you plan to see your aunt tonight?

  2. Flies and mosquitoes filled the air above the stagnant pond.

  3. The shoe polish was advertised as black, but it was really dark blue.

  4. April decided to leave the concert when some of the people near her

      sprayed insecticide at each other.

  5. Ten feet above the ground floated a hot air balloon with a huge

      smiley face on it.

B. In the space provided, indicate whether the underlined word is a noun (N), pronoun (Pro), verb (V), adjective (Adj), adverb (Adv), preposition (Prep), or conjunction (Conj).

  6. Gladys could <u>barely</u> see the trees through the fog.   _____

  7. Jack did not believe that the <u>unusual</u> seed pods came
      from outer space.   _____

  8. Mavis couldn't sleep, <u>so</u> she decided to read the latest
      Stephen King novel.   _____

  9. Bernard <u>will</u> miss the bus if he doesn't hurry.   _____

  10. The instructor reminded <u>everyone</u> to pack an extra
       parachute.   _____

C. In the following sentences, place all prepositional phrases in parentheses.

  11. Each of the girls stared at the trapeze artist.

  12. A large moth flew into the house and up the stairs.

  13. During his entire lecture, Mr. Stout kept staring over our heads.

14. Bill could hardly see without his glasses, so he asked his daughter to drive him to the store.

15. Ten people were surfing near the pier in spite of the storm warnings.

II. Chapter Two

A. Correct all fragments, comma splices, and fused sentences. If the sentence is correct, do nothing to it.

16. The mechanic, forgetting to put new oil in the car.

_____

_____

17. Roxanne lit her cigarette and inhaled deeply, then she began to cough and gasp.

_____

_____

18. Wondering where he was going, Faith watched as her husband walked into the forest.

_____

_____

19. Bette played the lottery she hoped she would win this year.

_____

_____

20. Steve watched helplessly as his computer monitor fell to the floor its screen broke into two large pieces.

_____

_____

21. Ever since you came back from your trip to Antarctica.

_____

_____

22. Lester was not a mason, however, he knew what a brick wall looked like.

_____

_____

23. Jennifer stared at the spider it did not look like a black widow.

_____

_____

24. Close the door.

_____

_____

25. Shaking his head in disbelief when the officer told him he had run two red lights and had nearly hit a pedestrian.

_____

_____

B. Compose simple, compound, complex, and compound–complex sentences according to the instructions.

26. Write a simple sentence that contains at least one prepositional phrase.

_____

_____

27. Write a compound sentence. Use a coordinating conjunction and appropriate punctuation to join the clauses.

_____

_____

28. Write a compound sentence. Use a transitional word or phrase and appropriate punctuation to join the clauses.

_____

_____

29. Write a complex sentence. Use *when* as the subordinator.

_____

_____

30. Write a compound–complex sentence. Use the coordinating conjunction *and* and the subordinator *who*.

_____

_____

III. Chapter Three

A. Correct any misplaced or dangling modifiers in the following sentences. If the sentence is correct, do nothing to it.

31. Hoping to win the race, Laura's skis nearly flew across the snow.

_____

_____

32. Tom's son carried a dog into the kitchen that was covered with fleas.

_____

_____

33. Startled by the loud noise, Chen's packages fell to the ground.

_____

_____

34. Cheryl only told her son he could have one doughnut, but he ate six.

_____

_____

35. Wondering if she would ever find her wallet, the entire house was thoroughly searched.

_____

_____

36. Yesterday in the park I saw a man smoking a cigar from my neighbourhood.

_____

_____

37. The Mazda Miata was almost going 140 km per hour when it passed the pickup.

_____

_____

38. Hearing that the riot was over, the mayor heaved a sigh of relief.

_____

_____

39. Hillary gave the ice cream to the customer covered in hot fudge.

_____

_____

40. Buried in ice for thousands of years, the archaeologist was amazed to find the Neanderthal man so well preserved.

_____

_____

B. Add phrases or clauses to the following sentences according to the instructions. Be sure to punctuate carefully.

41. Add a verbal phrase. Use the verb *hope*.
    Pete bought two lottery tickets.

_____

_____

42. Add an adjective clause.
    The ladder in the back of my garage used to belong to my father.

_____

_____

43. Add a present participial phrase to the beginning of this sentence. Use the verb *push*.
    Gladys tried to move the boulder.

_____

_____

44. Add an appositive phrase after one of the names in this sentence.
    Harold asked Dr. Robinson if she had ever met Ms. Stanfield.

_____

_____

45. Add an infinitive verbal phrase to this sentence. Use the verb *give*.
    She spent all day at the mall trying to find the perfect gift.

_____

_____

IV. Chapter Four

A. Correct any subject–verb agreement errors in the following sentences by crossing out the incorrect verb form and writing in the correct form above it. If the sentence is correct, do nothing to it.

46. Every person I have ever met in my trips to foreign countries have been friendly and courteous.

47. That group of tourists visit the same ski resort every year.

48. Do his employer or co-workers ever complain about his attitude?

49. A stray dog with its five pups have taken up residence in my backyard.

50. Anyone wanting to see the new foals need to go to the stables behind the barn.

51. Two kilograms of chocolate were all that Roy could manage to eat.

52. Rice or baked potatoes serve as a good side dish for many meals.

53. Someone from the ranches in the valley have agreed to act as mediator.

54. There seems to be at least two good reasons not to let you in.

55. One of the athletes competing in the track meet look like my older brother.

B. Correct any pronoun use errors in the following sentences by crossing out the incorrect pronoun and writing in the correct one above it. In some cases you may have to rewrite part of the sentence. If the sentence is correct, do nothing to it.

56. Before a person starts to jog, you should warm up with stretching exercises.

57. The owner of the trampoline factory told my sister and myself to leave.

58. Art put his paper in his briefcase, but later he couldn't find it.

59. Lester and May had both worked at the photo lab for two years, but Del could develop pictures much faster than she.

60. The windshield wipers needed to be replaced; this bothered Ken.

61. At Christmas, the Dewy Compost and Fertilizer Company gave all of their employees a bag of potting soil.

62. The new members of the math club wanted to solve the problem by themself.

63. Sarah beamed with pride when she heard that the winners of the sculpture contest were Randy and her.

64. The reporter asked Sarah how she felt about winning, which seemed silly to me.

65. At the hypnotist conference one of the participants could not keep their eyes open.

V. Chapter Five

A. Add commas to the following sentences where necessary. If the sentence is correct, do nothing to it.

66. No I did not eat your ice cream nor did I take the chocolate chips.

67. The maître d' adjusted his white gloves straightened his bow tie lifted his nose into the air and ignored the people waiting in line.

68. On March 31 1903 two thousand Barr colonists set sail from Liverpool.

69. Halitosis for example can spoil a date and ruin a relationship.

70. When he saw the torn tattered curtains Jake knew something was wrong.

71. The person who sold the painting to you has left town and will not return until Monday.

72. The orangutan one of the most intelligent apes is a friendly gregarious animal.

73. Because she had always loved the snow Beverly moved to Edmonton Alberta last year.

74. Julia please close the door turn on the heater and put away your sweater before you sit down.

75. Barry of course had already seen the movie but he would not tell anyone how it ended.

B. Correct any errors in the use of periods, exclamation points, question marks, semicolons, colons, quotation marks, or apostrophes in the following sentences. If the sentence is correct, do nothing to it. Do not add or delete any commas.

76. What part of Canada is called "Lotus Land?"

77. Rebecca said, We should have left ten minutes ago however, we can still make it

78. Maxwells list included the following items: a telephone in his shoe a pen with invisible ink and a secret agent trench coat.

79. Havent you ever wondered why the sky is blue? asked Linus.

80. Its too bad that you can afford only two dollars worth of gas.

C. Correct any errors in the use of capitalization, titles, or numbers in the following sentences. If the sentence is correct, do nothing to it.

81. The novel zero avenue is about a young housewife who is kidnapped and driven into the okanagan valley.

82. Cecil told his father to drive east on danforth avenue for 3 kilometres.

83. Orville brought 125 copies of saturday night and ten copies of holiday to his psychology class.

84. Some students in the literature class wondered if the poem my papa's waltz is about alcohol abuse.

85. My uncle in the maritimes recently mailed seven dollars and fifty-five cents to me.

VI. Chapter Six

A. In the following sentences correct any errors in the use of irregular verbs by crossing out the incorrect forms and writing in the correct ones above. If the sentence is correct, do nothing to it.

86. The clock setting on the mantle had not worked properly for years.

87. The alligator had swam nearly to the edge of the pond before the picnickers noticed it.

88. After lunch, Barbara laid down on the couch and took a nap.

89. I was surprised when Judy brang me a dead penguin.

90. After Butch had drank the entire quart, he lied the empty bottle down and passed out.

B. Correct any errors in word choice in the following sentences by crossing out any incorrect words and writing the correct words above. If the sentence is correct, do nothing to it.

91. Randy has always thought that the principle cause of his poor posture is that he is to tall.

92. If your sure you do not want the package, you should refuse to

    except it.

93. Each year less people visit the Queen Mary then the year before.

94. A blue hippopotamus lead the parade as it preceded down Main

    Street.

95. The personal of the company knew that they're jobs were in

    jeopardy.

C. The following sentences contain words or phrases that are inappropriate
    for college writing because they are slang, jargon, overly formal, or overly
    informal. Revise any words or phrases that are inappropriate for formal
    written Canadian English. If the sentence is correct, do nothing to it.

96. Eric's leg was kind of sore, but he did not think a lot about it.

    _____

    _____

97. A blue motor vehicle containing two adolescent male individuals
    travelled at an excessive rate of speed down the freeway.

    _____

    _____

98. Glenn was really bummed out because his place of residence had
    been forcibly entered by criminals.

    _____

    _____

99. His stereo and his audio/visual telecommunication device had been
    ripped off.

    _____

    _____

100. A lot of people get their kicks by bad-mouthing others.

_____

_____

Index

To the owner of this book

We hope that you have enjoyed *Inside Writing: A Writer's Workbook,* and we would like to know as much about your experiences with this text as you would care to offer. Only through your comments and those of others can we learn how to make this a better text for future readers.

School _____ Your instructor's name _____

Course _____ Was the text required? _____ Recommended? _____

1. What did you like the most about *Inside Writing?*

_____

_____

_____

2. How useful was this text for your course?

_____

_____

_____

3. Do you have any recommendations for ways to improve the next edition of this text?

_____

_____

_____

4. In the space below or in a separate letter, please write any other comments you have about the book. (For example, please feel free to comment on reading level, writing style, terminology, design features, and learning aids.)

_____

_____

_____

_____

Optional

Your name _____ Date _____

May Nelson Canada quote you, either in promotion for *Inside Writing* or in future publishing ventures?

Yes _____ No _____

Thanks!

- - - - - - - - - - - - - - FOLD HERE - - - - - - - - - - - -

MAIL POSTE

Canada Post Corporation / Société canadienne des postes

Postage paid
if mailed in Canada

Port payé
si posté au Canada

Business Reply

Réponse d'affaires

0107077099   01

Nelson

TAPE SHUT

TAPE SHUT

0107077099-M1K5G4-BR01

Nelson Canada
College Editorial Department
1120 Birchmount Rd.
Scarborough, ON M1K 9Z9

PLEASE TAPE SHUT. DO NOT STAPLE.